Borderlands

Archaeological excavations on the route of the
M18 Gort to Crusheen road scheme

Borderlands

Archaeological excavations on the route of the
M18 Gort to Crusheen road scheme

Shane Delaney, David Bayley, Ed Lyne,
Siobhán McNamara, Joe Nunan and Karen Molloy

with contributions by
Judith Carroll, Sarah Cobain, Jonny Geber, Eoin Grogan,
Stephen Mandal, Jacqueline MacDermott, Mary-Liz McCarthy,
Jim McKeon, Ellen O Carroll, Michael O'Connell, Ian Riddler,
Helen Roche, Farina Sternke and Nicola Trzaska-Nartowski

NRA SCHEME MONOGRAPHS 9

First published in 2012 by
The National Roads Authority
St Martin's House, Waterloo Road, Dublin 4
Copyright © National Roads Authority and the authors

Library of Congress Cataloging-in Publication Data are available for this book.
A CIP catalogue record for this book is available from the British Library.

Material from Ordnance Survey Ireland is reproduced with the permission of the Government of Ireland and Ordnance Survey Ireland under permit number EN0045206.

ISBN 978-0-9564180-6-7
ISSN 2009-0471
NRA Scheme Monographs 9

Copy-editing: Editorial Solutions (Ireland) Ltd
Cover design, typesetting and layout: LSD Ltd
Index: Julitta Clancy
Printed by: Nicholson & Bass Ltd

Front cover—Bone die from Ballyboy 1 ring-ditch, Co. Galway.

Back cover—Shale axehead from Caheraphuca 1 burnt mound, Co. Clare and (line drawing) cereal kilns at Curtaun, Co. Galway.

Frontispiece—Detail from a mural at Tubber National School, Co. Clare.

CONTENTS

CD CONTENTS

The CD accompanying this book contains the fully illustrated technical reports ('Final Reports') for all the archaeological excavations on the M18 Gort to Crusheen road scheme, in PDF format.

1. Explanatory note	
2. Excavation Final Report files	**Excavation directors**
Ballyboy 1 ring-ditch E3719.pdf	Siobhán McNamara
Ballyboy 2 ring-ditch E3718.pdf	Siobhán McNamara
Ballyline 1 and 2 burnt mounds E3717.pdf	Siobhán McNamara
Ballyline 3 burnt mound E3715.pdf	Joe Nunan
Caheraphuca 1 burnt mounds E3654.pdf	David Bayley
Caheraphuca 3–12 burnt mounds E3653.pdf	David Bayley
Clooneen 1 burnt mound E3722.pdf	David Bayley
Curtaun 1 and 2 burnt mound and cereal kilns E3721.pdf	Shane Delaney
Derrygarriff 1 burnt mound E3710.pdf	Joe Nunan
Derrygarriff 2 charcoal kiln and furnace E3711.pdf	Joe Nunan
Derrygarriff 3 burnt mound E3716.pdf	Joe Nunan
Drumminacloghaun 1 burnt mound E3720.pdf	Siobhán McNamara
Gortaficka 1 and 2 burnt mounds E3898.pdf	Joe Nunan
Gortavoher 1 burnt mound E3984.pdf	Shane Delaney
Monreagh 1 and 2 burnt mound E3712.pdf	Siobhán McNamara
Monreagh 3 burnt mound E4037.pdf	Shane Delaney
Rathwilladoon 2 and 3 prehistoric settlement E3656.pdf	Ed Lyne
Rathwilladoon 4 burnt mound E3655.pdf	Ed Lyne
Rathwilladoon 5 charcoal kiln E3657.pdf	Ed Lyne
Sranagalloon 1 burnt mound E3713.pdf	Joe Nunan
Sranagalloon 2 hilltop enclosure, well.pdf	Joe Nunan
Sranagalloon 3 burnt mound.pdf	Joe Nunan

FOREWORD

Ten years ago a map of infrastructural development projects in Ireland would have been dominated by the major inter-urban road projects, forming radial lines extending from Dublin to the provinces, like spokes in a giant wheel. In the intervening years, bit by bit, we have been building a great wheel-rim too, as sectors of the Atlantic Corridor have fallen into place. This is a very large-scale project that aims to link the towns and cities of the west and south coasts with each other, as well as with Dublin.

The M18 motorway is a central element in the Atlantic Corridor. It traverses the economic heartland of the West, linking its two major cities—Galway and Limerick—and passing by Shannon and Ennis among other places. But a better road does not set aside history to make a single region. The authors of this present volume remind us that the Gort to Crusheen sector of the M18 crosses the 'borderlands' between two provinces, two counties and also two historic territories. The contemporary motorist will hardly notice the boundary, as traffic streams north and south along a seamless new motorway. But it was once strongly defined in the landscape, by the Moyree River, and is still strongly defined in the imaginations of local people living on either side of the divide where Munster meets Connacht, Clare meets Galway and, in later medieval times, the old Gaelic kingdom of Thomond, in Clare, met conquered Norman lands to the north.

This latest in the NRA scheme monograph series tells some of the stories of the borderlands in prehistoric and historic times. At Rathwilladoon, the record of its settlement history goes back to Neolithic or Stone Age times, with the excavation of one of the earliest house sites in the region. By the Bronze Age, it had become a populous territory and fossil pollen analysis from Caheraphuca shows the extent of the human impact on the natural landscape in those years, with widespread woodland clearance for livestock pasture. Tillage grew in importance from one period to the next and the medieval cereal-drying kilns at Curtaun are an especially good example of their type.

It is the remains of people that most arrest our thoughts. The Iron Age people of the borderlands are represented in these pages by the cremated bones of their dead, discovered at Ballyboy, in the simple funerary monuments known as ring-ditches. A carved bone dice accompanied one of the ring-ditch burials. This is a poignant reminder of a very human circumstance: in all periods, and in every life, there is a degree of chance and a degree of choice, though the end is just the same. Along the way, we celebrate life while we can.

Once again, the NRA is very happy to bring the results of archaeological investigations on a national road scheme into public view with this handsomely produced archaeological monograph. Just as the new roads give improved public access between different regions, the books in this series are giving permanent public access to their history. We congratulate the authors and thank them for their work, and we hope our readers will enjoy the result.

Fred Barry
Chief Executive
National Roads Authority

ACKNOWLEDGEMENTS

The authors would like to express their sincere thanks to everyone who assisted in bringing the archaeological investigations on this scheme to completion. Martin Reid monitored the progress of the work for the National Monuments Service and Jerry O'Sullivan, NRA Archaeologist, acted as Project Archaeologist for Galway County Council. The Project Engineers at the Council were Jerry Dunne and Fintan O'Meara, supported by Ian Falconer, Martin Blackweir, David Lea and David Catley of Jacobs Engineering, consultants to the Council. The archaeology chapter in the Environmental Impact Survey (EIS) for the scheme was compiled by Johnny Dempsey of Jacobs Engineering and the geophysical survey at EIS stage was directed by Alister Bartlett of the Bartlett-Clarke Consultancy. Derry McCarthy, agricultural adviser, provided invaluable liaison with landowners along the scheme during the commencement of the work.

The field investigation team for Irish Archaeological Consultancy Ltd (IAC) included Shane Delaney, Senior Archaeologist and Site Director, Dave Bayley, Ed Lyne, Siobhán McNamara and Joe Nunan, Site Directors, and James Kyle, directing test excavations. Dave Swift gave logistical support on the ground and was responsible for implementing safe working practices. Specialist photography on site was by Gavin Duffy of AirShots Ltd and additional geophysical survey was by supplied John Nicholls of Target Archaeological Geophysics Ltd. The finds conservation was undertaken by Susannah Kelly and select artefacts illustration was by Alva MacGowan.

Dr Jim McKeon compiled a first full draft based on the individual Final Reports by the excavation directors. Dr Eoin Grogan provided academic comment on draft chapters. NRA Archaeologists Mary Deevy and Róisín Barton reviewed the final draft. Fintan Walsh provided assistance in managing the production of figures and in review and comment on the text. Paul Higgins and Graeme Kearney produced most of the illustrations. The Geographic Information System (GIS) figures were compiled by Kieron Goucher. Michelle Brick provided additional background research and Maeve Tobin provided additional editing. We would also like to acknowledge and thank Rob Lynch and Conor Gormley and all the office staff at IAC Ltd for assistance throughout the project and finally sincere appreciation to all the field crew, supervisors and site assistants that excavated the sites during the unforgiving wet winter of 2007 into 2008.

Dr Karen Molloy and Professor Michael O'Connell thank Pat O'Rafferty, Ingo Feeser, Ann Bingham and Beatrice Ghilardi for their assistance with pollen coring and analysis, and landowners Cronin and Margaret O'Keefe, and Terence Clarke, for access to pollen core sampling sites in Caheraphuca.

The archaeological investigations were commissioned by Galway County Council with funding from the NRA and were carried out under Ministerial Directions issued by the National Monuments Service, in consultation with the National Museum of Ireland.

1
INTRODUCTION

by Jim McKeon and Mary-Liz McCarthy

This book presents the results of archaeological investigations carried out in advance of the construction of the new M18 road between Gort, Co. Galway, and Crusheen, Co. Clare (Illus. 1.1 and 1.2). We have called the book 'Borderlands' because of the coterminous county, provincial and ancient borders traversed by the new road. Today this administrative border between Galway and Clare, and Connacht and Munster, is a peaceful and uneventful one, but this was not always the case. In the early medieval period it marked the political frontier between powerful Gaelic kingdoms, and in the later medieval period it divided Gaelic and Anglo-Norman Ireland. The land itself also represents a type of borderland, with the low-lying wetlands of County Clare to the south and the well-drained pastures of south Galway to the north, separated by a web of rivers and streams.

This chapter describes the landscape in the environs of the new road, and provides an historical and archaeological overview of the region. The background of the road scheme and the methodological approaches to excavation are then briefly described. Chapters 2–6 discuss the sites excavated in advance of the new road, and also the results of palaeoenvironmental research carried out in Caheraphuca Lough, Co. Clare (Chapter 4). Evidence of multiphase domestic settlement activity was discovered at Rathwilladoon, Co. Galway, including Neolithic, Bronze Age and Iron Age features (Chapter 2). Most of the sites identified on the scheme were prehistoric, with a particular preponderance of Bronze Age burnt mounds, or *fulachtaí fia*—11 of which were recorded in Caheraphuca townland alone (Chapter 3). At Ballyboy, Co. Galway, Iron Age funerary activity was revealed in the form of two ring-ditches containing multiple cremations and a quantity of high-status artefacts (Chapter 5). At Sranagalloon, Co. Clare, a Bronze Age cremation pit was discovered within a later enclosure, while Iron Age metal-working sites were found at Derrygarriff, Co. Clare, and Rathwilladoon, Co. Galway, (Chapter 6). Finally, a complex of three corn-drying kilns spanning the early and later medieval periods was excavated at Curtaun, Co. Galway, near a large bivallate ringfort on the edge of the road scheme (Chapter 6).

1.1—Landscape and geology

The new road between Gort and Crusheen traverses the inland rural and agricultural landscape of north Clare and south Galway (Illus. 1.3). The route runs north–south through a broad natural corridor that is framed to the east by the Slieve Aughty mountain range and to the west by the dramatic limestone uplands of the Burren (Illus. 1.4). It runs just west of the existing N18 road and the Athenry to Ennis railway line (see 'Post-medieval/early modern period', below). There is little

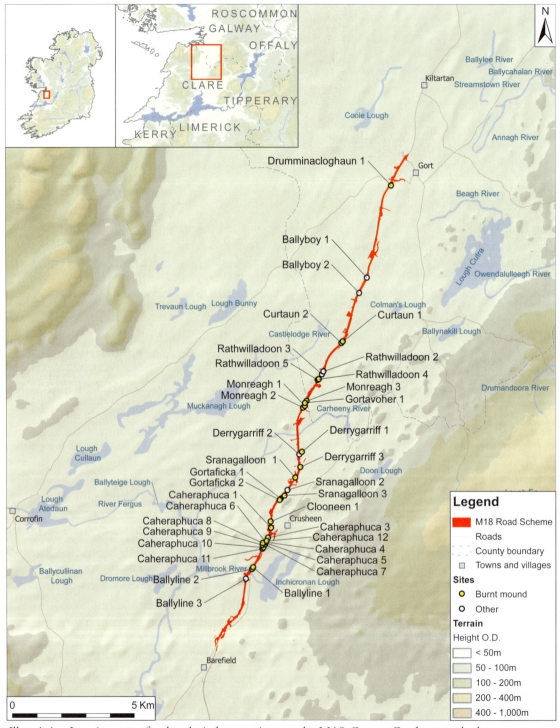

Illus. 1.1—Location map of archaeological excavations on the M18 Gort to Crusheen road scheme.

Illus. 1.2—Construction of an over-bridge at Gort. The road scheme involved construction of 22 km of new motorway forming part of the M18.

doubt that this natural path of least resistance in the modern era was equally attractive as a conduit between north and south—and Munster and Connacht—in antiquity.

The area exhibits many characteristics of the Burren, including thin soil cover, limestone rock outcrops and scrub regeneration, in a small-scale pattern interspersed between improved grassland, pockets of woodland, low hills and low-lying wetlands and lakes. In general the topography undulates gently within an average range of 20–30 m above Ordnance Datum (sea level). The two dominant rock types in the region are Carboniferous limestone, which underlies the entire length of the new road, and the Devonian Old Red sandstone which forms the Slieve Aughty range to the east (Herries Davies & Stephens 1978, 39–40; Illus. 1.5). The road predominantly overlies either limestone derived till and sandy till deposited during the most recent glaciation, or peat that has formed in low-lying, poorly drained areas where stagnant water and slow percolation causes thin layers of peaty soil to accumulate (Illus. 1.6). Some areas are represented by very thin to absent subsoils, while other areas along the road contain significant depths of subsoil, up to 13 m in places. Most of the low-lying areas along the route are towards the southern end of the scheme, in County Clare. This area is characterised by peat bogs and wetlands in glacially formed depressions and seasonal lakes known as turloughs. The higher ground, predominantly to the north, generally comprises well-drained, gently undulating pastureland with some uneven, hummocky till ridges of limestone epikarst and glacially formed drumlins.

Illus. 1.3—An aerial photo of part of the scheme corridor shows a landscape mosaic typical of the 'borderlands'. Fiddaun Castle (upper middle) occupies a defensible site between small lakes, on a low ridge where limestone bedrock protrudes at the surface (Ordnance Survey of Ireland 2010).

Curtaun ringfort (lower right) flanks a whale-back ridge of good farmland that is skirted by the new motorway and also the Ennis/Limerick railway, dividing the ridge from a peat bog in the lower ground to the east.

Illus. 1.4—Relief map of the region with places mentioned in the text. The M18 passes from Connacht into Munster between the uplands of the Burren and Sliabh Aughty (Ordnance Survey of Ireland).

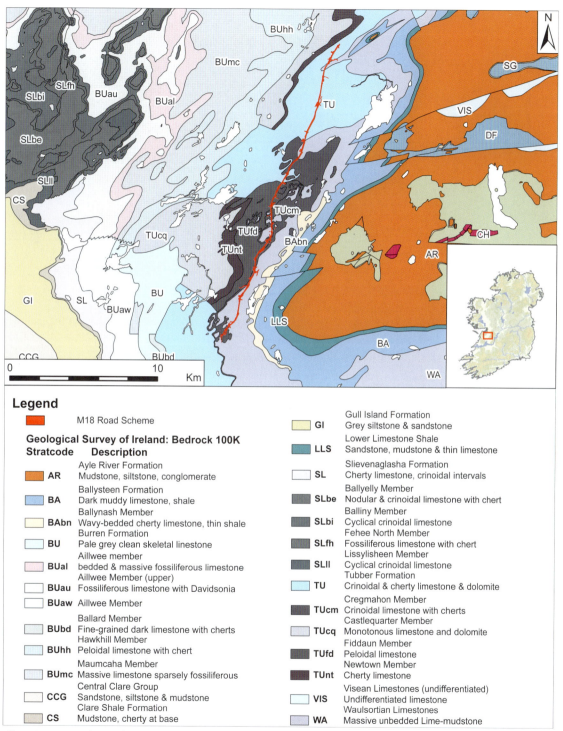

Legend

| | M18 Road Scheme |

Geological Survey of Ireland: Bedrock 100K

Stratcode	Description
AR	Ayle River Formation Mudstone, siltstone, conglomerate
BA	Ballysteen Formation Dark muddy limestone, shale
BAbn	Ballynash Member Wavy-bedded cherty limestone, thin shale
BU	Burren Formation Pale grey clean skeletal linestone
BUal	Aillwee member bedded & massive fossiliferous limestone
BUau	Aillwee Member (upper) Fossiliferous limestone with Davidsonia
BUaw	Aillwee Member
BUbd	Ballard Member Fine-grained dark limestone with cherts
BUhh	Hawkhill Member Peloidal limestone with chert
BUmc	Maumcaha Member Massive limestone sparsely fossiliferous
CCG	Central Clare Group Sandstone, siltstone & mudstone
CS	Clare Shale Formation Mudstone, cherty at base

Stratcode	Description
GI	Gull Island Formation Grey siltstone & sandstone
LLS	Lower Limestone Shale Sandstone, mudstone & thin limestone
SL	Slievenaglasha Formation Cherty limestone, crinoidal intervals
SLbe	Ballyelly Member Nodular & crinoidal limestone with chert
SLbi	Balliny Member Cyclical crinoidal limestone
SLfh	Fehee North Member Fossiliferous limestone with chert
SLll	Lissylisheen Member Cyclical crinoidal limestone
TU	Tubber Formation Crinoidal & cherty limestone & dolomite
TUcm	Cregmahon Member Crinoidal limestone with cherts
TUcq	Castlequarter Member Monotonous limestone and dolomite
TUfd	Fiddaun Member Peloidal limestone
TUnt	Newtown Member Cherty limestone
VIS	Visean Limestones (undifferentiated) Undifferentiated limestone
WA	Waulsortian Limestones Massive unbedded Lime-mudstone

Illus. 1.5—Geology of the study area (McConnell 2004: Geological Survey of Ireland). The road scheme traverses a bedrock foundation of limestone or cherty limestone.

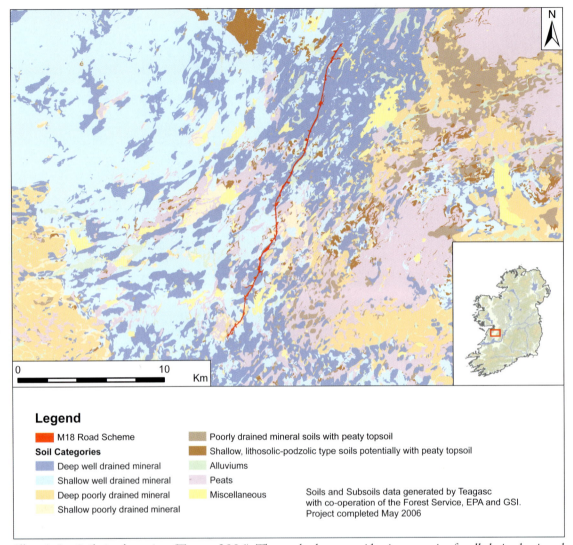

Illus. 1.6—Soils in the region (Teagasc 2006). The road scheme corridor is a mosaic of well-drained mineral soils and wet peat bogs.

On a provincial level the region is bounded by Galway Bay and the Atlantic Ocean to the west and north-west, and the River Shannon and Lough Derg to the east and south. In the more immediate study area, however, there are many lakes and wetlands, and a number of rivers and streams are crossed by the new road. While no fording points or other river crossings of known historic interest were identified, the importance of watercourses as territorial boundaries is markedly evident. Some act as townland and barony boundaries, and much of the county/provincial border between Clare/Munster and Galway/Connacht is delineated by rivers and streams. In the context of the road scheme, this occurs between the townlands of Gortavoher, Co. Galway, and Monreagh, Co. Clare, which are divided by the Scarriff Stream. This stream also marks the townland boundary between Gortavoher and Rathwilladoon. The Moyree River—which marks the provincial boundary just east of the scheme (before becoming the Carheeny River)—forms the townland boundary of Monreagh, separating it from Derrygarriff and Cappanapeasta (Illus. 1.7). Two other rivers of note that cross the path of the new road are the Millbrook and the Castlelodge. The Castlelodge River was partly straightened during the construction of the railway in the 19th century. The Millbrook ran through the demesne of Ballyline House (see 'Post-medieval/early modern period', below), and supported two mills.

Illus. 1.7—The Moyree river forms a county boundary between Galway and Clare and a provincial boundary between Connacht and Munster.

It is unlikely that the rivers located in the environs of the new road were navigable, and therefore would not have been used as a means of transport. However, they, along with the abundant lakes and wetlands, would have been exploited throughout history and prehistory, for fishing and hunting wild fowl, as a source of potable water, and for watering livestock. Indeed, evidence shows that Lough Inchiquin (c. 10 km north-west of Crusheen) in particular, was the focus of significant prehistoric activity, and Inchicronan Lake (just south of Crusheen) enjoyed similar attention throughout the medieval period. There are numerous turloughs and swallow-holes in the region and these were an important component of the early medieval, cattle-based economy (Delaney 2011, 47). Turloughs are seasonal lakes that are filled from the water table in winter and retreat in the drier summer months, leaving rich pasture. It has been suggested that whoever controlled the turloughs held the upper hand in the territorial power-struggles that were a defining characteristic of the period (Patterson 1994, 113).

Scattered among the low-lying wetlands and gently undulating improved agricultural lands, are pockets of coniferous woodland, particularly around the Castlelodge and Moyree rivers and south of the Derrygarriff stream. To the east of the scheme, on the Slieve Aughty range, plantations in the modern period have created one of the largest coniferous forests in Ireland. There is evidence, however, that this area was always forested to some degree: the 'Wood of Suidan' covered the border area between counties Galway and Clare in the 16th century (McCracken 1971, 43). Locally, some stands of mature deciduous trees are survivals of demesne planting in the 18th and 19th centuries around big houses like Ashfield, Ballyline and Cregg Demesne, in the road scheme corridor.

Today, the land in the region is predominantly used as grass pasture for cattle or sheep, in small fields bounded by drystone walls or embanked hedgerows, or a combination of the two. There are also some areas of improved land with larger fields bounded by post-and-wire fences. However, in many areas the land is of marginal or low agricultural capability. Dispersed rural dwellings and farms characterise this agricultural landscape. The town of Gort in the north and the village of Crusheen in the south are the largest nucleated settlements in the immediate vicinity of the road. The county town of Ennis, Co. Clare, lies approximately 8.5 km south of the scheme and the village of Ardrahan, Co. Galway, is c. 8 km to the north.

1.2—Archaeological and historical background

Mesolithic period (c. 8000–4000 BC)

Human occupation of Ireland first occurred in the Mesolithic period (c. 8000–4000 BC). Irish Mesolithic sites have been identified in low-lying locations near to coasts, rivers and lakes. This site distribution appears to reflect the fish-reliant economy of the semi-migratory Mesolithic communities, which supplemented their diet by hunting—particularly wild pig—and seasonal foraging for shellfish and wild plant-foods such as berries and hazelnuts (Jones 2004, 25).

No evidence of Mesolithic activity was found during excavations in advance of the new road. Indeed, no Mesolithic settlement sites have been identified to date in counties Galway or Clare, despite the presence of landscapes rich in staple foods such as shellfish beds in deep sea inlets and abundant hazel woods in the limestone lowlands. A Mesolithic presence, however, is attested in the general region by stray finds of stone tools at Killaloe and Lough Inchiquin (ibid., 26), c. 10 km north-west of Crusheen. Excavations in advance of the M6 motorway yielded stray Mesolithic stone tools at Barnacragh and Urraghry, near Ballinasloe (Tierney et al. 2009, 13–15) and Ballynaclogh, near Aughrim (Tierney & O'Dowd 2008, 5–6). Further isolated finds are also recorded in Galway City, Oranmore and Belclare near Tuam (Gibbons et al. 2004, 4–6) while a large assemblage of Mesolithic stone tools were recovered from the River Corrib and Lough Corrib, near Oughterard (ibid.).

While at present the Corrib and Suck environs seem the most likely locations for Mesolithic settlement, similar activity may have occurred in the low-lying and wetland areas between Gort and Crusheen, which include a number of streams, rivers and lakes (and peat-accumulated former lakes).

Neolithic period (c. 4000–2450 BC)

During the Neolithic period communities became less mobile as their economy became based on stock-rearing and cereal cultivation. Communities expanded and moved further inland and established permanent settlements. Agriculture demanded the altering of the physical landscape, and forests were rapidly cleared and field boundaries created. This transition was accompanied by major social change and a greater concern for territory (ibid.). This saw the construction of large ritual monuments such as megalithic tombs. Large rectangular houses were also characteristic of the Early Neolithic period, and over 90 examples have been identified in Ireland (Grogan 2002).

The earliest Irish pottery comes from this period, though traditions changed over time. Early Neolithic (c. 4000–3500 BC) pottery comprised mainly carinated bowls with everted rims, small step shoulders and deep, rounded body profiles (Grogan & Roche 2010, 27–9). The Middle Neolithic period (c. 3500–2800 BC) is characterised by the diversification of pottery forms—principally bipartite, broad-rimmed and globular bowls—and by the application of decoration, usually pressed into the pot surface (ibid., 29–33). The ceramic tradition of the Late Neolithic period (c. 2800–2450 BC) is dominated by Grooved Ware—bucket-shaped vessels with rounded, upright rims, straight or gently curved profiles and flat bases. These pots are commonly decorated with a groove, or grooves, on the inner surface beneath the rim (ibid., 34–5).

The Burren was a focus of activity throughout the Neolithic period, particularly towards its south-eastern extremity, on and around Roughan Hill. It is argued (Jones 2004, 30–54) that a sizeable, kin-based Neolithic society occupied this area, and was focused on a number of significant ritual/burial/territorial monuments. These include three chambered tombs at Parknabinnia, Ballyganner North and Leamaneh North; two portal tombs at Poulnabrone and Ballycasheen; and the Linkardstown cist cairn at Poulawack. Roughan Hill is just c. 15 km west of the M18 road scheme and, significantly, both the Ballycasheen and Poulnabrone portal tombs appear to have been deliberately situated along important routeways linking the Burren to the adjacent lowlands. This indicates that Neolithic activity extended beyond the Burren, and this is borne out by the distribution of find spots of stone axeheads. Neolithic stone axeheads (46) have been recovered from Lough Inchiquin, c. 10 km north-west of Crusheen, and from a number of riverine/wetland contexts across Clare, from the River Fergus to the Shannon, with over 750 from the fords at Killaloe/Ballina alone (Grogan 2005b, 106). Some of these implements may have been manufactured at Doolin, on the west coast of Clare, where a Neolithic/Early Bronze Age stone axe production site is recorded at the mouth of the Aille River (Jones 2004, 40).

An axehead recovered from a bog in Gortavoher townland in 1948 (Museum Files P1948:97) provides evidence of a Neolithic presence within the M18 road corridor between Gort and Crusheen. Another example was recovered from the bog at Monreagh during test excavations in advance of the new road, and Neolithic axeheads were also recovered during excavations at Sranagalloon 1, Caheraphuca 1 (Illus. 1.8) and Caheraphuca 8 (see Chapter 3). More significantly, archaeological investigations at Rathwilladoon, Co. Galway, found evidence of occupation during the Early Neolithic period—stone tools, diagnostic pottery and earth-cut features—suggestive of a settlement site (Chapter 2).

Illus. 1.8—Polished shale axehead (E3654:113:2) from a burnt mound at Caheraphuca 1, Co. Clare.

Chalcolithic period (Copper Age) (c. 2450–2200 BC)

The transitional period between the Late Neolithic period and the Early Bronze Age saw the first use of metal (copper) in Ireland. This Chalcolithic, or Copper Age, is also characterised by the introduction of new forms of funerary monuments (wedge tombs) and pottery types (Beaker Wares).

Beaker pots are usually S-shaped in profile with flat bases and, while plain examples are common, are typically decorated with horizontally arranged bands of incised, cord- or comb-impressed lines, blank zones, and panels filled with oblique, chevron or lattice ornament. The majority of wedge tombs, unlike the other, earlier classes of megalithic tombs, appear to have been built during this period—and continued into the Bronze Age. In general, wedge tombs are distributed in the west and south-west of Ireland. Isolated examples are dotted across south Galway, but apart from an outlying group in north Connemara, most are found on the flanks of the Slieve Aughty mountains. A large number are found throughout County Clare, concentrated particularly in the Burren, where around 80 have been identified (Jones 2004, 65), with outstanding examples at Roughan Hill, Parknabinnia and Creevagh, among others (Illus. 1.9). The cluster focused on Roughan Hill forms the densest concentration of wedge tombs in the country. A group of at least four farmsteads and associated field-systems survives on the hill at Parknabinnia. These may have been contemporary with the tombs, but represent a community whose origins lie further back in the Neolithic period (ibid., 56).

A wedge tomb in Caheraphuca townland, Co. Clare, stands c. 400 m east of the new road scheme (near Crusheen). It comprises a wedge-shaped chamber of five standing stones supporting

Illus. 1.9—Creevagh wedge tomb is one of many wedge tombs on the Burren, testifying to a high Late Neolilthic/Early Bronze Age population in the region (Carleton Jones).

two capstones, sitting on a low mound (Illus. 1.10). Five burnt mounds excavated between Gort and Crusheen returned radiocarbon dates that spanned or encroached into the Chalcolithic period (Drumminacloghaun 1, and Caheraphuca 5, 8, 9 and 11; see Chapter 3). Perhaps significantly, four of these sites were in close proximity to the wedge tomb. Significant quantities of Beaker pottery, representing at least 10 vessels, were recovered from a prehistoric settlement site at Rathwilladoon, Co. Galway (Chapter 2). These wares share similarities with sherds recovered from the settlement complex at Parknabinnia, Roughan Hill, on the Burren (Jones & Gilmer 2000).

The sheer number of Neolithic, Chalcolithic, and Early Bronze Age monuments in the Burren attests to a significant and organised population in the region throughout those periods. While the evidence suggests that a major focal point of those communities was Roughan Hill and the Burren in general, it is clear that funerary and settlement activity extended into the low-lying hinterland to the east and south. Only limited quantities of Beaker pottery have been recorded from the north Clare/south Galway region, so the evidence from Rathwilladoon, in particular, confirms and furthers our understanding of the Chalcolithic period in the general area, and specifically in the lands between Gort and Crusheen.

Bronze Age (c. 2200–800 BC)

The Bronze Age saw the earliest use of true copper-alloy technology (bronze) in Ireland, and with it came major changes in society, technology, ceramic and burial traditions. The physical expression

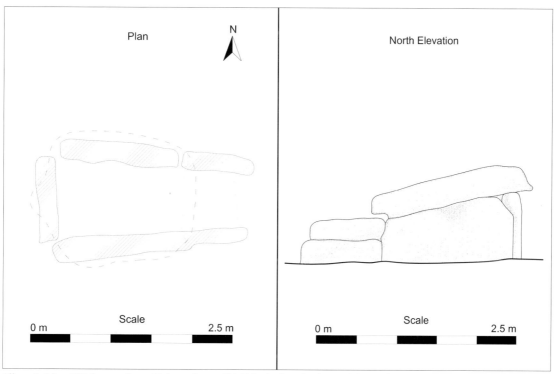

Illus. 1.10—Wedge tomb at Caheraphuca (IAC Ltd after Borlase 1897, Vol. 1, 82). The monument survives but is heavily overgrown.

of these changes is etched across the landscape. The final *floruit* of megalithic tomb building (wedge tombs) occurred during the Chalcolithic period and into the Bronze Age. After this, individual cist or pit burials emerged as the preferred method of laying the dead to rest, either in isolation or in small cemeteries. Different forms of the burial mounds known as barrows appear during this period, as well as ditched ceremonial enclosures known as henges. The Bronze Age landscape is also dotted with other monuments such as standing stones, stone rows and stone circles. Bronze Age settlement/occupation sites are well attested in the Irish archaeological record, including large hilltop enclosures (hillforts), some promontory forts, round-houses and burnt mounds, traditionally known as *fulachtaí fia*.

One of the characteristics of Bronze Age Europe was increased warfare, and in Middle–Late Bronze Age Ireland (c. 1500–800 BC) societies led by warrior élites dominated tribal regions (Jones 2004, 71). Ostentatious displays of wealth, gift-exchange, alliances and trade were all hallmarks of this period, as was the production, use and ritual deposition of weapons and personal ornaments of increasing sophistication, fashioned from bronze and gold. The powerful chiefdom societies of this period appear to have centred on large hillfort enclosures. Grogan (2005b, 123–4) argues that while these monuments were sites of strategic military importance, power and influence, they were also symbols of communal pride and cohesion, reflecting a sense of collective identity.

Grogan's (2005a & b) study of the spatial and social organisation of Bronze Age north Munster was focused particularly on the Bronze Age trivallate hillfort at Mooghaun, Co. Clare (Illus. 1.11). The study postulated a Bronze Age landscape of up to 450 sq km that was divided and sub-divided into a number of territories, ultimately dominated by the élite and powerful hillfort-dwellers of Mooghaun (Grogan 2005a, 79–101). The model is based on the distribution and perceived hierarchy of settlement sites within the region and on the artefactual record—particularly the presence of high-status goldwork. A hoard of gold objects discovered near Mooghaun in 1854 is one of the largest single discoveries of Bronze Age gold in Europe. Another significant find from north Clare was the Gleninsheen gorget, a large collar of hammered gold discovered in 1932. Grogan (2005a, 81) suggests that the prevalence, quality and regional character of goldwork found in north Munster shows a marked contrast with the rest of the country, and thereby provides evidence of a distinct regional identity and social cohesion. It is probable that a similar social structure operated on the Aran Islands (off the coasts of Clare and Galway), dominated by the multivallate hillfort of Dún Aonghasa, on Inishmore (ibid. 161–8).

While the area between Gort and Crusheen lies beyond the main North Munster Project study area, that territory may have come under the political influence of Mooghaun (c. 30 km south of Crusheen). Alternatively, the area may have operated within a similar spatial and social hierarchy, which had its own political focus elsewhere—perhaps at some as yet unidentified hillfort. Given the foci of monuments and importance of Roughan Hill in the Neolithic and Chalcolithic periods, it might seem the most likely candidate for a centre of power. However, the distribution of monuments in the region reveals that during the Bronze Age the population became more widespread on the Burren and expanded into south-east Clare (ibid., 71). Indeed, by the later part of the Bronze Age the lowland areas around Lough Inchiquin appear to have become the focus of activity, perhaps due to soil erosion on the increasingly exposed karstic limestone of Roughan Hill (Grogan 2005b, 107). It is possible that a large stone enclosure (c. 225 m diameter) on Turlough Hill, on the north-east edge of the Burren, was a Bronze Age hillfort that functioned in the same capacity as Mooghaun

Illus. 1.11—Late Bronze Age society in the West may have been organised around tribal 'capitals' like this hillfort at Mooghaun, Co. Clare (Con Brogan: National Monuments Service).

and Dún Aonghasa, and controlled the area between Gort and Crusheen, c. 14 km to the south-east. However, no excavation has been undertaken on the site, which could equally be a Neolithic ritual monument (Jones 2004, 42–5).

The landscape of County Clare is rich in sites dating to the Bronze Age, indicating that the area was widely inhabited at that time. Burnt mounds are the most frequent site recorded for this period. There are over 430 recorded in the county, with at least 22 Bronze Age examples identified within the Gort–Crusheen sector of the new M18 road (Illus. 1.12; Chapter 3). Only four burnt mounds were encountered in the northern, Galway stretch of the road, and fewer are recorded for that county as a whole. However, numerous examples have recently been excavated in advance of ongoing road projects in County Galway (and Clare), including eight along the Gort–Oranmore sector of the new M18 road—one at Ballyglass West, a cluster in Caherweelder townland and further examples in Moyveela and Coldwood (Delaney & Tierney 2011, 29–44). At least 15 were excavated in east Galway prior to construction of the M6 road (McKeon & O'Sullivan in press), two of which—in Killescragh townland—were associated with Bronze Age timber platforms and trackways. The ubiquity of this monument type within the narrow ribbons of land that are investigated prior to road developments indicates a populous Bronze Age landscape in south Connacht as well as north Munster.

In addition to burnt mounds, a number of other Bronze Age monuments have been recently discovered during infrastructural projects in the region. Funerary sites include a ring–barrow and an associated cremation pit identified during monitoring of the gas pipeline at Cloonagowan, Co. Clare (Dennehy 2002a). A second cremation pit was found nearby which contained a thumbnail scraper of Late Neolithic/Early Bronze Age type (Dennehy 2002b). Another cremation pit with associated industrial pits was identified during this project in Gortaficka, Co. Clare (Dennehy & Sutton 2002). Bronze Age cremation cemetery sites were excavated just south of Crusheen during advance works for the Ennis Bypass and the N85 Western Relief road: two in Manusmore townland and another at Killow, in close proximity to a burnt mound (Bermingham et al. in press). A ritual funerary deposition site was identified in Glencurran Cave on the Burren (Dowd 2007). A number of cremation burials were also found along the route of the M6 motorway in east Galway, in the townlands of Newford, Cross, Rathglass and Curragh More (McKeon & O'Sullivan in press). Bronze Age cist burials were also excavated during that road scheme, at Ballykeeran, and Treanbaun 3, and a possible Bronze Age ritual site was recorded at Treanbaun 1 (ibid.).

Evidence of Bronze Age settlement activity includes a round-house excavated at Barnhill, Dromoland, Co. Clare (Quinn 2007), and a probable habitation site at Ballaghfadda West, in advance of the Gas Pipeline to the West project (Halpin 2007, 169). Two sites in east Galway discovered

Illus. 1.12—Excavation of a burnt mound at Caheraphuca 1, Co. Clare. There were over 20 examples of this most common Bronze Age site type discovered on the scheme.

during work on the M6 road scheme—Mackney 1 and 2—were also interpreted as habitation sites but the most significant Bronze Age monument discovered during this, and other, road projects in the region was a large (c. 450 m diameter) multivallate hillfort at Rahally, near the village of New Inn (McKeown & Sullivan in press), c. 30 km north-east of Gort.

In the context of the new M18 road, the Bronze Age was represented by 22 burnt mound sites (Chapter 3), a cremation burial at Sranagalloon, Co. Clare (Chapter 6), and a probable house site at Rathwilladoon, Co. Galway (Chapter 2). The immediate area of the new road is framed by an intensively settled Neolithic/Chalcolithic landscape to the west, on the Burren, a highly structured Bronze Age chiefdom to the south, around Mooghaun hillfort, and probably a similar territory to the east, focused on the hillfort at Rahally, in east Galway. The excavated archaeological and visible upstanding evidence for the Gort–Crusheen area, particularly that provided by development-driven excavations, indicates that the area and its wider landscape were intensively inhabited throughout the Bronze Age. It is also probable that the area was organised within a spatial and social hierarchy, centred either on Mooghaun or another hillfort site.

Iron Age (c. 800 BC–AD 500)

The period defined as the Irish Iron Age saw the replacement of bronze with iron as the main metal used in the production of tools, weapons and personal ornaments. Inexplicably, it also saw the cessation of pottery production, and the apparent replacement of ceramic pots with wooden vessels and leather containers (Raftery 1995). The traditional view that these events did not occur until c. 600 BC is no longer acceptable, based on recent research in Ireland and Britain (i.e. Eogan 2010, 107; Grogan & Roche 2010, 41–3; Needham 1996; Needham et al. 1998). A start date of c. 800 BC for the introduction of iron technology is in keeping with the evidence, and the arrival of Christianity to the island in the fifth century AD marks an expedient end to the period.

Iron ore, unlike the more limited—and presumably controlled—supplies of copper and tin (used to manufacture bronze) was widely available in Ireland, not only from major sources such as the Antrim basalts and Wicklow pyrites, but also from rock outcrops and bogs (bog ores) across the country. The appearance of this new medium, and the changes in technology, society and language that accompanied it, have been the source of considerable debate in Irish archaeological and historical studies. These changes have been commonly classified in terms of a pan-European (non-Roman) 'Celtic' culture, which attained a perceived identity through contemporary Greek and Roman writings and later Irish and Welsh heroic literature (Waddell 2000, 288–90; Raftery 2000, 9–16). This 'Celtic' identity was further defined through archaeology, by the discovery of characteristic artefacts that were used to divide the Iron Age into two main phases: the earliest phase based on finds from Hallstatt, near Salzburg, in Austria, and the later phase—most prevalent in Ireland—named after a large assemblage of metal-work discovered at La Tène, on Lake Neuchâtel, in Switzerland. The appearance of a 'Celtic' social and material culture in Ireland, despite its distinct insular expression, was traditionally explained in terms of conquest and colonisation (e.g. Ó Corráin 1989, 1–3). However, current thinking promotes social/economic interaction and the diffusion of ideas, rather than the movement of people, as the main catalysts for technological, cultural and linguistic changes in Iron Age Ireland (Jones 2004, 79–81; Waddell 2000, 289; Raftery 2000, 224–6).

In contrast to the Bronze Age, evidence for Iron Age activity in Ireland has been somewhat scarce (particularly between c. 700–400 BC); indeed, the later first millennium BC and the early centuries AD are among the most obscure in Irish prehistoric archaeology. A number of high-profile 'royal' sites enjoyed significant Iron Age activity and have been discussed, such as Dún Ailinne, Co. Kildare, Emain Macha (Navan Fort), Co. Armagh, Rathcroghan, Co. Roscommon, and Tara, Co. Meath (Waddell 2000, 325–53; Raftery 2000, 64–83). In contrast, Waddell (2000, 319) could state that 'domestic occupation sites remain virtually unknown and our understanding of settlement, economy and social structure in the period from 600 BC to the early centuries AD is meagre in the extreme'. However, recent infrastructural projects across the country are uncovering Iron Age sites in increasing numbers and are beginning to fill the gaps. The Gort–Crusheen road scheme joins a number of recent large-scale road projects in the region that have included archaeological excavations. These include additional works elsewhere on the M18 road to the north and south, and the Gas Pipeline to the West, which runs mostly parallel to and just west of the new road. These projects have yielded evidence—albeit limited—for Iron Age settlement and activity in the region (Delaney & Tierney 2011; Grogan et al. 2007).

A potential Iron Age site located in Drumminacloghaun, Co. Galway towards the northern end of the route is no longer extant. A large and prominent 'hillfort' at Newtown, located 4 km north of Gort, has not been excavated and a definitive date is unknown for the site. Excavations at hilltop enclosures have produced evidence for activity in the Bronze Age and Iron Age (Raftery 2000, 58–62; Grogan 2005b, 130–1). It should be noted, however, that excavations have shown hillforts to be primarily Bronze Age occupation sites, and although they often include an Iron Age horizon, this represents small-scale and apparently non-domestic activity.

A concentration of funerary barrows is known to the north of the Gort–Crusheen scheme (to the east and north-east of Ardrahan), some of which have been dated to the Iron Age. One excavated example at Grannagh, Co. Galway, consisted of a ring-ditch containing pockets of cremated bone and a variety of finds, including glass and dumb-bell-shaped beads and bone pins (Waddell 2000, 367). Another ring-ditch, complete with cremation deposits, was excavated at Oran Beg, near Oranmore (Rynne 1970). Over 80 glass beads were recovered during the excavation, and some of these appeared to have been fused in a cremation pyre. South of the Gort–Crusheen road scheme there was evidence for Iron Age funerary activity recovered from excavations along the N18 Ennis Bypass (Bermingham et al., in press). At Manusmore, Co. Clare, 27 burial pits returned radiocarbon dates spanning the Neolithic period to the Iron Age, although the later pits contained burnt animal bone that may not be specifically related to the cremations. Another Iron Age pit burial was located nearby. At Killow, Co. Clare, cremation pits returned Iron Age radiocarbon dates of 750–390 BC (Beta-211589) and 390–180 BC (Beta-211592), and a wooden (ash) bowl found in nearby peat returned a radiocarbon date of 777–407 BC (UB-6287). An Iron Age ring-ditch was also excavated during that scheme that produced cremated bone and artefacts, including glass beads and fragments of quartz. Most of the Iron Age sites identified within close proximity to the new road relate to the funerary deposition of cremated bone, either in ring-ditches or in pits. At most of these sites the cremated remains did not represent complete individuals. This may indicate the practice of placing token deposits within the monuments. These burials demonstrate a remarkable similarity to Late Bronze Age funerary traditions and suggest an element of continuity with past practices.

Two Iron Age ring-ditches were excavated in advance of the M18 Gort–Crusheen road in

Ballyboy, Co. Galway. They included 'token cremations' and a significant quantity of glass and amber beads. These were 'truncated' monuments, with no surviving surface expression, but may once have had surrounding banks or central mounds (Illus. 1.13 and 1.14; Chapter 5). Domestic activity was indicated at Rathwilladoon 3, Co. Galway, by the foundation trench of a light structure that dated to between the first and second centuries BC (Chapter 2). Evidence for an Iron Age metal-working furnace and a possibly contemporary charcoal-production kiln were found in nearby Rathwilladoon 5, while an iron-working furnace was discovered at Derrygarriff 2 (Chapter 6).

We know little of everyday life during the Iron Age, as few domestic structures or artefacts have been identified. The discoveries along the new road are therefore important, primarily in helping to map the Iron Age geography of western Ireland—particularly that of north Munster/south Connacht—but also in providing clues to everyday activities. Archaeological excavations are beginning to uncover an Iron Age landscape that reflects the lives of ordinary people in the period.

Illus. 1.13—This barrow burial monument from Monksfield, near Gort, in Co. Galway is a glimpse of the likely original appearance of 'ring-ditches' excavated on the road scheme at Ballyboy.

Illus. 1.14—Excavation of an Iron Age ring-ditch with cremated human burials at Ballyboy 2, Co. Galway. The charcoal-rich ditch fills appear as a dark circular soil mark in the foreground.

Early medieval period (c. AD 500–1100)

The only early medieval features newly identified during excavations between Gort and Crusheen were cereal-drying kilns located beside a bivallate ringfort in Curtaun, Co. Galway (Illus. 1.15; Chapter 6). It is clear, however, from the historical and archaeological records, that the region was a hive of activity at that time. The political and territorial frontier between Connacht and Munster, through which the new road passes, would have been a hotly contested and busy one during that period.

According to Ó Cróinín (1995, 12), during the early medieval period 'change was constant, sometimes rapid, and often fundamental'. The period saw significant changes to political organisation, settlement forms, art, land-use and technology. This was also the beginning of history in Ireland, so the written word can also be used to help inform our understanding of the period. The defining aspect of early medieval Ireland, however, was the conversion from paganism to Christianity, which began some time during the fifth century AD. The new religion was accepted—slowly at first—before spreading across the country and growing in influence throughout the period.

The early Church has left an abiding monumental imprint on the landscape. The earliest churches would have been wooden and none survives, but from as early as the ninth and 10th centuries there are little stone churches surviving in the region. Early monastic sites could include church buildings, burial grounds, round towers, high-crosses and holy wells, and were usually surrounded by curvilinear enclosures, or *valla*. The footprint of these enclosures is sometimes preserved in the street patterns of modern towns, as at Armagh, and Tuam, Co. Galway. Despite the unwelcome attentions of Viking raiders in the eighth and ninth centuries—another significant aspect of the period—the Church flourished, and by the 10th century, nucleated settlements, or 'proto-towns', had developed around some of the larger monastic sites (Edwards 1990, 104–21).

In this period Ireland was not a united country but a patchwork of petty kingdoms scrambling for dominance, with their borders changing as alliances were formed and battles fought. Towards the end of the period, powerful dynasties such as the *Uí Néill* in the north and the *Éoganacht* in the south dominated expanding territories at the expense of the lesser kingdoms (Ó Cróinín 1995, 41–62; Edwards 1990, 8). The basic territorial unit of the tribal kingdoms was the *túath* and over 150 of these existed across the country during the early medieval period.

Illus. 1.15—Excavation of medieval corn-drying kilns at Curtaun, Co. Galway. The kilns were located on a hillslope between a ringfort on higher ground and a peat bog (left).

With the exception of the monastic 'proto-towns' and Viking towns that developed in the latter centuries of the period, settlement in Ireland was rural in character. The most common settlement type was the ringfort. Thousands once dotted the Irish landscape, but in recent decades many have been destroyed by agricultural improvements. Ringforts normally survive as roughly circular, earthen bank-and-ditched (raths) or drystone-walled (cashels) enclosures that were predominantly built and occupied by Gaelic chiefs, lesser nobles and free farmers. Earthen ringforts are found throughout the lower-lying environs of the road scheme, like the example immediately adjacent to the new road at Curtaun (Chapter 6), but stone-walled cashels are more typical of the nearby Burren uplands that overlook the scheme corridor (Illus. 1.16). They often included internal structures—houses, cattle-pens and souterrains—and while they vary in size, form and function, the majority probably represented semi-defended farmsteads.

The other main settlement type of the period is the *crannóg*, which is essentially a wetland adaption of the ringfort. The organisation of labour needed to construct these latter monuments, and the prestigious artefacts that they often yield, suggest that they were occupied only by the higher echelons of Gaelic society (Edwards 1990, 34–41).

New evidence from recent, development-led excavations, however, is revealing a number of atypical and more complex early medieval settlement sites that would traditionally be considered ringforts. At Roestown 2, Co. Meath, for example, a D-shaped 'ringfort' was excavated in advance of the M3 road (O'Hara 2009). That site yielded evidence of craftworking—particularly fine metal-work—and

Illus. 1.16—Enclosed farmsteads were the dominant settlement type of the early medieval period. The stone-walled types known as cashels are abundant on the Burren, with earthen ringforts more common in the low-lying environs of the road scheme. Caherconnel cashel, Co. Clare (Con Brogan: National Monuments Service).

large-scale animal husbandry in external enclosures. The presence of imported pottery revealed trade links with the wider world, and ultimately the site may have functioned as an estate centre where tribute and food rent was received and processed. Another emerging 'ringfort' site is the 'cemetery-settlement' (Ó Carragáin 2009, 339), or 'secular-cemetery' (Stout & Stout 2008, 75). In these sites a burial ground forms a significant portion of a circular enclosure—commonly the south-east quadrant—and has no apparent ecclesiastical associations. The documentary evidence for kindred burial grounds, that did not form part of churchyard cemeteries, was first considered by O'Brien (1992; 2003). This has been strongly endorsed in recent years by field evidence. At first these cemetery-settlements seemed to be a phenomenon of the fertile, low-lying parts of eastern Ireland, but examples have recently been excavated in advance of road projects west of the Shannon, in County Galway: at Carrowkeel, Treanbaun and Owenbristy (Lehane et al. 2010; McKeon & O'Sullivan in press).

The portion of the new M18 road that lies in County Galway was within the kingdom of *Aidhne* or *Uí Fhiachrach Aidhne*. This territory was defined to the east by the Slieve Aughty Mountains, to the south by County Clare, and to the west by the Burren and Galway Bay. The town of Gort, or *Gort Inse Guaire* ('island field of Guaire'), is named after Guaire, who had a fortress there. The *Uí Fiachrach* claimed descent from Fiachra, an older half-brother of Niall Noígiallach (Niall of the Nine Hostages). The *Uí Fhiachrach Aidhne* were at the height of their power in the seventh century when Guaire Aidhne became King of Connacht in c. AD 655 (Grey & McNamara 2000, 53–6). By the end of the eighth century the *Uí Briúin Seola* had become the dominant sept in the region (Ó Cróinín 1995, 61).

The southern end of the study area (north Clare) was dominated by a loose federation of families known as the *Eoghanacht*. Before the eighth century the area around modern County Clare was inhabited by two main sub-groups of that federation: the *Corcú Modruadh* and the *Corcú Baiscinn*. Around this time, a group known as the *Deis Tuaisceart* began to push their way into the territories of the *Corcú Modruadh* and the *Corcú Baiscinn* and by the middle of the eighth century had succeeded in forcing them out (ibid., 58). The *Deis Tuaisceart* grew in power and later became known as the *Dál gCais* (then *Uí Briain*, or O'Brien), ultimately the most influential Gaelic power in the Munster region (Ó Murchadha 1992, 6).

Ringforts dominate the early medieval landscape of the new road. They are particularly prevalent along the Galway section of the route, becoming less frequent as the road moves southwards into County Clare. This may be related to the quality of the land as bogs and areas under peat become more common. A cashel is recorded in the townland of Caheraphuca, Co. Clare, c. 150 m west of the new road, and two others were excavated beyond the southern end of the scheme in the townlands of Carrowdotia and Cahircalla More, Co. Clare (Bermingham et al. in press). There are also 21 unclassified enclosure sites in the area, at least some of which may be ringforts or early medieval monuments. One of these enclosures was excavated just beyond the southern end of the scheme, at Killow, Co. Clare, but did not reveal any trace of early medieval activity (ibid.). Three souterrains are also found in the general vicinity of the new road.

Ecclesiastical activity is well represented in the area. There is considerable toponymic evidence for early churches and places dedicated to saints/holy men in the townland names and settlements across the region. Numerous instances of the prefix 'kil' (church) are found, such as Killinny, Co. Galway, where the ruins of a small church survive, c. 6 km north-west of Gort (Illus. 1.17). The important monastic site of Kilmacduagh is c. 5 km south-west of Gort (Illus. 1.18). A monastery was originally founded here in the seventh century by St Colman, son of Duagh, on land granted by King Guaire. The site comprises a group of mainly later medieval small churches, but its 10th-century round tower, at 33.5 m (110 feet) high, is one of the finest examples in the country, and the primary elements of the much-modified principal church—*Teampall Mór MacDuach* (Illus. 1.19)—can also be dated to the 10th century by its surviving architecture (ibid., 32–40). Kilmacduagh was raided twice by the Vikings in the early medieval period in 866 and 922. In the later medieval period it became a cathedral centre and enjoyed continuing patronage from local Gaelic aristocratic families. Approximately 9 km north of Gort, in the village of Ardrahan, there is the base of a round tower in the graveyard of the later church. The monument marks the site of an early medieval monastery, which was probably associated with the O'Heynes family—descendants of King Guaire—who had their chief settlement there from the 10th to the 13th century (ibid., 281). In County Clare, a hermitage is said to have been founded on Inchicronan lake, just south of Crusheen, in the sixth century by St Cronan (Spellissy

2003, 95). Approximately 1 km north of Crusheen (*Croisín*, the little cross), also in the parish of Inchicronan, is the probable site of a church also founded by the saint in the sixth century. While no trace of the church survives, it is thought to have stood on the site now occupied by Kilawinna/Killaveiny cemetery—locally thought to have been used as a children's burial ground (Coffey 1993, 69). Another children's burial ground is situated in the townland of Rathwilladoon, c. 60 m west of the new road. It is located within an oval enclosure which may represent the

Illus. 1.17—The earliest surviving churches are simple stone buildings like Killinny church, near Gort, in County Galway.

remnants of an earlier ecclesiastical site. A number of holy wells dot the landscape, many of which would have been venerated during the early medieval period, and perhaps earlier. One lies just west of the new road near Gort (Ballylennan townland), and is marked as both 'Cloghannanack Well' and 'Tobermacduagh Well', the latter being a dedication to St Colman MacDuagh.

Illus. 1.18—Kilmacduagh, near Gort in County Galway, was an important early monastery in the region, enjoying the patronage of several Gaelic families.

Illus 1.19—Teampall Mór MacDuach, the principal church of Kilmacduagh, was a cathedral in medieval times and a burial place of the O'Shaughnessys.

23

Later medieval period (c. AD 1100–1600)

The defining point for this period was the arrival of the Anglo-Normans in 1169 and their subsequent colonisation of most of the country. Their arrival, however, must be viewed in the context of an ongoing power struggle among the major Gaelic provincial powers for political domination of the island, and an equally disharmonious reformation of the Irish Church that had begun in the early 1100s (O'Keeffe 2000, 12; Simms 1989, 54–7). The years spanning the late 12th and later 13th century saw the Anglo-Norman colonists spread across much of the country, making and breaking alliances with the Gaelic aristocracy and forcing the indigenous Irish into more marginal lands. While nominally they swore fealty to the English King, the Anglo-Normans essentially represented just another tribe, or rather tribes, trying to win political and territorial gains, more often than not by the sword. By the mid 13th century the native Irish were making ever-increasing attacks on Anglo-Norman settlements and by the 14th century the colony was in crisis (Simms 1989, 82–6). Cultural assimilation was also taking place by this time, with many descendants of the original colonists adopting the customs, language and sympathies of the native Irish. Colonial families, such as the Butlers of Ormond and the FitzGeralds of Desmond and Kildare, had become 'Gaelicised' by this time. By the close of the 15th century, only Dublin and its surrounding area—the Pale—supported a significant population of subjects loyal to the English Crown. By the mid 16th century, however, the English—now under the rule of Henry VIII—were regaining control. From the 1540s the Irish monasteries were dissolved. In the 1550s Laois and Offaly were planted with loyal settlers, and in the 1580s an ultimately unsuccessful attempt was made to do the same in Munster.

The archaeological landscape of medieval Ireland is dominated by the settlement forms and monuments of the colonists. As they fought their way across the island they established boroughs and towns, many of which were surrounded by imposing stone walls. These towns included parish churches, abbeys, hospitals, and often a castle. Castles, both urban and those dotted across the countryside, were a hallmark of the medieval period, and the Anglo-Norman colonists. Their form, use and evolution in Ireland have been well rehearsed (e.g., Sweetman 1999; O'Conor 1998, 17–39; McNeill 1997), from the initial earth-and-timber mottes and ringworks to the fortified houses of the late/post-medieval period, with a range of great stone fortifications—hall-keeps, keepless castles and later tower-houses—in between. Another semi-defensive monument introduced by the Anglo-Normans was the moated site, which generally survives today as a rectangular earthwork bounded by banks and ditches (O'Conor 1998, 58–69; Holland 1994).

Little is known about the settlement patterns of the native Irish in the medieval period. Few castles were built by Gaelic kings and lords until the 15th century, at which time they began to construct tower-houses. These tall, narrow, forbidding buildings are especially numerous in the environs of the road scheme, in south Galway and north Clare. However, it has been shown that ringforts and *crannóga* continued to be occupied throughout this time in areas under Gaelic control, and that some moated sites were also of Irish creation (O'Conor 1998, 73–106).

The Church made a great impact on the social geography and architecture of medieval Ireland. New religious orders arrived during this period: the Cistercians and Augustinians arrived around the mid 12th century, followed by others, including the Carmelites, Franciscans and Dominicans. These orders were given land to build abbeys, and were patronised by both Anglo-Norman and Gaelic lords. The abbeys and churches were embellished with the latest architectural styles—Romanesque then Gothic—from Britain and the European mainland, with often a distinctive insular flavour of their own (O'Keeffe 2000, 132–57). Following the dissolution of the monasteries in the 16th century, many abbeys were granted to secular lords, some of who developed them for domestic or individual use. Some abbey churches continued in use as parish churches and, particularly in the West of Ireland, clergy are often recorded still in residence at abandoned abbeys. During the Cromwellian period (mid 17th century) many abbeys were plundered and left to ruin, and it is in this condition that most survive in the landscape today.

The only medieval features identified during excavations between Gort and Crusheen were a 13th-century corn-drying kiln (Chapter 6) and a 14th-century pit beneath a modern burnt mound at Derrygarriff 1 (Chapter 3). The corn-drying kiln is a significant discovery, as it was the latest in a series of three kilns—the other two of early medieval date—found in close proximity to a bivallate ringfort at Curtaun. This hints at either the continuous occupation of the ringfort into the later medieval period, or its reoccupation in the 13th century.

Despite the Norman presence, south Galway was dominated by the Gaelic clans of the *Uí Fhiachrach Aidhne* for much of the medieval period, with the O'Heynes and later the O'Shaughnessys emerging as two of the principal families. It is recorded that in 1207 Murtogh Muimhneach, son of Turlogh Mor O'Brien, attacked *Uí Fhiachrach Aidhne* and plundered 15 towns and villages (Fahey 1893, 145). Inter-clan hostilities were common, first between the O'Heynes and the O'Connors, and later with the O'Briens of Thomond, and by the mid 13th century the O'Heynes power was greatly diminished (Grey & McNamara 2000, 64–5). The O'Shaughnessys became dominant in the 13th century after defeating another prominent family—the O'Cahills (Spellissy 1999, 389). The cathedral church at Kilmacduagh became their hereditary burial place (Illus. 1.19). They built a number of castles, including the 16th-century tower-house at Fiddaun. Fiddaun Castle lies just west of the new M18 road and functioned as a frontier castle: it guarded the western limits of O'Shaughnessy territory. With its gatehouse and masonry evidence for halls and kitchens in the bawn, it is the outstanding example among many fine tower-houses in the region (Illus. 1.20 and 1.21). (The family held their lands until the 1690s, when these were confiscated for supporting the Jacobite cause against William of Orange.) New churches and a fortified 'bishop's house' were built at Kilmacduagh in the 13th century, while earlier churches were modified and enlarged. These works were a response to destruction caused by the O'Conors, the O'Briens and William de Burgh in the early 13th century, and also to the arrival of the Augustinians sometime before 1227.

The Anglo-Normans also became heavily involved in the affairs of the region. William de Burgh had received a speculative grant of Connacht in 1194, and wasted little time in devastating the land and destroying many churches (Grey & McNamara 2000, 64). His son Richard conquered much of the province in 1235, and soon established towns at Galway and Loughrea. His chief vassal, Meiler de Bermingham, founded the town of Athenry. Closer to the road scheme, the Anglo-Norman lord, Maurice Fitzgerald, built a castle in Ardrahan, c. 1238, which soon developed into a sizeable settlement—Ardrahan had been the chief residence and inaugural seat of the O'Heynes in *Uí Fhiachrach Aidhne* until they were driven out by the de Burghs (Spellissy 1999, 281–2). Richard de Burgh built Ballinamantain Castle (also called Kiltartan Castle) in Castletown, just north of Gort. The castle was strategically located to control the pass between the Burren and the Slieve Aughty mountains, and the important routeways from Portumna in the east and Munster to the south. The

Illus. 1.20—Fiddaun Castle, Co. Galway, was a lordly seat of the O'Shaughnessys and is an outstanding example of a later medieval tower house.

Illus. 1.21—The ruinous condition of Boston tower-house, near Tubber, reveals some architectural details of a tower-house interior.

de Burghs may have also built Ballylee Castle (now known as Thoor Ballylee), c. 3 km north-east of Gort. The style of the castle (tower-house), however, would suggest a later, 15th- or 16th-century date. Although the castles at Ballinamantain and Ballylee lie beyond the immediate environs of the new road, their presence reveals the political and social atmosphere on the border of Connacht/*Uí Fhiachrach Aidhne* and Munster/Thomond throughout the medieval period.

While south Galway was dominated by the clans of the *Uí Fhiachrach Aidhne*, north Clare was dominated by the clans of the *Dál gCais*. This was the name given to the grouping of clans that Brian Boru led to military and political dominancy in Ireland at the end of the 10th and early 11th centuries (Ó Murchadha 1992, 6). They came to rule an area of north Munster that became known as *Tuamhumhain*, or Thomond. By the early 12th century, this consisted of much of Clare, Limerick and Tipperary, and parts of Offaly. Thomond fluctuated in size over the centuries and by the later 12th century was confined to the area of modern County Clare, due to pressure from the Anglo-Normans in the south and the O'Conors of Connacht in the north. Indeed, in the knowledge that he would soon lose his power-base to the Anglo-Normans, in c. 1208–1216 the O'Brien chief Donnchadh Cairbreach moved his principal residence from Limerick to *Inis Cluain Rámh Fhada* (island of the long rowing), later to become Ennis Clonroad and eventually Ennis (Spellissy 2003, 15). The 13th and early 14th centuries are characterised by internecine fighting and fluctuating alliances/hostilities with

Illus. 1.22—Inchicronan Priory was an Augustinian foundation endowed by the O'Briens on an 'island' promontory of Inchicronan lake.

the Anglo-Normans, which culminated in a battle near Dysart O'Dea in 1318. Murtagh O'Brien, along with Felim O'Conor, Loughlin O'Hehir and Conor O'Dea, defeated the Anglo-Norman army led by Richard de Clare, and Murtagh became the undisputed king of Thomond. After that pivotal battle Thomond remained free of Anglo-Norman or English involvement until the mid 16th century (Nicholls 2003, 184). In the 1540s the O'Briens accepted the English title of Earl of Thomond under the 'surrender and regrant' policy of Henry VIII. This paved the way for an influx of English colonists and transformed Thomond from a Gaelic kingdom into an English county.

During their rule over Thomond the O'Briens granted significant lands to the Church, including land in the vicinity of the new road. The island hermitage on Inchicronan Lake was granted to the Augustinian canons of Clare Abbey—another O'Brien endowment, near the town of Ennis—in 1189 by Donald Mór O'Brien (Illus. 1.22 and

Illus. 1.23—A round-headed window in the east end of the church at Inchicronan Priory hints at its origins as an early medieval hermitage.

1.23). Inchicronan was the site of an Augustinian priory until it was dissolved in 1577, along with Clare Abbey (Coffey 1993, 47–58). The ruins of two castles also stand on the banks of Inchicronan Lake: O'Brien's Castle stands in the townland of the same name and the other is referred to as Caisleán an Oileán (O'Donovan & Curry 2003, 181; Lewis 1998, 52). Both were probably built by the O'Briens in the later medieval period.

Post-medieval/early modern period (c. AD 1600–1900)

The reformation of Church and State begun by Henry VIII in the first half of the 16th century, and enforced more vigorously by Elizabeth I in the latter half, paved the way for over a century of social unrest, political turmoil and open warfare in Ireland, most of which revolved around matters of religion, but also land and wealth. While England had—for the most part—adopted the new Protestant faith, the majority of Ireland had not. Significantly, this majority did not just include the Gaelic Irish, but also the 'Old English' lords of Anglo-Norman descent that were essentially *de facto* rulers of much of the island. The refusal of these previously loyal lords to acknowledge the authority of the Crown in spiritual as well as temporal affairs rendered them ineligible for administrative positions within the colony. Consequently, these government positions were awarded to English-born Protestants who had no real concern for the welfare of the community and advocated penal legislation against Catholics, including the dispossession of their lands (Canny 1989, 114–17).

Ultimately, by the close of the 16th century—and throughout the 17th century—Ireland was a country divided along religious and political lines: on one side were the Protestant officials trying to implement the policies and State religion of the English Crown; on the other were the 'Old English' and Gaelic aristocracy, priests and communities, resisting government authority in an attempt to uphold their way of life and the Catholic cause. These internal divisions within Ireland had implications on a broader stage. England was under threat from the other major European power, Spain, a Catholic country. A Spanish invasion of Ireland would therefore be welcomed—and was indeed courted—by the Catholic majority, and would provide a perfect springboard from which to mount an attack on Britain (ibid., 128).

This was the context for the events of the late 16th and 17th centuries that fill the pages of countless works on Irish history (e.g. Canny 1989, 125–60; Lennon & Gillespie 1997, 53–77; Killeen 1994, 22–35) and set the tone of Anglo-Irish relations to the modern day: the plantations of Munster, Connacht and particularly Ulster; the rebellion of Hugh O'Neill culminating in the Nine Years War, the battle of Kinsale (1601) and the 'flight of the Earls'; the horrors of the Cromwellian campaign (1649–54); the Williamite wars in Ireland (1688–91); and the anti-Catholic Penal Laws of the late 17th and 18th centuries.

The English conquest of Ireland was complete by the end of the 17th century, and as a result the 18th century was, by comparison, relatively peaceful and uneventful. The Irish economy, and population, boomed under the administration of an ascendant Protestant élite that ensured their dominance over the Catholic majority through a series of penal laws. Between c. 1700 and 1850 the island saw an eightfold increase in population and a huge increase in lands under arable cultivation (O'Sullivan 2009, 37–41). Much of the Gaelic population remained poor, downtrodden and often hungry, and in 1798—inspired by discontent and the republican ideals of the French Revolution—rebellion broke out. What began with the honest idealism of the United Irishmen (Protestant and

Catholic) soon descended into a sectarian war, with atrocities carried out on both sides. While the rebellion was swiftly quashed and reprisals made, the events of the final years of the 18th century heralded a new era of Irish nationalism, which was to dominate the political horizon of the island throughout the modern period.

By the early 17th century the trading merchant families of Galway, or Tribes, owned large areas of land in County Galway and surrounding counties, particularly the Clanricard Burkes (formerly de Burghs) (Mulloy 1996, 213–14). The remnants of some old Gaelic lordships also survived—the O'Kellys, O'Flahertys, O'Shaughnessys and O'Maddens retained vestiges of their old privileges but suffered declining fortunes during the 17th century (ibid.). In 1543 Dermot O'Shaughnessy had an estate of 16,800 acres in and around Gort, but these O'Shaughnessy lands were confiscated in 1697 following the Williamite War, as members of the family had fought for the Jacobites at the battles of the Boyne and Aughrim (Grey & McNamara 2000, 79–84). The surrender of Murrough O'Brien and other Gaelic chieftains to the English Crown in 1543 had opened the way for Protestants in County Clare. Clare, which had been in Connacht province, remained so until 1576 when it was returned to Munster (Coffey 1993, 119). In the first half of the 17th century the Earl of Thomond was inviting English Protestants to settle on his considerable estates across the county, but they were still heavily outnumbered by Irish Catholics. In 1651 the Earl owned 10 townlands in Inchicronan alone, the rest being mainly in the possession of the O'Gradys, McNamaras, O'Briens, MacBrodies, MacQuins and O'Roughans (ibid., 119–21).

Galway was the last town to surrender to Cromwell's Parliamentarian army, in April 1652. A decision was then made to confiscate all Catholic estates in the country and to resettle those landowning Catholics that had not been involved in the rebellion into Connacht and Clare. The settlement area was cut off from foreign contact by a colony of soldier-settlers, who were to occupy a four-mile strip along the coast and the river Shannon. In Connacht there emerged a concentration of minor Catholic landowners resulting from the influx of transplanters who joined the existing occupiers of the land (Mulloy 1996, 219). Many of the prominent Galway merchants (Tribes) kept their lands at this time, and some, including Dominick Browne, Patrick French, and members of the Kirwan and Lynch families, increased their landholdings. Even the Earl of Clanricard, who had fought for the losing (Catholic) side, managed to keep most of his estates through 'negotiations with the enemy' (ibid., 221–3). Many new families were transplanted into Clare at this time, including 'innocent papists' such as the Butlers, who were dispossessed 'Old English' Catholics that were given the choice of 'Hell or Connacht' (Coffey 1993, 122). The Butlers emerged as one of the biggest landowners in and around the region of the new M18 road, with landholdings in Crusheen, Sranagalloon, Gortaficka, Ballyline and Inchicronan, among others. By 1781 Cornet James Butler held c. 13,800 acres of land across 36 townlands in counties Clare and Galway (ibid., 106–10). The penal laws that followed the Williamite War dramatically reduced the amount of land owned by Catholics in Ireland as a whole, but as a result of the earlier transplantations, County Galway had one of the highest proportions of Catholic landholders in the country, at least until the larger landlords, such as the Burkes, Clanricards and Martins, adopted the Protestant faith during the 18th century (Mulloy 1996, 227).

Following the troubled years of the Cromwellian campaign, Ireland witnessed a growth in purely domestic unfortified houses. From the 1660s onwards, the older mosaic of lordships and feudal landholdings that had dominated Ireland was swallowed up by a centralising State, and was replaced by a commercial system of landed estates (Whelan 1997, 68). There was a consequent restructuring of rural settlement and society around the new principal components of landed estates centred on mansion houses—demesne settings or parks. Many of the field divisions that continue to characterise the rural landscape today date to this period—large rectangular pasture fields defined by drystone walls—and are a result of agricultural improvements associated with these large estates and the predominantly English-speaking Protestant landlords that controlled them.

Ashfield House, Co. Galway, was the focus of a demesne located just west of the new M18 road. Little remains of the house or demesne but it is marked on the Grand Jury Map of 1787, though the extent of the estate is not given. It was the residence of John Blakeney in 1783 (Kelly 1996, 253), but it is unclear when the house was built. The road scheme does not impact on the estate—as indicated on the first-edition Ordnance Survey map (1840)—but will pass through land associated with another house marked on the map, Rosehill House. This house did not have an associated demesne, and was no longer extant at the time of the second-edition Ordnance Survey map (1899). The demesne of Ballyline House, Co. Clare, is affected by the new road. The Butler family was given lands in Ballyline under the Cromwellian settlement of the 17th century. However, the area—as depicted in the Down Survey map—does not equate to the townland boundaries indicated on the Ordnance Survey maps, and it appears that the boundaries in this area were altered between the 17th and early 19th centuries. Ballyline House was built c. 1763 by the Butler family and was originally called Millbrooke House, due to the mill that stood nearby (Coffey 1993, 95–6). The house remained the seat of the Butler family until the early 19th century, during which time it was renamed Ballyline House. The house was demolished in the 1920s, but the original piers of the entrance gateway—though altered—are still *in situ*, and some outbuildings and a walled garden survive. The first-edition Ordnance Survey map shows a nursery within the demesne, the site of which will be crossed by the new road (Illus. 1.24). The nursery contained a concentration of trees flanking a narrow laneway, but this was gone by the time of the second-edition Ordnance Survey map. A little further east of the scheme, Cregg Demesne has fared better and the current owners are restoring some of its parkland features (Illus 1.25).

While the affluent classes of the early modern period built mansions and held sway over ordered demesnes, the settlements of the rural poor typically comprised informal clusters of drystone cabins, or *clachans*. These agricultural settlements dotted the Irish landscape and were commonly located on more marginal land, and while many are marked on the first-edition Ordnance Survey maps, they have left little trace on the landscape today. There are a few *clachans* marked in close proximity to the new road on the first-edition maps (1840), in the townlands of Sheeaun, Lurga, Curtaun and Rathwilladoon—all in County Galway. Following the Famine in the 1840s many of these settlements were abandoned, and this is apparent on the late 19th-century second-edition Ordnance Survey maps, by which time many had disappeared or significantly reduced in size. More substantial, mortared and slate-roofed buildings appear at this time, forming dispersed farmsteads. A comparison of the first and second-edition maps also reveals increased land enclosure in County Galway during this period.

There are no *clachans* marked on the first-edition Ordnance Survey maps in the immediate environs of the new road in County Clare. Furthermore, little change was noted in the layout of field boundaries in the county between the earlier and later Ordnance Survey editions. However, the post-Famine landscape in Clare showed a decrease in the number of houses in the study area.

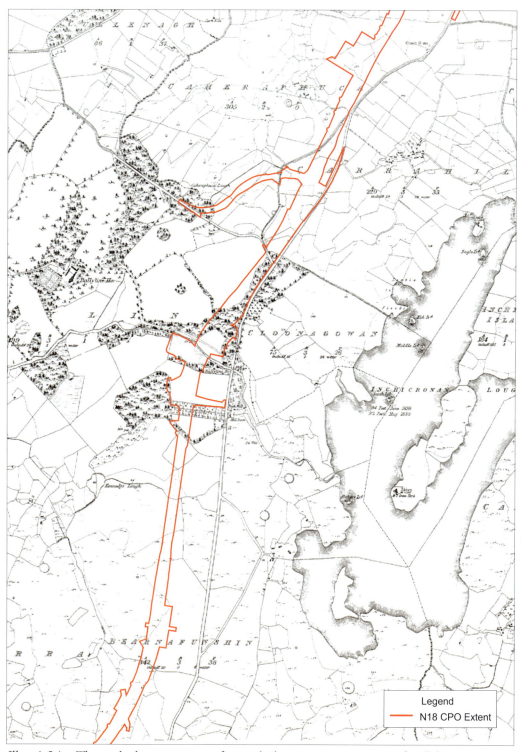

Illus. 1.24—The road scheme traverses a farmtrack that was once an avenue of Ballyline House, now demolished. The first edition of the Ordnance Survey records the house and its demesne landscape (left).

Illus. 1.25—Gate lodge and entrance to Cregg Demesne, east of the road scheme, on the old Gort to Crusheen road.

The townland of Gortaficka, for instance, was more densely inhabited on the first-edition map than on the second-edition, with individual houses shown dotted throughout the townland. By the end of the century, many houses had disappeared while others were shown as open rectangles, indicating that they were no longer roofed.

Finally, one noteworthy feature of 19th-century Ireland that had a direct impact on the area surrounding the new road was the arrival of the railways. Their construction made a lasting impact on the architectural heritage and landscape of the island, comprising an array of engineering works including cuttings, embankments, bridges, viaducts, keepers' cottages, engine sheds, water towers, stations and, of course, railway tracks. The tracks of the 'Athenry and Ennis Junction Railway' lie just to the east of the new road for its entire course, and they almost converge as they pass through the townlands of Curtaun, Lurga and Derry. The line formed part of the 'Waterford Limerick and Western Railway' until 1901 when it amalgamated with the 'Great Southern and Western Railway' (www.westontrack.com/history). After closing in 1963, the line reopened in 2010. A handsome masonry road bridge in rusticated ashlar crosses the tracks at Rathwilladoon, and the nearby railway station is now a private dwelling house (Illus. 1.26). Another, conjoined bridge carries the railway line across the Castlelodge River and a road at Lurga, and a bridge carries the line across the existing N18 road just south of Crusheen.

Illus. 1.26—The 'borderlands' have been a transport and communications corridor in all periods. Rathwilladoon Station, on the original 'Waterford and Limerick Western Railway', is now a private house.

We have characterised the landscape traversed by the new road scheme as 'borderlands' but that is not to suggest that it is merely a no-man's land. The landscape today is peppered with farmsteads and new rural dwelling houses. Apart from major population centres north and south of the scheme, in Ennis and Gort, there are along the way smaller, local communities whose identity is strongly felt and vibrantly expressed in sport, music, seasonal festivals and other voluntary community activities (Illus. 1.27 and 1.28). Some artefacts from the archaeological investigations on the road scheme were exhibited in Clare Museum over several months in 2011 (Illus. 1.29). This book is a further contribution to the shared identity of the communities in the 'borderlands' and to the history of the landscape they inhabit.

1.3—Circumstances and methods

The M18 Gort to Crusheen scheme involved the construction of 44 km of road, including mainline roadworks (22 km), associated side roads (10 km) and access tracks (12 km). The new road is a four-lane motorway with a central barrier. The road bypasses to the west of the town of Gort, Co. Galway and the village of Crusheen, Co. Clare. A total of 43 new structures are proposed for the scheme. These consist of nine road over-bridges, one road under-bridge, two accommodation road over-bridges, two

Illus. 1.27—Community identity is strongly felt in the 'borderlands': detail from the entrance to Crusheen GAA club.

Illus. 1.28—A mural on Tubber National School celebrates the natural and built heritage of the area in vibrant colours.

Illus. 1.29—Archaeological investigations on the new road scheme have contributed to shared identity and history in the region: opening night of a scheme exhibiton in Clare Museum, March 2011 (John Rattigan).

river bridges, a wildlife underpass, and 24 culverts running under the roads. The new route traverses 23 townlands and commences just north of Gort, where a new roundabout has been constructed at Ballinger's Corner, Glenbrack, to connect the bypass to the existing N18. At its conclusion to the south, the new road ties into the Ennis Bypass scheme in Carrowdotia townland, Co. Clare.

The proposed M18 was subjected to an Environmental Impact Assessment by Jacobs Babtie Engineering. The archaeology and cultural history section was compiled by Rob McNaught (Babtie Pettit 2006), which included a full scale geophysical survey carried out by RSKENSR (Bartlett 2004) in addition to the standard paper and field surveys. The paper survey identified 28 sites of potential cultural heritage significance located within c. 100 m of the centreline of the road of which 12 were directly impacted by the road scheme.

The geophysical survey involved magnetometer and magnetic susceptibility surveys along all accessible areas of the route. The survey included recorded coverage of an initial 15 m-wide magnetometer sample strip, and two parallel lines of susceptibility readings. Thirty-seven areas of archaeological potential were identified as part of this geophysical survey. These anomalies were specifically targeted during subsequent archaeological testing (see below). Two similar archaeological sites—ring-ditches—were identified on a long (c. 2 km), whale-backed ridge in Ballyboy (Chapter 5), and it was considered that the ridge potentially contained more sites. A supplementary geophysical survey was carried out on the ridge by Target Geophysics Ltd, but no additional sites were identified.

As a result of the paper survey, field inspections, geophysical survey, and archaeological testing, a total of 22 fully recorded manual licensed excavations were carried out over 36 sites on this section of the M18 route. The archaeological investigations were conducted by Irish Archaeological Consultancy Ltd on behalf of Galway County Council and the National Roads Authority, with Ministerial Directions administered by the National Monuments Service for the (then) Department of Environment, Heritage and Local Government, in consultation with the National Museum of Ireland (Illus. 1.30).

Illus. 1.30—The archaeological investigations were subject to 'Ministerial Directions' in accordance with the National Monuments Acts. Excavation Director Joe Nunan makes an interpretive point on site to Martin Reid of the National Monuments Service.

Phase 1 of the investigations consisted of earthwork, building, and metal-detecting surveys, and test excavations by hand on sites of known or suspected archaeological interest. Test excavations were undertaken by machine at locations of geophysical anomalies of possible archaeological origin. This involved the stripping of 37 areas of up to 50 sq m (15,025 sq m in total). Machine-cut linear test excavations were carried out in all remaining greenfield areas where there was a potential for archaeological features to be found. A total of 137,000 sq m of trenches was mechanically investigated, using 20-tonne excavators under close archaeological supervision. The trenches were generally arranged in a standard testing pattern—i.e. a linear trench along the proposed road centreline with offsets excavated every 10–12.5 m on alternate sides of the centre trench. The test trenches were excavated to determine, as far as reasonably possible, the location, extent, date, character, condition and significance of any surviving archaeological remains impacted by the proposed development. This programme of testing revealed 35 previously unknown archaeological sites, and investigated the three previously recorded monuments (in the *Record of Monuments and Places*) impacted by the new road. These consisted of an enclosure (CL018-017) at Sranagalloon, Co. Clare, a bivallate ringfort (GA128-043) at Curtaun, Co. Galway, and a burnt mound (CL02-143) at Caheraphuca, Co. Clare. Sixteen of these sites were fully investigated during testing and required no further investigation.

Phase 2 of the investigations consisted of excavations to fully investigate any significant archaeological features or deposits discovered during Phase 1. At most of the sites the ground surface was reduced to the interface between natural subsoil and topsoil using a 20-tonne excavator equipped with a flat toothless bucket. The remaining topsoil was removed by the archaeological team with the use of shovels, hoes and trowels in order to expose and identify the archaeological remains. Approximately half of the previously recorded enclosure at Sranagalloon (CL018-017) lay within the footprint of the new road. This area was excavated by hand (Chapter 6). The burnt mound at Rathwilladoon 4 was also dug manually (Chapter 3). A small portion of the outer earthwork of the ringfort at Curtaun (GA128-043) was truncated by the road scheme. (At this point the road passed through the narrow space between the ringfort and the adjacent railway line and hence the unavoidable impact on the ringfort.)

Phase 3 comprised post-excavation analyses and conservation work arising from the investigations and the production of illustrated reports on this work. Radiocarbon dating was carried out by means of AMS (Accelerator Mass Spectrometry) dating of recommended charcoal samples. (AMS dates in this publication are calibrated dates, quoted to a two-sigma or 96% degree of statistical confidence.) Palaeoenvironmental research on a peat core from Caheraphuca Lough was undertaken by Dr Karen Molloy and the Palaeoenvironmental Research Unit, School of Natural Sciences (Botany), at the National University of Ireland, Galway (Chapter 4).

2
MULTIPHASE PREHISTORIC SETTLEMENT AT RATHWILLADOON

by Ed Lyne

with contributions by S Cobain, J Geber, F Sternke, E Grogan and H Roche

Four distinct phases of prehistoric settlement were identified at Rathwilladoon 2 and 3, Co. Galway, represented by a number of earth-cut features, artefacts and palaeoenvironmental remains. A series of radiocarbon dates placed this activity in the Neolithic period, the Chalcolithic period (Copper Age), the Late Bronze Age and the Iron Age.

Rathwilladoon is located in County Galway, just north of the county border with Clare, and the provincial border between Connacht and Munster. The excavation site was about 6.5 km NNE of Crusheen and c. 0.5 km south-east of Tubber, on the south-east-facing slope of a well-drained, low hill. It overlooked low-lying wetlands (formerly a shallow lake) and was sheltered from the prevailing winds by the ridge of the hill rising behind the site (Illus. 2.1). This topographical setting would have

Illus. 2.1—Rathwilladoon 2: general view of the site, looking south-east across the neighbouring wetland area.

Illus. 2.2—Rathwilladoon 2: topsoil from test-pits across the site was sieved to sample for chipped stone tools and other smaller objects.

been conducive to settlement, and undoubtedly accounts for the repeated selection of the site for habitation throughout prehistory. A ringfort (GA128-070) and a cemetery (GA128-069) situated just beyond the limits of excavation, share this hillside location.

The excavation site comprised two areas: Rathwilladoon 2 encompassed an area c. 60 m by 50 m, and contained three chronologically discrete concentrations of features while Rathwilladoon 3 consisted of an area of 20 sq m—approximately 100 m south-west of Rathwilladoon 2—and included a single, isolated feature. Two further archaeological sites were identified in the townland that are discussed elsewhere: a burnt mound at Rathwilladoon 4 (Chapter 3) and an Iron Age metal-working site at Rathwilladoon 5 (Chapter 6).

Before excavations began, 147 test pits (1 m by 1 m) were hand dug across the site of Rathwilladoon 2. These pits were dug until either natural geology or the surface of archaeological features was reached. The removed topsoil was dry-sieved on site and all finds were recorded (Illus. 2.2). A total of 80 prehistoric artefacts were recovered from the test pits, comprising 70 pieces of chert (including seven scrapers), nine pieces of flint, and one piece of possible prehistoric pottery. Most of the stone assemblage comprised waste or debitage items, and the bias towards chert was not surprising given the scarcity of flint in the area. In addition to the prehistoric finds, 159 post-medieval/modern artefacts were recovered from the test pits: these were mainly ceramics, glass and iron objects such as corroded nails.

2.1—Rathwilladoon 2 and 3: excavation results[1]

Phase 1—Neolithic period

The earliest human activity was represented by four pits and a post-hole, clustered together at the eastern edge of the site (Area 3; Illus. 2.3). The principal feature appeared to be the largest pit (Pit M), which contained a significant quantity of worked chert and flint tools and waste material, and sherds of prehistoric pottery. These artefacts were diagnostic of the Early Neolithic period (see 'Artefacts', below). The pit was irregular in shape—possibly due to disturbance by roots—and measured roughly 3 m long by 1.3 m wide and 0.6 m deep. It was probably used for the disposal of waste, perhaps from a nearby stone-working area where tools were being produced. While the smaller pits and the post-hole were probably associated with the large pit, their function is unclear and, collectively, they formed no discernable pattern. Only one of the smaller pits contained artefacts, comprising three chert flakes. No material suitable for radiocarbon dating was recovered from these features.

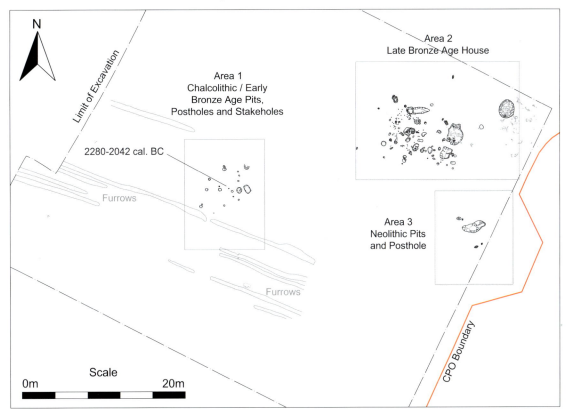

Illus. 2.3—Rathwilladoon 2: plan of excavated features in Areas 1–3.

Phase 2—Chalcolithic period (Copper Age)

The second phase of activity was indicated by three small pits and a series of eight small post-holes and 11 stake-holes (Area 1; Illus. 2.3). While their spatial arrangement revealed no clear pattern,

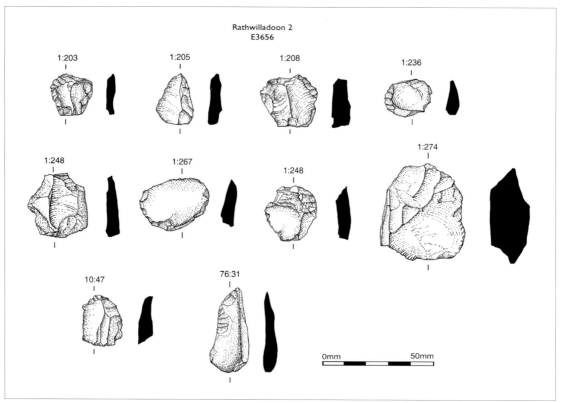

Illus. 2.4—Rathwilladoon 2: selection of chipped stone objects recovered from topsoil (E3656:1), the fill of Pit A (E3656:10) and Pit M (E3656: 76) (Alva MacGowan).

it is tentatively suggested that they represent the earth-cut remains and associated features of a lightly built, oval or sub-rectangular post-built structure. One of the pits (Pit B) had a charcoal-rich primary fill, and was interpreted as a possible hearth. This shallow pit was sub-rectangular in plan, measured c. 1 m long by 0.6 m wide, and contained no artefacts. In contrast, a small, oval pit (Pit A) just west of Pit B produced 58 sherds (representing three vessels) of prehistoric pottery and worked stone—chert flakes, blades, debitage and three convex scrapers (Illus. 2.4)—as well as significant quantities of charred hazelnut shells. Similar material in smaller quantities was found in Pit C—a small, circular pit just north of Pits A and B—and in three of the post-holes and one stake-hole, suggesting that the features were contemporaneous. The majority of the pottery recovered from the various features was identified as Beaker Ware, though some, presumably residual, possible Neolithic sherds were also present.

A radiocarbon date of 2280–2042 BC (UBA-12736) was returned for a charred hazelnut shell in the upper (secondary) fill of Pit A. This date range spans the final years of the Chalcolithic period and the Early Bronze Age. Most of the pottery in both the primary and secondary fills of Pit A was identified as Beaker Ware, but while the upper (secondary) fill also contained 36 pieces of worked chert and debitage, the primary (lower) fill included just a single chert scraper. This indicates two discrete episodes of deposition in the pit: the primary layer only contained domestic waste, while the second layer included both domestic debris and material consistent with an episode, or episodes, of stone tool production. To date, Irish Beaker Ware has only been recovered from Chalcolithic (c. 2450–2200 BC) contexts (Grogan & Roche 2010, 36–8), so it would appear that both episodes of activity at Pit A occurred in the latter years of that period. Ultimately, the features in Area 1 appear to represent a small-scale, Chalcolithic, domestic habitation site.

Phase 3—Late Bronze Age

Late Bronze Age activity was identified at the north-eastern end of the site (Area 2; Illus. 2.3) and consisted of a probable rectangular house and associated features, including a central hearth. The house was represented by a group of eight post-holes that appeared to define the limits of a rectangular space, measuring approximately 5.5 m north-east/south-west by 3.5 m (Illus. 2.5 and 2.6). Charcoal recovered from these (and other) post-holes indicates that the structure was predominantly constructed from oak and ash, and yielded radiocarbon dates of 913–807 BC (UBA-12733) and 928–825 BC (UBA-12734). A further eight post-holes and 78 stake-holes were identified in the interior of the house. The post-holes possibly held roof supports or other internal fixtures, while the stake-holes may have supported part of the wall structure between the posts. Some may have supported internal divisions within the structure or even held timber fixtures or fittings, such as raised sleeping platforms. The stake-holes were mostly arranged inside the proposed

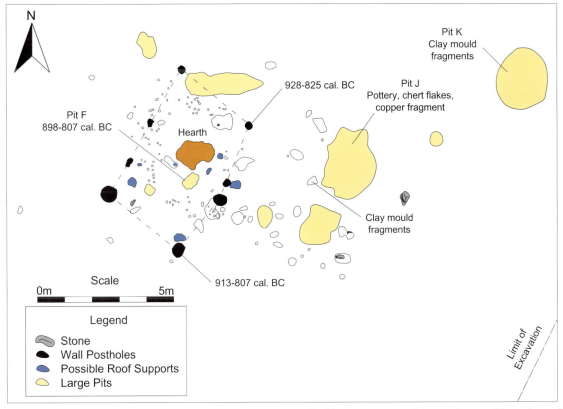

Illus. 2.5—Rathwilladoon 2: plan of the Late Bronze Age building in Area 2, showing the possible outline of a rectangular house (black), a central hearth (red) and associated pits (yellow), post-holes and stake-holes.

Illus. 2.6—Rathwilladoon 2: outline of the Late Bronze Age house superimposed on the ground surface, as indicated by the arrangement of post-holes, looking south.

north-west, north-east and south-east wall-lines, with a notable absence along the south-west wall. The central hearth-pit measured 1.25 m by 0.6 m in plan and was 0.4 m deep (Illus. 2.5). It was identified by its charcoal-rich fills and clear evidence of *in situ* burning, in the form of a burnt clay base. Five small pits were situated within the structure. One of these (Pit F) contained a rubbing stone that appeared to have been deliberately placed, face down, in the pit. Charcoal from this pit returned a radiocarbon date of 898–807 BC (UBA-12732). A further six post-holes and three stake-holes were situated in close proximity to the rectangular structure externally, and may have held additional wall or roof supports. Alternatively, these may have held a free-standing windbreak, or part of an external superstructure ancillary to the main building—i.e. a lean-to or a roofless pen. A limited amount of worked chert, mainly debitage, was recovered from the structure, along with burnt animal bone, charcoal and charred cereal grains/hazelnuts.

Further features were found in the environs of the house, in the form of dispersed stake-holes and post-holes and a series of three large and 13 small pits (Illus. 2.5). These features are likely to have been associated with the house, or with activities carried out around it. Some probably functioned as waste or storage pits. Two of the large pits contained significant finds. Prehistoric pottery fragments, chert flakes and a small copper fragment were recovered from the charcoal-rich fill of Pit J, while a chert flake and five clay mould fragments were identified in Pit K. A further two possible clay mould fragments were recovered from one of the small pits (C134), along with fragmented animal bones.

The recovery of a copper fragment and a number of clay mould fragments may suggest that metal-working was carried out on site.

Phase 4—Iron Age

A shallow curvilinear cut with a charcoal-rich fill was identified at Rathwilladoon 3. This isolated feature—approximately 100 m south-west of Rathwilladoon 2—may represent part of the footing trench for a lightly built circular structure, but its full extent could not be ascertained due to modern agricultural activity in the area that had destroyed most of the site. The feature measured 5.7 m long, 0.3 m wide and 0.09 m deep (Illus. 2.7), but it is projected that the original structure would have had a diameter of at least 10 m, based on the curve of the surviving cut.

No artefacts were recovered from the feature, but charcoal consisted of hazel, alder/hazel, ash and Maloideae species (hawthorn/rowan/crab apple). Hazel and ash were commonly used as structural timbers—for wattling or light posts—while hawthorn, rowan, and crab apple are more likely to have been selected as firewood. The mixture of typical building materials and firewood in the charcoal assemblage raises the possibility that the structure was burned down, either accidentally or perhaps deliberately as part of a ritual act. The symbolic firing of a domestic residence as a 'deliberate act to end the life of the building' has been argued for a number of Bronze Age houses in England (Brück 1999, 154). It is also suggested that, given the variety of species, the charcoal assemblage may

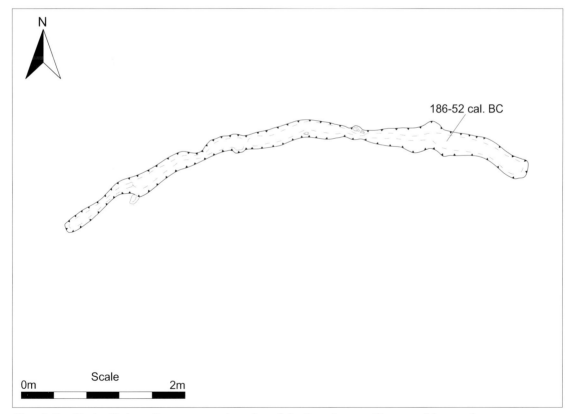

Illus. 2.7—Rathwilladoon 3: post-excavation plan of the Iron Age curvilinear cut/slot trench.

represent rake-out material from a domestic hearth that found its way into the foundation trench of the structure (see 'Charcoal and plant macrofossil remains', below). Given the quantity of charcoal in the trench, however, this could only have occurred after the superstructure had been removed.

A charcoal sample returned a radiocarbon date of 186−52 BC (UBA-12731), placing the feature in the La Tène Iron Age. The exact nature of the structure is unclear, but it may have been a domestic or ritual building.

2.2—Artefacts

The most significant artefacts recovered from Rathwilladoon were worked stones and pottery sherds. The stone assemblage was dominated by chert flakes and included a significant quantity of debitage, indicative of on-site stone tool production. Most of the worked stone was diagnostic of the earlier Neolithic period, but some Late Neolithic/Chalcolithic/Early Bronze Age pieces were identified, and a few possibly date to the Mesolithic period. Neolithic and Beaker pottery was found in significant amounts, with at least 13 individual vessels represented. The pottery assemblage is particularly important as few prehistoric wares have been recorded in this region. Clay moulds were also recovered, suggestive of on-site metal-working activities. A number of post-medieval/modern artefacts were also recovered, mainly from the topsoil, including ceramics, clay pipes and metal finds. These are not discussed further here but are catalogued in the CD that accompanies this book.

Worked and chipped stone
by Farina Sternke

A total of 266 lithics were retrieved during excavations at Rathwilladoon. These consisted of 161 pieces of worked chert, 33 pieces of worked flint, six flakes of quartz crystal, five of siltstone/mudstone, and two used pieces of sandstone. In addition, 58 unworked pieces of chert and one of flint were recovered. The worked assemblage comprises seven cores, nine chunks, 12 blades, 86 flakes, 75 pieces of debitage, 16 retouched artefacts, and two macro tools—a fragmented hammer stone and a broken and burnt rubbing stone, or 'mano'. The retouched artefacts include nine convex end scrapers, a possible concave end scraper, two abandoned arrowhead preforms and one possible invasively retouched form or backed blade. The lithics survive in variable conditions—46 were incomplete and 84 cherts and 12 flints bore the remnants of a cortex. The lustre observed on 12 artefacts is a result of their exposure to heat: they were not directly burnt in a fire but were possibly strewn around a hearth. Many of the topsoil finds included plough damage, making a positive identification of retouched artefacts problematic.

Almost half of the assemblage was recovered from topsoil; however, 95 pieces derived from two Neolithic pits (Phase 1; Area 3); 44 came from Chalcolithic/Early Bronze Age (Phase 2; Area 1) pits, post/stake-holes and a possible hearth (Pit B); and nine pieces were retrieved from features associated with the Late Bronze Age house (Phase 3; Area 2).

The majority of the assemblage is typologically and technologically diagnostic and predominantly dates to the first half of the Neolithic period. Among these Neolithic artefacts were three flakes from a polished mudstone axehead and two attempted arrowheads—one of chert that was converted to a convex end scraper and another leaf-shaped flint example that was left unfinished. The macro tools—hammer stone and mano—probably also date to this period. At least one bipolar pebble flint core and two small scrapers appear to date to the Late Neolithic/Early Bronze Age (or Chalcolithic period). It is possible that one dual opposed platform core and several blades and flakes, as well as an invasively retouched form or backed blade, represent residual Early Mesolithic material.

The significant quantity of debitage present—predominantly in the Neolithic pits (Phase 1)—indicates that *in situ* knapping and tool resharpening took place at the site. The rubbing stone/mano may form the upper, grinding element of a saddle quern, like the example that was found in the nearby townland of Monreagh (Chapter 3), and indicates small-scale cereal processing. Indeed, the stone artefacts recovered from Rathwilladoon are probably associated with domestic tasks carried out in and around the environs of a prehistoric house or houses.

Prehistoric pottery
by Eoin Grogan and Helen Roche

The site produced 86 sherds of prehistoric pottery (plus 29 fragments), which represent at least three Early Neolithic vessels, 10 Chalcolithic Beakers, and fragments of a clay mould. The pottery was recovered from pits and post-holes and constitutes domestic debris.

Early Neolithic pottery
The three Early Neolithic vessels were represented by 22 sherds and three fragments, weighing 195 g. These comprised two rim-sherds, six neck sherds, one shoulder sherd and 13 body sherds. The 13 sherds from Vessel 1 were retrieved from the fill of a large pit (Pit M) in Area 3 (Illus. 2.3) and are generally well preserved, although there is a reddish, iron-rich deposit on the surfaces and edge breaks. This deposit was not noted in the pit so it appears that the pottery had been in a layer/midden subject to percolating, iron-rich water for some considerable time prior to its redeposition in the pit. The hillside site in Rathwilladoon is generally well drained, so this contact with percolating mineral water presumably occurred elsewhere, probably in the wetlands at the foot of the hill. Vessel 1 is a large, Early Neolithic carinated bowl of fine, dark grey fabric with quartzite inclusions. It has a rounded everted rim; a high (at least 53 mm) concave neck and small step shoulder, and had an external rim diameter of 270 mm (maximum). These forms (Case 1961: 'Dunmurry-Ballymarlagh styles'; Sheridan 1995: 'classic' carinated bowls) are widely dated to c. 4000–3600 BC.

The remainder of the Early Neolithic pottery (Groups X and I) was in a fragmentary and worn or much worn condition, with no feature sherds preserved (i.e. rims, bases or shoulders). It came from the fills of a stake-hole and a pit (Pit A) in Area 1. Both of these features also contained Beaker pottery and a Chalcolithic/Early Bronze Age radiocarbon date of 2280–2042 BC (UBA-12736) was returned for a charred hazelnut shell in Pit A. It should be noted that the condition of these fragments prevented a definitive identification and, while their fabric and firing are more typical of Early Neolithic pottery, it is possible that they derive from Beaker-period vessels. A single sherd of Early Neolithic pottery, possibly from Vessel 1, also came from the topsoil.

There is little recorded Early Neolithic pottery from the region, although extensive Neolithic settlement is indicated by the distribution of megalithic tombs and stone axeheads (see Chapter 1 'Neolithic period'). A small pottery assemblage came from the court tomb at Parknabinnia on the

Burren, Co. Clare (Jones & Gilmer 2000), and there are two sherds from the hillfort at Mooghaun, Co. Clare (Grogan 2005a, 323–7). All of the Early Neolithic pottery from Rathwilladoon represents domestic debris, and sooting on the outer faces of some Vessel 1 sherds indicates that the pot was probably used for cooking. One sherd (Group X) included more definite cooking evidence in the form of a blackened accretion on its inner surface, perhaps suggesting another function for the pot, such as a brazier or even a means to transport fire or hot embers.

Beaker pottery

The site yielded 62 sherds of Chalcolithic pottery, representing at least eight fine Beakers and two domestic Beaker vessels. These included 10 neck sherds, one base-angle sherd, one belly sherd and 47 body sherds (plus 26 fragments) with a total weight of 189 g. The bulk of the assemblage (67%) came from two fills of Pit A, in Area 1. Sherds representing three vessels were retrieved from the two fills, which also produced what appears to be Early Neolithic pottery (see above). The remaining Beaker pottery came from the fills of four nearby post-holes and a pit (Pit J) in Area 2 (Phase 3).

The pottery is well fired and of good quality, consisting of worn or much worn sherds. It comprises cream-to-red buff-coloured fabric, commonly with a darker core, which is typical of much Beaker pottery. Fine inclusions of crushed quartzite occur in all of the vessels. The presence of so many vessels represented by a small assemblage (6.2 sherds per pot) is indicative of domestic activity, and evidence of burning on some of the sherds suggests that the pots were used for cooking. Again, this sooting occurred on the inner surface of the sherds so might represent an alternative function.

Although only limited reconstruction is possible, the fine vessels appear to have soft S-shaped profiles. One of the vessels (Vessel 3) was decorated with scored horizontal lines alternating with blank zones. This arrangement forms one of the most common Irish Beaker designs. Examples have been found at Knowth, Co. Meath (Eogan 1984, 266–80, figs 94 and 100–1), Dalkey Island, Co. Dublin, (Liversage 1968, 72, fig. 8), and various sites at Lough Gur, Co. Limerick (Ó Ríordáin 1954, 277–8, pls 36–7; Grogan & Eogan 1987, 407, fig. 46). The only other decoration is a possible lozenge motif on one group of sherds (Group IV). These forms and decorative styles have generally been assigned to Clarke's European Bell Beaker, or his Wessex/Middle Rhine types (Clarke, D L 1970). More recently, following reviews by, for example, Lanting & van der Waals (1972), there has been a greater recognition of the regional development of Beaker Ware (Grogan & Roche 2010, 36–8). Case's (1993; 1995) simpler threefold scheme, and its specific application to the Irish material, provides a straightforward medium for insular comparison. The formal horizontally zoned decoration on Vessel 3 suggests that the Rathwilladoon pottery belongs to his 'Style 2' and should date to c. 2450–2300 BC.

There is little recorded Beaker pottery from this region. An extensive settlement complex at Parknabinnia, Roughan Hill, on the Burren, Co. Clare, produced a small assemblage of both fine and domestic vessels (Jones 1998; Roche 1999). At least one fine vessel is comparable to Vessel 3 from Rathwilladoon. Limited quantities of Beaker also came from Mooghaun, Coolnatullagh, and the portal tomb at Poulnabrone, all in Co. Clare (Grogan 2005a, 323–7; Eogan 1998; Lynch 1994).

Clay moulds and metal-working

Fragments of shaped and fired clay were recovered from the fills of two pits (Pit K and C134) just east of the Late Bronze Age structure in Area 2 (Phase 3; Illus. 2.5). These appear to be the outer casings of clay moulds, however, only very small areas of the finer inner matrix—that might indicate the type of artefact being cast—is preserved. This technology was principally for the manufacture of copper-alloy artefacts. It was introduced in the latter part of the Middle Bronze Age (c. 1400–1300 BC) for casting rapiers, but was not in general use for other objects until the Late Bronze Age (c. 1100 BC). The technical process did not develop significantly until the medieval period and, as there are no diagnostic features on these pieces, it is not possible to indicate their date. Perhaps, significantly, a small amorphous copper-alloy fragment was recovered from another pit (Pit J), also east of the structure. The fragment (7 mm by 5.5 mm) formed no identifiable object, but was retrieved from the same context as a Beaker sherd and a chert flake. The identification of a copper-alloy fragment and clay moulds indicates that metal-working was being carried out on, or near to the site over a long timeframe as, while the copper-alloy fragment and the pot sherd could be contemporary, the Beaker sherd and the clay moulds are not from the same period.

2.3—Environmental remains

Environmental evidence in the form of charcoal, plant macrofossil remains and animal bone was recovered from archaeological features in all four phases of activity at Rathwilladoon 2 and 3. This evidence provides insights into building materials and fuel sources, the diet of the occupants, and the composition of local woodlands.

Charcoal and plant macrofossil remains
by Sarah Cobain

A total of 51 bulk soil samples were analysed for charcoal remains and six for plant macrofossil species. Two of the Neolithic pits (Phase 1, Area 3) had relatively charcoal-rich fills that contained inclusions of oak, ash, elder, alder/hazel, hazel, yew, elm, wild/bird cherry and blackthorn/sloe (Table 2.1). This probably represents hearth rake-out material that was deliberately discarded into waste pits.

The three Chalcolithic pits that contained charcoal (Phase 2, Area 1), had a mixed assemblage of oak, ash, hazel, elm, alder/hazel, yew, elder and alder—but only oak and ash were present in all three pits. Hazelnut shells were recovered from two of those pits, while one contained a single grain of wheat (Table 2.1). This charcoal and macrofossil material is again indicative of rake-out waste from a domestic hearth, which has been disposed of in pits.

A number of features associated with the Late Bronze Age house contained charcoal (Phase 3, Area 2), including post-holes, stake-holes, pits and a hearth (Table 2.2). Oak, ash and alder/hazel were represented in all of those features, while most included yew, hazel and Maloideae species (hawthorn, rowan and crab apple). Elm and alder were also present to a much lesser degree. (Disease may have caused periodic decreases in elm throughout prehistory, though none is as strongly defined as the 'Elm Decline' of the early fourth millennium BC.) The widest variety of wood types came from the post-holes that defined the rectangular structure, and included charcoals from Scots pine, wayfaring tree, wild/bird cherry and spindle tree. Those post-holes also contained two carbonised grains of barley, one hazelnut shell and a bird cherry pip, as well as evidence of nodding smartweed.

Table 2.1—Wood types present in charcoals sampled from Rathwilladoon 2 and 3 (Maloideae species include hawthorn, rowan and crab apple), and plant macrofossils recovered (by number of specimens).

Charcoal type	Neolithic pits (Phase 1)		Chalcolithic pits (Phase 2)			Iron Age ditch (Phase 4)
	Pit L	**Pit M**	**C5**	**C7**	**C9**	
Ash	Yes	Yes	Yes	Yes	Yes	Yes
Oak	Yes	Yes	Yes	Yes	Yes	—
Hazel	Yes	Yes	—	—	Yes	Yes
Elm	Yes	Yes	Yes	—	—	—
Alder/hazel	—	Yes	—	Yes	—	Yes
Yew	—	Yes	Yes	—	Yes	—
Elder	—	Yes	—	Yes	—	—
Alder	—	—	—	Yes	—	—
Wild/bird cherry	—	Yes	—	—	—	—
Blackthorn/sloe	—	Yes	—	—	—	—
Maloideae species	—	—	—	—	—	Yes
Macrofossil species						
Hazelnut shells	—	—	3	—	108	—
Wheat	—	—	1	—	—	—

Carbonised cereal grains of indeterminate species and a wild cherry pip were found in a post-hole just east of the structure, and blackthorn/sloe charcoal was recovered from a nearby pit. Most of the charcoal and macrofossil material in the post-holes and stake-holes was probably deposited through a combination of natural silting and deliberate backfilling after the posts/stakes had been removed. Two post-holes, however, contained charcoal from single species—100% oak and 100% ash—suggesting that the posts that had stood within them were burnt *in situ*. It is likely that these posts formed part of a structure, as both oak and ash are anatomically dense woods with a fine grain, making them strong and tough. These wood types were commonly sought for construction purposes. The feature interpreted as a hearth was located centrally within the structure and comprised a scorched clay surface. The charcoal-rich fill of this feature included main fuel types (oak and ash) and several minor species, which could have served as kindling (hazel, yew, Maloideae), which may support its identification as a hearth. Several pits were located within the structure, each of which contained fewer than 35 fragments of charcoal. This low charcoal count suggests that they may have been storage pits that were subsequently backfilled when the structure went out of use. During this process residual charcoal from within the structure could have accumulated/silted into the pits. A similar course of events may account for limited quantities of charcoal finding its way into some of the external pits, although others had charcoal-rich fills that suggest they were waste pits for rake-out material from hearths.

The curvilinear Iron Age cut (Rathwilladoon 3; Illus. 2.7) yielded charcoals of ash, hazel, alder/hazel and Maloideae species from its only fill (Table 2.1). This charcoal assemblage included a

Table 2.2—Wood types present in charcoals sampled from the Late Bronze Age structure and associated features at Rathwilladoon 2 (Phase 3) (Maloideae species include hawthorn, rowan and crab apple), and plant macrofossils recovered (by number of specimens).

Late Bronze Age structure (Phase 3)							
Charcoal	External post-holes	Internal post-holes	Structural stake-holes	Internal hearth	Internal pits	Other post-holes/ stake-holes	Other pits
Ash	Yes	Yes	Yes	Yes	Yes	Yes	Yes
Oak	Yes	Yes	Yes	Yes	Yes	Yes	Yes
Alder/hazel	Yes	Yes	Yes	Yes	Yes	Yes	Yes
Yew	Yes	Yes	—	—	Yes	Yes	Yes
Maloideae species	Yes	—	Yes	Yes	—	Yes	Yes
Hazel	Yes	—	—	Yes	Yes	Yes	—
Elm	Yes	—	—	Yes	—	—	—
Alder	Yes	—	—	—	—	—	Yes
Wild/bird cherry	Yes	—	—	—	—	—	—
Scots pine	Yes	—	—	—	—	—	—
Wayfaring tree	Yes	—	—	—	—	—	—
Spindle tree	Yes	—	—	—	—	—	—
Blackthorn/ sloe	—	—	—	—	—	—	Yes
Macrofossil species							
Hazelnut shells	1	—	—	—	—	—	—
Barley	2	—	—	—	—	—	—
Indet. grain	—	—	—	—	—	5	—
Nodding smartweed	2	—	—	—	—	—	—
Wild cherry	—	—	—	—	—	1	—
Bird cherry	1	—	—	—	—	—	—

dominant fuel wood (ash) and probable kindling material, and possibly represents rake-out waste from a domestic hearth which was disposed of in the foundation trench of the possible structure. This could only have occurred, however, after the superstructure had been removed. Alternatively, a structure built from ash and hazel may have burnt *in situ*. This may have occurred accidentally due to the spread of fire from a domestic hearth, or may have been a deliberate act.

The charcoal remains suggest that the woodland surrounding the site would consist of an oak-ash climax community consisting of hazel, birch, oak, ash, wayfaring tree, Scots pine, Maloideae species (hawthorn/rowan/crab apple), wild/bird cherry, blackthorn/sloe, elm and yew. The evidence of alder and elder charcoal indicates a more wetland environment, possibly downslope in the same location as the present day wetland.

The plant macrofossils indicate possible cereal processing to produce food such as bread, porridges and stews (though a larger assemblage of seeds would be required to create a more accurate picture).

The presence of carbonised hazelnut shells and wild and bird cherry pips indicates the hand collection and consumption of fruits and nuts, which would have added extra nutrients, and especially vitamins, to the diet.

Animal bone
by Jonny Geber

A total of 1,135 burnt animal bone fragments (383.95 g) were found in 22 features at Rathwilladoon 2 (none from Rathwilladoon 3, Phase 4), but only 88 fragments (108.06 g) could be identified. These were dominated by cattle bones (81 fragments; 79.08 g), followed by caprovines (sheep/goat) (six fragments; 27.95 g) and pig (one fragment; 1.03 g). The majority of the bones were found in the fills of post-holes and stake-holes (264.04 g), followed by pits (78.34 g) and hearths (41.57 g). The presence of bones in these types of features have previously been interpreted as remnants of discarded food waste from occupation on the site, which have percolated into the soil due to human and/or animal activity within the structure they supported. Alternatively, they may represent ritual deposits in the structural foundations.

2.4—Discussion

The archaeological features recorded at Rathwilladoon represent four discrete phases of settlement activity dating from the Neolithic, Chalcolithic, Late Bronze Age and Iron Age periods, reflecting the repeated selection of the site for human settlement throughout prehistory. This was presumably due to the suitability of the site for habitation—on the south-east-facing slope of a hill overlooking a shallow lake (now wetland), and sheltered from the prevailing winds.

Phase 1—Neolithic period

The first phase of activity consisted of four pits and a post-hole (Area 3). The key feature in this group was the largest pit (Pit M), which contained a large quantity of worked stone and some pottery. These artefacts were typologically and technologically diagnostic of the early part of the Neolithic period and, in the absence of any material suitable for radiocarbon testing, provided the date for this archaeological horizon.

The large amount of debitage, in addition to broken axehead fragments in Pit M, suggests that it was used for dumping waste material from a nearby stone-working site. This indicates the presence of a Neolithic settlement in close proximity. Sternke (above, 2.2) argues that the lithics are probably associated with domestic tasks carried out in and around the environs of a prehistoric house. Such a settlement was not found within the confines of the new road, but probably lies just beyond, perhaps to the south-east, closer to the edge of the former lake. The pottery from Pit M derives from a large, Early Neolithic carinated bowl, dating to c. 3900–3600 BC. Some sherds included blackened accretions indicative of cooking, further supporting the argument for a nearby Early Neolithic domestic settlement. Of note is the apparent redeposition of the pottery sherds into the pit. The surfaces and broken edges of the pot (Vessel 1) were coated with an iron-rich deposit that appears to have formed due to water percolation while the sherds were in a highly organic and/or wet soil environment for a considerable period of time. Evidently the pottery was later removed from this original, mineral-rich context/midden and redeposited in the pit.

One interesting aspect of the investigations at Rathwilladoon concerns the overall lithic assemblage retrieved from across the various areas of excavation. The majority of diagnostic pieces recovered from the excavated features in all areas (including topsoil and test-pits) were characteristic of the Early Neolithic period. This could imply that the later inhabitants of Rathwilladoon used relatively few stone tools, or were perhaps disposing of them more carefully. Alternatively, perhaps they were re-using Neolithic tools that they found in the environs of their settlement, providing an early example of opportunistic recycling.

Prior to this excavation, little evidence for Neolithic settlement activity had been recorded in the environs of the new M18 road—the nearest being on and around Roughan Hill in the Burren (Jones 2004, 51–4; see Chapter 1 'Neolithic period'). Consequently, this site makes a significant contribution to our knowledge of the period in the north Clare/south Galway region.

Phase 2—Chalcolithic period

The second phase of activity was represented by three small pits and a series of small post-holes and stake-holes (Area 1). A radiocarbon date range of 2280–2042 BC (UBA-12736) from a charred hazelnut shell spanned the Chalcolithic period and the Early Bronze Age. However, the artefacts recovered from these features (Beaker Ware), appear to favour the earlier part of this date range.

The post- and stake-holes, while reflecting human activity, did not make up any obvious pattern, though it is tentatively suggested that a north/south aligned oval or sub-rectangular structure is discernible. This structure would have measured c. 3.2 m wide and 4.9 m in length. The limited artefactual material recovered from the post-holes suggests that they may represent the remains of a lightly built Chalcolithic period structure. If the post-holes do define such a structure, then all of the nearby pits were located outside the building on its eastern side. One of the pits (Pit B) was rich in charcoal and may represent the remains of an outdoor hearth.

Another of the pits (Pit A) produced significant quantities of pottery fragments and worked stone—chert flakes, blades, debitage and three convex scrapers—as well as large amounts of charred hazelnut shells. Similar material in smaller quantities was found in some of the other features. Most of the pottery was identified as Beaker Ware, with only a few possible Neolithic sherds present. However, most of the worked stone would not be out of place in a Neolithic assemblage. This may reflect the fact that many of the pieces were not particularly diagnostic or—as discussed—may indicate the recycling of abandoned Neolithic tools at a later time. It has been established that Early Neolithic activity had occurred virtually on the same site (c. 30 m east), so it is plausible that residual material from this earlier horizon was scattered about the later site, and subsequently found its way into later contexts.

Pit A included two distinct fills that reflected two discrete episodes of use or dumping, and a clear division was observed in the type of stone artefacts recovered from each (the pottery from both fills represented three vessels). The primary fill yielded a single chert scraper and 30 sherds of pottery. The secondary fill, however, produced 36 pieces of chert—flakes, blades, scrapers and debitage—and 28 sherds of pottery. It would appear then, that the primary layer only contained domestic waste, while the second layer included material consistent with an episode, or episodes, of stone tool production—i.e. industrial waste in addition to domestic debris.

The environmental remains from this area (Area 1) were indicative of rake-out from a domestic hearth, which had been disposed of into the pits. There was evidence to suggest that wheat and hazelnuts formed part of the diet of the inhabitants, however, as only one carbonised wheat grain was recovered, it would appear that cereal processing was taking place elsewhere. Hazelnuts would have been gathered from the surrounding area and either eaten raw or mixed into salads or porridges (Mabey 2007, 44).

In conclusion, the features and finds in this area probably represent the remnants of a Chalcolithic house/hut site. Broad regional comparisons can be made with Ross Island, Co. Kerry; Lough Gur, Co. Limerick and particularly Parknabinnia, in the Burren, Co. Clare, about 15 km WSW of the site. Parknabinnia produced sherds of a fine pot that was very similar to one of the vessels (Vessel 3) from Rathwilladoon. That site consisted of a field system, wedge tombs and at least one Beaker-period farmstead (Jones & Gilmer 2000) and provides a window into the broader Chalcolithic landscape of north Clare/south Galway beyond the immediate environs of the excavation area.

Phase 3—Late Bronze Age

The third phase of activity comprised a large and complex arrangement of post-holes, stake-holes and pits (Area 2) that appear to represent a rectangular domestic structure (5.5 m by 3.5 m) with a central hearth and associated internal and external features. Charcoal from three of these features provided dates ranging between the late 10th and the late ninth centuries BC (UBA-12732–4), placing the activity in the Late Bronze Age.

While the clearest pattern that emerges from the cluster of post- and stake-holes appears to be a defined rectangular space, this is by no means certain. It must be considered that the post-holes could all have been internal with perhaps an outer wall of mud, which of course would not survive. In this case the structure could originally have been larger, and might even have been circular or oval in plan, as would be more typical at this time. However, as no evidence remains for this, our interpretation can only be based on the surviving post-holes, and these suggest a rectangular plan as the most likely. As a site with a rectangular Bronze Age structure Rathwilladoon (Area 2) is unusual but not unique. Doody's (2000) study of excavated Bronze Age houses in Ireland found that 87% of his sample were round, but that leaves 13% that were not.

One of the pits within the house contained what appeared to have been a deliberately deposited rubbing stone, or mano, which would have been used with a saddle quern, suggesting that small-scale food processing (grain, seeds or nuts) was carried out on site. This object may have been deliberately left behind when the house was abandoned, perhaps symbolising the end of the lifecycle of the building. It may be significant that the rubbing stone was placed with its working face down. This is a trend noticed at a number of other sites, including a Late Bronze Age enclosure at Stamullin, Co. Meath (Ní Lionáin 2007). Of four saddle querns recovered at this site, three appeared to have been deliberately deposited face down, suggesting that this form of symbolic deposition was an accepted and widespread way of decommissioning grinding stones. With the aid of ethnographic studies, research in England (Brück 1999) has explored the relationship between the lifecycles of Bronze Age houses and their inhabitants, evidenced by the deliberate deposition of 'odd objects' within those structures, not only at key moments in the lifecycle of the house—i.e. construction, renovation and abandonment—but also as the demographic, social and economic circumstances of a site's occupants changed over time—e.g. birth, marriage or crop failure. Among the more common objects used for these symbolic depositions were quern-stones and rubbing stones—essential for the production of food and therefore a potent symbol of life, fertility and productivity—although stranger depositions recorded in England include the skeleton of a pregnant cow, a group of five dog skulls and a chalk phallus. While some 'odd objects' were buried in pits and post-holes, others were left on the ground surfaces of abandoned huts. Brück (1999, 154) argues that, rather than forming an inadvertent component of abandonment refuse, these artefacts provide evidence for culturally specific abandonment practices, in which special 'closing deposits' were made as a means of formally ending or transforming the relationship between the building/its dead inhabitant(s) and the rest of the settlement's kin group.

A wide range of wood species was identified in the charcoal assemblage from the post-holes that defined the structure. Two post-holes, however, contained just one species each (ash and oak) suggesting that those posts may have burnt *in situ*. Both of these species were popular for construction material in prehistory, being strong, tough timbers that would form sturdy structures with considerable life spans. While the apparent burning of the structure may have been accidental, it could also have formed part of a closing rite, a 'deliberate act to end the life of the building', as has been postulated for a number of English Bronze Age houses (ibid.).

Two charred grains of barley, a bird cherry pip and a charred hazelnut shell were recovered from the site, in addition to burnt cattle and caprovine bones. This suggests that beef, lamb/mutton and barley products—bread, porridge, stew thickeners—formed at least part of the diet, supplemented by the seasonal collection of cherries and nuts. Barley could also have been used to make beer which, in addition to its calorific and mineral properties, would have been consumed for social purposes, just as it is today (Galloway 1991, 87).

The recovery of clay mould fragments suggests that copper/bronze objects were being cast on site, although the moulds were not complete enough to suggest what these items were. Bronze casting in clay moulds is a feature of the Late Bronze Age, but only a small number of metal-working sites have been identified. During the period many high-quality weapons and ornaments of bronze and gold were being produced across Ireland. The final part of this period is sometimes referred to as the Dowris Phase, named after the Dowris hoard from County Offaly (Eogan 1964; Waddell 2000, 225). One characteristic feature of this phase is production, dispersal and deposition—sometimes in hoards—of high quality metal-work. The evidence for metal-working at Rathwilladoon (Area 2) was slight, but the site may have been involved in the small-scale production of copper/bronze artefacts for local use.

Phase 4—Iron Age

The final phase of prehistoric activity consisted of a single isolated archaeological feature (Rathwilladoon 3) radiocarbon-dated to 186–52 BC (UBA–12731) in the La Tène Iron Age. This feature consisted of a shallow curvilinear cut with a charcoal-rich fill. This is possibly the surviving part of a footing trench for a lightly built circular building. Based on an extrapolation of the existing curve, the diameter would have been at least 10 m. Alternatively, the trench may not have formed a complete circle, and perhaps represents a less permanent structure such as a windbreak or a drying rack. Charcoal from the cut included a variety of wood species, and may represent rake-out from a domestic hearth that was disposed of and silted into the foundation trench following the abandonment of the building and the removal or decay of its superstructure. The presence of both structural and hearth/kindling wood types in the charcoal assemblage may, however, indicate the deliberate or accidental destruction of the structure by fire. Those wood types, in conjunction with the curvilinear trench, present a case for the structure having been a domestic house, but the disturbed nature of the site makes any interpretation tentative.

Little is known of Iron Age buildings or domestic activity in Ireland, though more evidence is emerging due to the increasing number of excavations in recent decades. Recent research (Becker et al. 2008) identified only 16 sites of Iron Age date in County Clare, and just seven in County Galway, but none of these could be described as definite habitation sites as they include no evidence for structures. The paucity of evidence emphasises the importance of Rathwilladoon 3, despite the limited information that could be gleaned from the site. A metal-working site of similar Iron Age date was also identified during excavations in the townland (Rathwilladoon 5; Chapter 6), and it is possible this was associated with the activity at Rathwilladoon 3.

Taking the phases of Rathwilladoon individually, each of them contributes significantly to our understanding of the prehistory of the north Clare/south Galway region where, to date, relatively few prehistoric habitation sites are known. Taken collectively, these four separate phases of activity comprise a rare example of a single location being re-inhabited over a period of some 4,000 years. This would imply that the site continued to be a suitable location for habitation over the millennia, and stresses the importance placed on site selection. If one takes into account the possible Mesolithic tools found on the site and the ringfort and cemetery located just beyond the limits of excavation, that time-span stretches considerably.

Notes

1   Excavation No. E3656; Director Ed Lyne; NGR 141360 194246 & 141275 194125; height 28–31 m OD; parish of Beagh; barony of Kiltartan; County Galway.

3
BURNT MOUNDS: KITCHEN SINKS OF THE BRONZE AGE?

by Shane Delaney, David Bayley, Ed Lyne, Joe Nunan and Siobhán McNamara
with contributions by S Mandal, E O Carroll, S Cobain, J Geber and F Sternke

Burnt mounds are not as visibly appealing as the megalithic tombs, ringforts and castles that dot the Irish landscape. They are, however, the island's most commonly excavated monument, and the number of identified examples increases significantly every year. Few major road projects are completed without encountering one, or often several, of these enigmatic monuments. The Gort to Crusheen section of the M18 road was no exception. In total, 26 burnt mound sites were excavated along that route, some of which included more than one mound (Illus. 3.1). But what are burnt mounds? What do they look like? Where are they found? When were they built, and why? These general questions are addressed, before discussing the evidence for the burnt mounds excavated between Gort and Crusheen.

Illus. 3.1—Caheraphuca 1: burnt mound site during excavation looking south-west (AirShots Ltd).

3.1—Burnt mounds: what, where, when and why?

Over a decade ago upwards of 7,000 burnt mounds were recorded in Ireland (Power et al. 1997), and in excess of 1,000 more have since been excavated, mostly during development-led archaeological investigations. Despite the information gleaned from these excavations, no definitive, or universally accepted, interpretation of their function has been forthcoming.

Ó Néill (2004, 82) identified burnt mounds as the apparatus and by-product of pyrolithic technology. This technology involved heating or boiling water by placing fire-heated stones into troughs of water. Surviving burnt mounds usually contain thousands of stones, but experiments have shown that only about 60 fist-sized stones are needed for each episode of use—i.e. to boil c. 350 litres of water in a trough and keep it hot for an hour or two (Billy Quinn, pers. comm.). The large quantity of stones found at these sites indicates that burnt mounds were used on multiple occasions.

Burnt mounds are usually located in areas where there is a readily available water source, often in close proximity to a river or stream or in places with a high water table (Illus. 3.2). They are commonly found in clusters, and they typically survive in the landscape as low, horseshoe- or kidney-shaped, grass-covered mounds (Illus. 3.3). These 'classic' shapes were formed when, over a period of time, used stones were removed and thrown to the side of the trough after each episode of use. When the topsoil is removed, this waste material survives as a spread/mound of black, charcoal-rich soil

Illus. 3.2—Sranagalloon 3: due to the low-lying, wetland locations of burnt mounds, sites are often waterlogged and challenging to excavate.

Illus. 3.3—Rathwilladoon 4: (top) looking south-east, the classic horseshoe-shaped, grass covered burnt mound as it appeared prior to excavation; and (bottom) a section through the burnt mound revealing the black, charcoal-rich soil and heat-shattered stones that are characteristic of these sites.

and heat-shattered stones. One or more earth-cut troughs are often found beneath the stones, and sometimes these are lined with timber, clay or, more rarely, leather or stone. Other associated features include pits and gullies. These are usually interpreted as water management features, such as wells and cisterns. Sometimes a hearth is identified, indicating the place where the stones were heated. Post- and stake-holes are occasionally identified on burnt mound sites, and these may represent the remains of small structures or windbreaks. In general, burnt mounds are, usually, artefact poor, and only limited plant remains and animal bones are recovered.

Burnt mounds are predominantly Bronze Age monuments, and it has been argued (Brindley et al. 1990, 25–33; Corlett 1997) that they reached their pinnacle of use in the Middle/Late Bronze Age. Earlier sites, such as Enniscoffey Co. Westmeath (Grogan et al. 2007, 96), have been dated to the Neolithic period, and later sites, such as Peter Street, Co. Waterford (Walsh 1990, 47), have been dated to the medieval period. So while burnt mounds are generally characteristic of the Bronze Age landscape, the use of pyrolithic technology has a long history in Ireland.

Although there is a general consensus that burnt mounds are the result of pyrolithic technology for heating water, the precise function of these sites has not been agreed. The most enduring theory is that burnt mounds were used as cooking sites. O'Kelly (1954) and Lawless (1990) have demonstrated how joints of meat could be efficiently cooked in troughs of boiling water, and animal bone is one of the few persistent, if occasional, finds associated with burnt mounds. Though limited in quantity, animal bone was recovered from 10 of the 26 sites between Gort and Crusheen. The use of burnt mounds for bathing or as saunas has been suggested as an alternative function (Lucas 1965; Barfield & Hodder 1987; Ó Drisceóil 1988; O'Neill 2010, 38–9). This proposal is largely influenced by references in early Irish literature to sites of a similar character—*fulachtaí fia*—and is difficult to prove. The name *fulachtaí fia* was first coined in the 17th-century manuscript *Foras Feasa ar Éirinn* and does not appear as a complete term until that time (Ó Néill 2004). The presence of stake-holes arranged around a trough might indicate that a light structure, such as a sweat house, once existed there. However, the sheer number of burnt mounds would suggest that if bathing was the primary reason for these sites, the people of Bronze Age Ireland must have been obsessed with personal hygiene. There are other alternatives. Jeffrey (1991) argued that burnt mounds may have been centres of textile production for the fulling or dyeing of cloth. Also, recent demonstrations have shown that troughs could have been used for brewing beer (Quinn & Moore 2009; 2007). This last theory has its critics (McClatchie et al. 2007, 46), due to the absence of cereal remains from most sites. But in response, it is argued (Quinn & Moore 2009, 52) that uncharred grain would not survive the attentions of insects, birds and vermin or the ravages of time. Ultimately, it is possible that some burnt mounds were used for brewing beer. Other burnt mounds may have been ritual sites. The general lack of environmental and artefactual remains might be interpreted to mean that some form of ritual cleansing or purification took place after the site was used (though this clearly did not extend to clearing away burnt stones). However, any theory based on an absence of evidence is difficult to argue and almost impossible to prove. The debate concerning the function of these enigmatic monuments is set to continue but, ultimately, burnt mounds are the by-product of producing hot or boiling water, and this water was undoubtedly put to a number of different uses, just as it is today. The evidence suggests that burnt mounds were multifunctional, 'the kitchen sinks of the Bronze Age' (ibid., 53), with many conceivable uses.

3.2—Burnt mounds: Gort to Crusheen

Over 430 burnt mounds were recorded in County Clare by the start of the century (Grogan 2005a, 107), and three were recently excavated just south of the Gort–Crusheen road scheme, on the route of the Ennis Bypass (Bermingham et al. in press). Far fewer have been identified in County Galway, but numerous examples have been excavated in advance of recent road projects. These include eight along the Gort–Oranmore sector of the new M18 road (Delaney & Tierney 2011), and at least 15 along the route of the M6 road between Galway City and Ballinasloe (McKeon & O'Sullivan in press). All but four of the 26 burnt mound sites excavated between Gort and Crusheen were in County Clare (Table 3.1), where the land is more low-lying than in the Galway section of the new road, and where large areas of peat bog have formed in what were once lakes. A cluster of burnt mounds were found in close proximity to the site of a previously known Recorded Monument at Caheraphuca (CL02-143), but it was unclear which of these was the known monument.

In the following account of the excavated sites on the present route, the chronology of the burnt mounds is discussed first, before addressing the spatial/temporal distribution of the sites and the apparent clustering of these monuments. The main ingredients of a burnt mound are stones and the wood that was used to heat water, so following a brief outline of some of the features found at the sites, the stones and charcoal are discussed, in addition to plant macrofossil remains and unburnt timber. The faunal and artefactual assemblages are then assessed. Finally, the 26 burnt mound sites excavated between Gort and Crusheen are individually described.

Chronology

With the exception of one medieval burnt mound (Derrygarriff 1), one of unknown date (Gortaficka 1), and three with radiocarbon dates encroaching into the Iron Age (Drumminacloghaun 1, Sranagalloon 3, Caheraphuca 7), all of the sites included a Bronze Age horizon: 13 returned Early Bronze Age dates, nine dated to the Middle Bronze Age, and seven saw activity in the Late Bronze Age (Table 3.1). Five sites returned radiocarbon dates that extend back to the Chalcolithic and/or Late Neolithic period (Drumminacloghaun 1 and Caheraphuca 5, 8, 9 and 11). Five sites returned radiocarbon dates from two distinct phases of activity, and at Drumminacloghaun 1, these phases were potentially separated by up to 1,800 years.

Spatial/temporal distribution

Isolated burnt mounds were identified at Rathwilladoon 4, Drumminacloghaun 1 and Clooneen. As the route of the new road travels south it tends to cross marginal wetland and stream valleys, and the burnt mounds appear to become more clustered. This clustering of sites was identified at Curtaun, Gortavoher/Monreagh, Derrygarriff, Sranagalloon/Gortaficka, Ballyline and, particularly, Caheraphuca. A similar pattern of clustered burnt mounds to the south, in County Clare, and fewer in County Galway, was also observed during the construction of the Bord Gáis Éireann pipeline (Grogan et al. 2007). One must be careful, however, not to confuse 'clustering' with contemporaneity. Just because a number of similar sites are found in close proximity to one other, it does not necessarily mean that they were all in use at the same time and that the area was a hive of cooking, bathing,

Table 3.1—Overview of the burnt mounds, showing features, finds and periods of use. LN=Late Neolithic period; Chal.=Chalcolithic period; BA= Bronze Age; EBA=Early Bronze Age; MBA=Middle Bronze Age; LBA=Late Bronze Age; Iron=Iron Age.

Site	County	Trough	Timber (in situ)	Other features	Artefacts	Animal bone	Period
Drumminacloghaun 1	Galway	1	No	No	No	Yes	Chal.–EBA & LBA–Iron
Curtaun 1 and 2	Galway	3	No	Yes	No	Yes	MBA
Rathwilladoon 4	Galway	No	No	Yes	No	No	EBA–MBA
Gortavoher 1	Galway	No	No	No	No	No	EBA
Monreagh 3	Clare	1	No	No	No	No	EBA & LBA
Monreagh 1 and 2	Clare	6	No	Yes	Yes	Yes	MBA & LBA
Derrygarriff 1	Clare	1 (poss.)	No	No	Modern	No	Medieval & modern
Derrygarriff 3	Clare	2	No	Yes	No	Yes	LBA
Sranagalloon 1	Clare	1	Yes	Modern	Yes	No	MBA
Sranagalloon 3	Clare	3	Yes	Yes	Yes	Yes	MBA & LBA–Iron
Gortaficka 1	Clare	No	No	No	No	Yes	Unknown
Gortaficka 2	Clare	3	Yes	Yes	No	Yes	EBA & MBA
Clooneen	Clare	1	Yes	Yes	No	No	EBA
Caheraphuca 1	Clare	≥3	No	Yes	Yes	Yes	EBA & MBA
Caheraphuca 3	Clare	No	No	No	Yes	No	prob. BA
Caheraphuca 4	Clare	1	Yes	No	No	Yes	MBA
Caheraphuca 5	Clare	No	No	No	No	No	Chal.–EBA
Caheraphuca 6	Clare	1	Yes	Yes	No	Yes	LBA
Caheraphuca 7	Clare	1	No	Yes	Yes	No	LBA–Iron
Caheraphuca 8	Clare	2 (poss.)	Yes	Yes	Yes	No	LN–Chal. & EBA
Caheraphuca 9	Clare	No	No	Modern	No	No	LN–Chal.
Caheraphuca 10	Clare	No	No	No	No	No	EBA
Caheraphuca 11	Clare	1	No	No	Yes	No	LN–Chal.–EBA
Caheraphuca 12	Clare	1 (poss.)	No	No	Yes	No	MBA
Ballyline 1	Clare	5	No	Yes	No	No	EBA
Ballyline 2	Clare	3	No	Yes	Yes	No	EBA
Ballyline 3	Clare	No	No	Modern	No	No	EBA

tanning or brewing activity. Using the 'cluster' of 10 burnt mounds in Caheraphuca as an example, five returned Chalcolithic/Early Bronze Age radiocarbon dates, three dated to the Middle Bronze Age, and two were used in the Late Bronze Age (Table 3.1). The Chalcolithic/Early Bronze Age sites alone spanned as much as 860 years, with the earliest site (Caheraphuca 8) returning a radiocarbon date of 2480–2300 BC (UBA-12725), and the latest (Caherapuca 1) producing a radiocarbon date of 1877–1620 BC (UBA-12745). (To put this in perspective, 860 years ago from now, the Anglo-Normans had not yet arrived in Ireland!) It must also be remembered that only a narrow corridor of land was required and subsequently investigated in advance of the new road. Apparently isolated sites might also belong to 'clusters' of burnt mounds that lie outside the landtake for the road. The grouping of burnt mounds does, however, reveal the continued presence of a Bronze Age community and the persistent use of an area for the same set of activities over a considerable period of time. Those areas clearly remained conducive to the construction and use of burnt mounds over thousands of years.

Troughs and other features

At 19 of the sites, earth-cut troughs were recorded, with at least 40 troughs identified in all (Table 3.1). Numerous pits and earth-cut features of unclear function were also identified at many of the burnt mounds: the sites at Caheraphuca 1 and Gortaficka 2, for example, included multiple troughs, drains, hearths and possible preparation areas with stake-lined pits, perhaps suggesting a more industrial purpose than the other sites. The troughs at Curtaun 1 and 2, Caheraphuca 1 and Gortaficka 2 (Illus. 3.4), displayed evidence for a timber lining through the presence of stake-holes for upright supports, while at Clooneen, Caheraphuca 4, Sranagalloon 1, Sranagalloon 3, Gortaficka 2 and Caheraphuca 6, remains of a timber lining survived. These wood-lined troughs were preserved to various degrees, with the best example surviving at Clooneen, Co. Clare (Illus. 3.5). At Caheraphuca 6, a roughly linear setting of 24 large, flat, limestone flags formed a work surface, or platform, just north of a timber trough (Illus. 3.6); and at Caheraphuca 8, a series of timbers appeared to form the vestigial remains of a platform or a possible structure. These oak and alder timbers were positioned on a former lake shore, between the waterlogged peat and the dry, natural subsoil. Another possible platform was identified at Caheraphuca 8, consisting of a series of longitudinally placed alder tree trunks. These timbers extended towards an adjacent woody root mass and, although there was no physical relationship between the two, it is possible that they combined to form a surface, or platform, on the peat. While apparently a natural formation, the system of intertwining roots appeared to have been consolidated by at least one wooden peg (Illus. 3.7). A similar arrangement of worked timber platforms and naturally occurring wood/roots was revealed at a burnt mound site in Killescragh, Co. Galway, during excavations in advance of the Galway to Ballinasloe sector of the M6 motorway (McKeon & O'Sullivan in press).

Stone
by Stephen Mandal

A total of 38 bulk samples of stone were examined from the 26 burnt mounds, in order to establish whether specific types were preferred and hand-picked. In 24 of the samples, limestone and/or cherty limestone was the principal stone type. Eight of these limestone-dominated samples also

Illus. 3.4—Gortaficka 2: post-excavation view of the trough (C39), with stake-holes around the interior edge.

Illus. 3.5—Clooneen: a fine example of a timber-lined trough, being recorded by Elaine Tobin.

Illus. 3.6—Caheraphuca 6: timber trough and stone platform/work surface.

contained quartzite, three contained sandstone, and one included both quartzite and sandstone. A total of 11 bulk samples contained quartzite as their primary stone. Three of these samples also contained limestone, one contained sandstone, and three included both. Finally, three samples contained sandstone as the primary stone type. One of these (Gortaficka 1) also contained chert, and one (Gortaficka 2) included limestone (Table 3.2). Ultimately, 19 of the 26 burnt mounds between Gort and Crusheen contained limestone.

Coarse-grained sandstone and quartzite are typical of burnt mound material. However, despite the fact that most of the burnt mound sites contained limestone, this stone is generally atypical of these monuments: fine-grained rock types such as limestone do not absorb heat as efficiently as coarse rock types such as sandstone. Limestone bedrock forms the underlying geology of the region, and was presumably preferred to other materials due to the ease with which it could be sourced, either directly from bedrock or as inclusions in the glacial till/subsoil. It should be noted, however, that a trough surrounded by burnt granite cobbles was excavated at Dún Aonghasa, on the Aran Islands, Co. Galway (Cotter 1993, 13). The Islands are a geological extension of the Burren, and consist almost entirely of limestone. Given the lack of granite there, it appears that a lot of effort was taken to source those stones, and to avoid using stone that was readily available (Quinn & Moore 2009, 48). Perhaps the burnt mound users in the lands traversed by the M18 road scheme were less discerning with regard to the stone they used to heat their water, or perhaps limestone was suitable for their purposes.

Table 3.2—Stone types identified in the burnt mounds. The assigned periods are from radiocarbon dates recovered from charcoal at the sites and do not specifically relate to the collected stone samples. LN=Late Neolithic period; Chal.=Chalcolithic period; BA= Bronze Age; EBA=Early Bronze Age; MBA=Middle Bronze Age; LBA=Late Bronze Age; Iron=Iron Age.

Site	Period	Limestone	Sandstone	Chert	Quartzite	Quartz inclusions
Drumminacloghaun 1	Chal.–EBA & LBA–Iron	Yes	—	—	—	—
Curtaun 1 and 2	MBA			Not sampled		
Rathwilladoon 4	EBA–MBA	Yes	Yes	Yes	Yes	Yes
Gortavoher 1	EBA	—	Yes	—	—	—
Monreagh 3	EBA & LBA	Yes	Yes	—	Yes	—
Monreagh 1 and 2	MBA & LBA	Yes	—	—	Yes	—
Derrygarriff 1	Medieval & modern	Yes	—	—	—	—
Derrygarriff 3	LBA	Yes	—	—	—	—
Sranagalloon 1	MBA	Yes	—	—	—	—
Sranagalloon 3	MBA & LBA–Iron	Yes	—	Yes	—	—
Gortaficka 1	Unknown	—	Yes	Yes	—	Yes
Gortaficka 2	EBA & MBA	Yes	Yes	Yes	Yes	Yes
Clooneen	EBA	Yes	—	—	Yes	—
Caheraphuca 1	EBA & MBA	Yes	—	Yes	—	—
Caheraphuca 3	prob. BA	Yes	Yes	Yes	Yes	—
Caheraphuca 4	MBA	Yes	Yes	—	Yes	—
Caheraphuca 5	Chal.–EBA	—	—	—	Yes	—
Caheraphuca 6	LBA	Yes	Yes	Yes	Yes	Yes
Caheraphuca 7	LBA–Iron	Yes	Yes	—	—	Yes
Caheraphuca 8	LN–Chal. & EBA	Yes	Yes	Yes	Yes	Yes
Caheraphuca 9	LN–Chal.	—	—	—	—	—
Caheraphuca 10	EBA	Yes	Yes	Yes	Yes	Yes
Caheraphuca 11	LN–Chal.–EBA			Not sampled		
Caheraphuca 12	MBA	—	—	—	Yes	—
Ballyline 1	EBA	Yes	Yes	Yes	Yes	Yes
Ballyline 2	EBA	Yes	—	Yes	Yes	—
Ballyline 3	EBA			Not sampled		

Illus. 3.7—Caheraphuca 8: part of a natural root system appears to have been held in place by at least one wooden peg.

The stone samples indicate that limestone continued to be selected as the primary material in the Chalcolithic period, throughout the Bronze Age and into the Iron Age, at most of the burnt mounds. There was, for example, no shift from limestone to another stone type (i.e. sandstone) observed between the earlier and later sites. Firstly, this indicates that the water-heating process was successful using limestone. It may also suggest that this stone was deliberately sourced for a specific function that remained the same throughout prehistory. Irrespective of what it was used for, the bias towards limestone observed at most of the burnt mounds between Gort and Crusheen and, significantly, its absence from others, suggests that particular stone types were deliberately selected for specific purposes. This is all the more apparent when the evidence from these sites is contrasted with the burnt mound at Dún Aonghasa, where limestone appears to have been deliberately avoided, despite its local abundance.

Wood and charcoal
by Ellen O Carroll (wood) & Sarah Cobain (charcoal)

Wood was a vital and widely used raw material from prehistoric to medieval times, but its importance is rarely reflected in the analysis of archaeological assemblages due to its perishable nature. People in prehistoric (and medieval) communities were dependent on woodland resources for the construction of buildings, the manufacture of most implements, and to fuel the fires that

Table 3.3—Charcoal samples and/or unburnt wood (including worked wood and also natural fallen wood and roots) recovered from burnt mounds (Maloideae species = hawthorn, rowan and crab apple)

Site Name	Alder/hazel	Alder	Hazel	Oak	Ash	Maloideae species	Yew	Elm	Birch	Poplar/willow	Wayfaring tree	Blackthorn/sloe	Wild/bird cherry	Traveller's joy	Holly	Pine	Elder
Drumminacloghaun 1	Y	–	–	Y	Y	Y	Y	Y	–	–	–	–	–	–	–	–	–
Curtaun 1 and 2	–	Y	Y	–	Y	–	–	–	Y	–	–	–	–	–	–	–	–
Rathwilladoon 4	Y	–	Y	Y	Y	Y	–	Y	–	–	–	–	–	–	–	–	–
Gortavoher 1	Y	–	Y	Y	Y	Y	Y	Y	Y	Y	Y	Y	–	–	–	–	–
Monreagh 3	Y	Y	Y	Y	Y	Y	–	Y	Y	–	–	–	–	–	–	–	–
Monreagh 1 and 2	Y	Y	Y	Y	Y	Y	Y	–	Y	–	–	Y	Y	–	–	–	Y
Derrygarriff 1	Y	Y	Y	Y	Y	–	–	–	Y	Y	–	–	–	–	–	–	–
Derrygarriff 3	Y	–	Y	Y	Y	Y	–	Y	Y	Y	–	–	Y	–	–	–	–
Sranagalloon 1	Y	Y	Y	Y	Y	Y	–	Y	Y	Y	–	–	–	Y	–	–	–
Sranagalloon 3	Y	Y	Y	Y	Y	Y	Y	Y	Y	Y	–	Y	Y	–	–	Y	–
Gortaficka 1	Y	–	Y	–	Y	–	–	–	–	–	–	–	Y	–	–	–	–
Gortaficka 2	Y	Y	Y	Y	Y	Y	Y	Y	Y	Y	Y	–	–	Y	–	–	–
Clooneen	Y	Y	Y	Y	Y	–	–	–	–	Y	–	–	–	–	–	–	–
Caheraphuca 1	Y	–	Y	Y	Y	Y	–	Y	Y	Y	–	–	–	–	–	–	–
Caheraphuca 3	Y	–	Y	Y	Y	–	–	–	–	–	–	–	–	–	–	–	–
Caheraphuca 4	Y	Y	Y	Y	Y	Y	–	Y	Y	Y	–	Y	–	–	–	Y	–
Caheraphuca 5	Y	–	Y	Y	Y	Y	Y	–	Y	Y	–	–	–	–	–	–	–
Caheraphuca 6	Y	Y	Y	Y	Y	–	–	Y	Y	Y	–	–	Y	Y	–	–	–
Caheraphuca 7	Y	–	Y	Y	Y	Y	–	Y	Y	Y	–	–	Y	Y	–	–	–
Caheraphuca 8	Y	Y	Y	Y	Y	Y	Y	–	Y	Y	–	–	–	–	–	Y	–
Caheraphuca 9	–	Y	–	–	Y	–	–	–	–	–	–	–	–	–	–	–	–
Caheraphuca 10	Y	–	–	Y	Y	Y	–	–	–	–	–	–	–	–	–	–	–
Caheraphuca 11	Y	–	–	Y	–	–	–	Y	–	–	–	–	–	–	–	–	–
Caheraphuca 12	Y	Y	Y	Y	Y	Y	Y	Y	–	–	–	–	Y	–	–	–	Y
Ballyline 1	Y	–	–	Y	Y	Y	–	–	–	Y	–	–	–	–	–	–	–
Ballyline 2	Y	–	–	–	Y	Y	–	–	–	–	–	–	–	–	–	–	–
Ballyline 3	Y	–	–	Y	Y	Y	–	–	Y	–	–	–	–	–	–	–	–

cooked their food and provided a source of heat. Industrial activities (i.e. metal-working, pottery production and cereal drying) were also dependent on fire, and, in the context of burnt mounds, it was used to heat the stones for boiling water. The woods in a surrounding catchment area were exploited, and often managed, to provide an essential raw material for the community. The

Table 3.4—Carbonised plant macrofossil remains; also unburnt blackberry and stone bramble seeds

Site	Hazel shell	Yellow water–lily seed	Mustard/ cabbage seed	Tufted vetch seed	Water pepper seed	Blackberry seeds (unburnt)	Stone bramble seeds (unburnt)
Drumminacloghaun 1	—	Yes	—	—	—	—	—
Sranagalloon 3	Yes	—	—	—	—	—	—
Rathwilladoon 4	Yes	—	—	—	—	—	—
Gortavoher 1	—	—	Yes	Yes	Yes	—	—
Monreagh 3	Yes	—	—	—	—	Yes	Yes
Caheraphuca 3	Yes	—	—	—	—	—	—
Caheraphuca 8	Yes	—	—	—	—	—	—

economic importance of wood cannot be over-estimated, and a study of the range of species on an archaeological site offers an indication of the composition of local woodland in its period of use, as well as wood selection and use for specific functions.

Structural timbers and natural wood were recovered from seven burnt mounds and associated peat bogs, in addition to one wooden artefact fashioned from yew. Alder and oak dominated the assemblage and were the preferred woods used for the lining of troughs, although at two sites (Sranagalloon 3 and Clooneen) ash was also used. Based on analysis from other infrastructural schemes (i.e. the Gas Pipeline to the West, Grogan et al. 2007) it is apparent that alder, ash and oak were the most frequent species used in the construction of plank-lined troughs while hazel and ash were selected for posts also used in the construction of wattle troughs. One fragment of holly brushwood also lined a trough (C50) at Sranagalloon 3, and pine formed part of the natural wood assemblage from Caheraphuca 4 and 8, though this was not dated and may be relatively modern. Although much of the timber was poorly preserved, tool-marks were evident on some pieces and many had been deliberately split (tangentially, radially, half- and quarter-split). The tool-marks or facets recorded on many of the worked timbers were narrow and long, which suggests that a number of narrow bladed axeheads were used, most notably at Sranagalloon 3. In addition the analysis of the wood assemblage also showed that the inhabitants had the knowledge and skill in timber splitting, as demonstrated by the different conversion methods and split types used to make the timbers that lined the troughs.

A carved yew club or possibly a handle was recovered from beneath a redeposited layer in the bottom of a timber-lined trough at Sranagalloon 3, and appeared to have been deliberately placed there (Illus. 3.8). The object was almost 1 m in length. It measured 0.065 m in diameter at its widest point and 0.034 m at its tip. The rod was rounded at one end and slightly pointed at the opposite end, and looked as if it had been used for pounding or mashing as it was frayed and slightly degraded. There were hundreds of small slightly concave facets (0.01 m by 0.02 m) along one end of the shaft (Illus. 3.9). The centre of the club did not contain as many facets as the two ends, but it was clear that branches had been stripped away, particularly in the central area. There were raised signatures (0.001 m wide) present on some of the facets indicating that there was a nick in the axe that cut them.

The original function of the yew artefact from Sranagalloon may have varied and similar objects have been found at Corlea, Co. Offaly (Raftery 1996, 260), and at Edercloon, Co. Leitrim (Cathy

Table 3.5—Wood types (unburnt) identified from the burnt mounds and adjacent wetlands. Alder would have been selected from close to the site as the natural habitat of alder wood is in a wetland environment. The oak and ash would have grown in a drier terrain, possibly as the main tall canopy formers with holly as an understorey tree or scrubland wood.

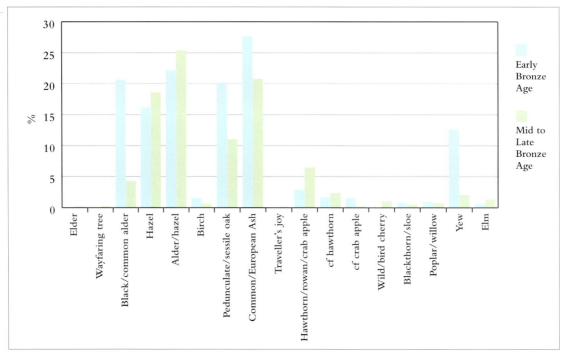

Moore, pers. comm.), where 'rods' of comparable size and shape including similar facets were recovered. Yew wood is strong and durable, and objects made from yew rarely warp or crack. The wear marks on one end suggest it may have been used for pounding food. Stunning animals is an alternative use. A wooden paddle or 'stirring stick' would also have formed part of the equipment needed to brew beer, and in Scandinavia and the Orkneys tradition states that early brewers placed great value on these 'wands' and may even have imbued them with magical or spiritual properties (Quinn & Moore 2009, 46–51).

The yew object may have been deposited ritually under the trough as an offering to the gods. Parallels for the deposition of wooden objects in burnt mound troughs can be seen at excavations along the N5 Charlestown Bypass, Co. Mayo, where a carved yew club was recovered from a trough at Fauleens II (Kerrigan & Gillespie 2010, 147). An oak paddle, or shovel-shaped object, was recovered from a wattle-lined trough at Caraun More 3, Co. Galway (McKeon & O'Sullivan in press), during excavations along the M6 Galway to Ballinasloe motorway, and wooden 'shovels' were also recovered from burnt mounds at Ballyvollane, Co. Limerick (Coyne 2002), and at Ballybar Lower, Co. Carlow (Hackett 2007). The deposition of the yew club/handle from Sranagalloon 3 underneath the trough suggests a ritual act. It has been argued (Brück 1999, 154) that 'odd objects' may have been deliberately left behind in Bronze Age houses when they were abandoned, perhaps symbolising the end of the lifecycle of the buildings. If this theory is accepted for houses, then it may also be pertinent to other Bronze Age monuments, including burnt mounds.

Illus. 3.8—Sranagalloon 3: a carved yew club/handle/stirring stick (E3897:82:1) recovered from the base of a timber-lined trough. Beside it is a modern pick-axe handle for comparison.

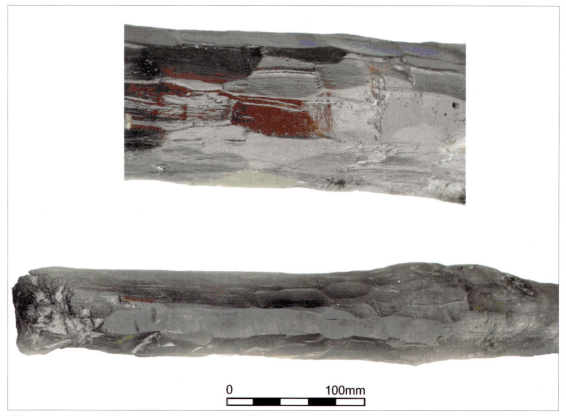

0   100mm

Illus. 3.9—Sranagalloon 3: the yew club/handle/stirring stick (E3897:82:1) had been stripped of branches and had hundreds of axe facets along one end; (inset) detail of the facets showing the raised signatures.

All of the burnt mounds (with the exception of Caheraphuca 3) contained moderate to large quantities of charcoal, comprising a wide range of tree species (Table 3.3). Charcoal represents the firing debris from fuel used in the hearths that heated the stones. Limited quantities of plant macrofossil remains were also identified (Table 3.4). Carbonised hazelnut shells were recovered from five sites, and may represent the remains of food consumed on-site. Alternatively, they could be the remains of nuts that were attached to hazel branches used as firewood. The vetch, mustard/cabbage, yellow water lily and water pepper can all be consumed (see below), but the small quantities in which they were recovered suggests that they were possibly accidental inclusions (lost during harvesting, burning weeds or dropped by animals/birds) rather than indicators of food production. The unburnt blackberry and stone bramble seeds from the trough at Monreagh 3 almost certainly represent material that was deposited by birds/animals.

The woodland species exploited for fuel were similar throughout the Bronze Age. The main fuels used as firing material were ash, oak and elm. There was a high proportion of charcoal fragments from these species that did not show obvious curved growth rings: therefore it is likely the wood was derived from larger branches or stem (trunk) wood, which would have been deliberately cut with the intention of burning, rather than opportunistic gathering of brushwood. A proportion of the oak and ash charcoal did exhibit curved growth rings, and is likely to represent smaller branches. Ash, oak and elm would have been chosen as they have dense heartwood with good ventilation, and therefore burn slowly and maintain an even temperature (Cutler & Gale 2000, 120, 205; Stuijts 2005, 145). This is essential for a fire being used to heat stones, as it would require constant heat for relatively long periods of time. As wood collection is a labour-intensive activity, selection of species according to their burning properties would have been commonplace.

There was also a high percentage of hazel and alder/hazel charcoal from all of the sites. Hazel is a reasonably good fuel wood and was widely available within oak woodlands, particularly on the fringes of cleared areas. It is possible that hazel was used as a dominant fuel where oak and ash were not available.

The remaining charcoal comprised alder, birch, Maloideae species (hawthorn, rowan, crab apple), elder, wayfaring tree, traveller's joy, wild/bird cherry, blackthorn/sloe, poplar/willow and yew. The majority of the charcoal from these species exhibited curved growth rings, which suggests they derived from roundwood lateral branches rather than stem/trunk wood. It is likely, therefore, that these branches were collected as deadwood and used within brushwood bundles as kindling for the fire. Alder, elder, birch and poplar/willow are species that are ideal for kindling. They are all anatomically less dense than, for example, oak and ash, and burn quickly at relatively high temperatures (Cutler & Gale 2000, 34, 50, 236). The high temperatures produced would have been needed to encourage the oak and ash to start to burn. Hawthorn, rowan, crab apple, yew, wild/bird cherry and blackthorn/sloe have a more close-grained anatomical structure and, as a result, make reasonably good firewood (Cutler & Gale 2000, 196; Stuijts 2005, 144). However, the majority of charcoal from these species originated from small twigs, which indicates that, rather than being the dominant fuels, they were used as kindling. Wild/bird cherry and blackthorn/sloe can be slow to ignite and therefore need assistance from other species such as alder or birch, which burn at high temperatures. Traveller's joy and wayfaring tree are good fuel woods, but as they are both small shrub species and were only present in small quantities, it is likely that they were collected incidentally while gathering other twigs/roundwood for brushwood bundles (Stuijts 2005, 145; Cutler & Gale 2000, 80).

There were some slight percentage changes in species noted between the Early Bronze Age burnt mounds and the Middle/Late Bronze Age sites. (While these trends have been observed, they must be interpreted with caution because the percentage fragment count cannot be used to deduce the actual abundance of these species within the woodland.) The most noticeable change was the decrease in oak, ash, and yew from the Early to Late Bronze Age. This can be attributed to the increase in deforestation throughout the Bronze Age—to make way for settlement and agriculture—which resulted in oak, ash, and yew becoming less widely available. This trend is mirrored in pollen core results from Caheraphuca Lough (Chapter 4), and was also noted in a pollen study at Sheeauns Lough, Co. Galway, in Connemara (Molloy & O'Connell 1991, 79, 102).

The large number of burnt mounds identified in Ireland indicates that significant quantities of wood would have been needed to fuel the fires that heated the stones. This would have had an impact on local woodlands. Bronze Age communities were undoubtedly aware of the impact of deforestation, and coppicing may have been introduced to manage and retain this valuable resource. The high volume of hazel and alder roundwood identified, particularly in the charcoal assemblage, is indicative of woodland management by coppicing. This would have been achieved by cutting the tree to a stump every five to seven years and allowing it to regenerate. The new stems produced were harvested and used for fuel or for craft and construction purposes (van der Verf 1991, 97; Rackham 1980, 103).

Herbaceous plants were often used in cooking or eaten raw, adding flavour and providing vitamins, minerals and additional fibre. Cabbage/mustard, as identified at Gortavoher 1, was eaten raw as salad, boiled down and used in stews and soups, and as a vegetable similar to spinach (Behre 2008, 67–8). Vetches were also retrieved at Gortavoher 1, and would have been used to thicken stews. Water pepper was also present, and while it has an acrid taste, its seeds have been used for spices in food (Timson 1966, 817). Hazelnuts would have provided valuable vitamins and minerals, and could be eaten raw or crushed and added to stews (Pearson 1997, 13). While these nuts and seeds may represent accidental inclusions, it cannot be ruled out that some were being exploited and consumed.

Based on the assumption that communities will collect wood from the closest possible source (Scholtz 1986) and, in particular, the collection of economically less important kindling wood, the unburnt timber and charcoal assemblages from the burnt mounds suggests that they were located close to a wetland environment. The characteristic woodland in this environment would have consisted of alder, willow and poplar. These are all trees which thrive in waterlogged and damp soils, particularly in areas close to streams or with a high water table. Elder is an understorey shrubby plant/small tree that can grow in similar conditions. Birch is a tree that can tolerate both dry and damp soils and would most likely have been located in marginal areas between the damp, waterlogged soil and drier areas, upslope from the burnt mound sites.

The oak, ash and elm would have grown in a drier terrain, possibly on raised areas/slopes close to the sites. These would have been the dominant large tree species and the main canopy formers. On the marginal areas of oak–ash woodlands or in clearings, yew, rowan, hazel, hawthorn, crab apple, wild/bird cherry and blackthorn all thrive. These species are all lower-level woodland species and will grow in shaded conditions. However, they are usually located where there is a moderate level of light, in order for flowers and fruits to develop. Traveller's joy is an understorey shrub that clings to trees within oak woodlands.

Faunal remains
by Jonny Geber

Limited animal bone was recovered from 10 sites (Table 3.6). With the exception of a sheep/goat bone from Caheraphuca 1, none of the bones showed evidence of having been butchered. At Drumminacloghaun 1, there was just a single unidentified bone from the burnt mound deposit, and at Derrygarriff 3, fragments of undiagnostic, burnt animal bone were retrieved from a trough. The tusk of a wild pig/boar was recovered from a pit in Curtaun 1 and 2, and a single tooth/tusk from a wild pig/boar was found in peat near the mound at Gortaficka 1. Cattle bones were recovered from a pit in Gortaficka 2, and one cattle bone was identified in a pit in Sranagalloon 3. At Monreagh 2, 29 fragments of unidentifiable mammal bone (9.34 g) were recovered from a trough, two of which were burnt. Also at Monreagh 2, two burnt fragments of an unknown mammal were retrieved from a well, and a pit contained a fragment of a sheep/goat tooth. At Caheraphuca 4, 104 fragments (950 g) of cattle bone were recovered from a natural deposit of peat near the burnt mound. The bones belonged to the same, infant animal (5–6 months), that probably died prematurely, and was disposed of at the site. A cattle bone was retrieved from the smaller of two burnt mounds at Caheraphuca 4, and the larger mound contained a sheep/goat bone and seven adult cattle bones (394 g). A total of 13 bone fragments was recovered from a layer of redeposited peat beneath the timber trough at Caheraphuca 6. Five of these were unidentified and burnt, and eight were sheep skull bones, probably from the same animal. At Caheraphuca 1, three burnt fragments of indeterminable mammal species came from the fill of a pit, and 27 unburnt fragments (957 g) came from a burnt mound deposit (11 of which were from indeterminate large mammals). These included 13 cattle bones, one sheep/goat bone, a horse bone and a red deer antler. The cattle bones consisted mainly of meat-rich body regions. Butcher marks were noted on the sheep/goat fragment, where three parallel knife-cut marks were noted on the inferior margin of the neck portion of the bone, showing where the humerus was separated from the joint. The shoulder height of the horse could be estimated from the metacarpal, which gave a stature of 152 cm.

Not enough data was available for any assessment of husbandry, economy or age-at-slaughter strategies. Cattle bones dominated the assemblage, with skeletal elements from both meat-rich and meat-poor body regions. The sheep/goat, horse, red deer and pig/boar elements were all meat-poor. While the assemblage is limited, the overall anatomical distribution suggests that hides from at least sheep/goat, horse and red deer—with the skull and feet still attached—may have been brought to the sites to be processed within a tannery industry. This is consistent with animal bones finds found at a number of other burnt mounds (Tourunen 2007, 70–1).

Chipped and worked stone objects
by Farina Sternke

Burnt mounds are commonly artefact poor, but a limited number of prehistoric finds was recovered from 10 sites (Table 3.1), including 41 chipped and worked stone objects. Many of these came from unstratified, disturbed or modern contexts, and appeared to be residual finds. Most were typologically of Neolithic date. Almost all were fashioned from chert, 10 of which were identified as natural chunks.

Table 3.6—Animal bone recovered from burnt mounds

Site	Cattle	Sheep/Goat	Horse	Pig/Boar	Red Deer	Unidentified
Caheraphuca 1	13 frags: vertebrae, ribs, scapulae, humerus, ulna	1 scapula frag (butchered)	1 right metacarpal	—	1 antler frag	11 frags
Caheraphuca 4	104 frags: right maxilla & zygomatic, right mandible, a cervical vertebra, 6 thoracic vertebrae, 21 ribs, scapulae, right humerus, ulnae, right metacarpal, coax, femora, tibiae, right metatarsal, 2nd phalanx. 7 frags: molar tooth, rib, scapula, left radius, diaphyses of a left & right femur, diaphysis of right tibia, 1 right metatarsal	1 metacarpal	—	—	—	—
Caheraphuca 6	—	8 skull bones: occipital, sphenoid, left maxilla, horn core, mandible, styloid process of the hyoid	—	—	—	5 burnt frags
Monreagh 2	—	1 incisor tooth frag	—	—	—	29 mammal frags, 2 burnt
Gortaficka 1	—	—	—	1 tooth/tusk	—	—
Gortaficka 2	1 rib frag; 9 cranial frags	—	—	—	—	—
Sranagalloon 3	1 frag of the acetabulum of right coxae	—	—	—	—	—
Derrygarriff 3	—	—	—	—	—	Burnt frags
Curtaun 1 & 2	—	—	—	1 tusk	—	—
Drumminacloghaun 1	—	—	—	—	—	1 bone.
TOTAL	128	11	1	2	1	>46

A large shale axehead was recovered during test excavations at Monreagh 1, and a quartzite saddle quern of Neolithic or Bronze Age type (Illus. 3.10) was found on the surface of the peat that overlay the site. Part of a polished, mudstone axehead or adzehead, dating to the Late Mesolithic or Neolithic period, was recovered from the gravel surface at Sranagalloon 1. A chert bipolar blade and bipolar flake of Neolithic type were recovered from a prehistoric layer at Sranagalloon 3, but were not associated with the burnt mound. At Caheraphuca 1, two Neolithic stone axeheads (Illus. 1.8 and 3.11) were retrieved from the burnt mound, while a chert, plano-convex knife (Illus. 3.11) and two chert flakes were recovered from the interface between the peat and the burnt mound deposit. The flakes were produced using platform core technology, diagnostic of the Late Neolithic period, while the plano-convex knife is characteristic of the Late Neolithic/Chalcolithic/Early Bronze Age. Also at Caheraphuca 1, a fragment of a sandstone rubbing stone was recovered from a trough that had been cut by a modern field drain. At Caheraphuca 3, a bipolar flake and a flake produced from a platform core (both chert) were recovered from modern field drains. They are of Late Neolithic or Early Bronze Age type. Artefacts recovered from the peat surrounding Caheraphuca 8 included a mudstone axehead (Illus. 3.12), a chert, convex end scraper, a chert flake, all of Neolithic type, and also a natural chert chunk. (The leather sole of an early modern/modern shoe was also recovered here, suggesting somebody became stuck in the bog and lost their shoe in the relatively recent past.) Also at Caheraphuca 8, a chert blade and a flint, hollow-scraper fragment were recovered from a spread of charcoal-rich clay and heat-affected stones. Those artefacts are typologically consistent with a Neolithic, Chalcolithic or Early Bronze Age date. At Caheraphuca 11, the surrounding peat

Illus. 3.10—Monreagh 1 and 2: a quartzite saddle quern-stone (E3712:1:1) was found during test-excavations on the surface of the peat that overlay the site.

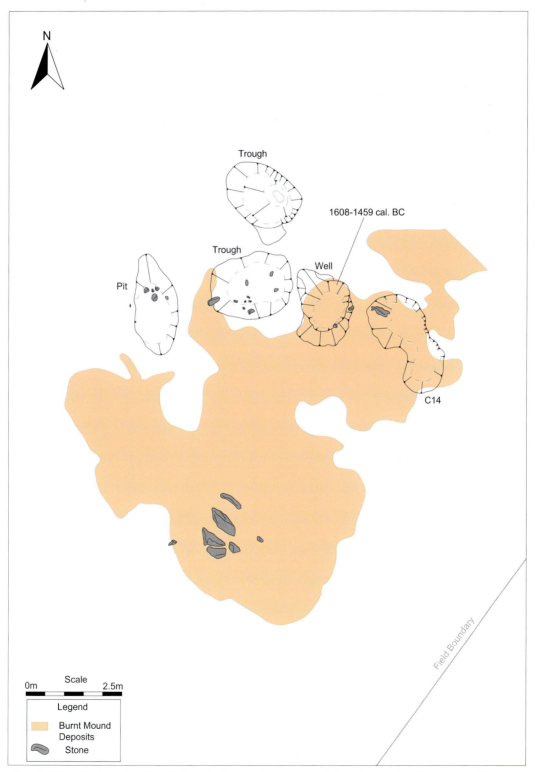

N

Trough

1608-1459 cal. BC

Trough

Well

Pit

C14

Scale
0m   2.5m

Legend

Burnt Mound
Deposits

Stone

Field Boundary

Illus. 3.14—Curtaun 2: plan of Area 2, showing burnt mound deposit, troughs, pits and a well.

which took place between the months of November and January. This, and its location adjacent to the troughs, suggests that it may have functioned as a well or a sump. Hazel charcoal from the base of one of the pits returned a radiocarbon date of 1608–1459 BC (UBA-12708), indicating Middle Bronze Age activity. Other charcoals were recovered from this pit (Table 3.3), in addition to the tusk of a (probable) wild boar.

3.5—Rathwilladoon 4[4]

A burnt mound was located on the edge of wetland in Rathwilladoon, Co. Galway, c. 0.8 m south-east of Tubber. The site was overlooked to the west by the steep slope of a north/south ridge. On the first-edition Ordnance Survey map, the area is on the edge of a small lake (now bog) called Loughannirra. A little further south is Scarriff Lough, and this whole low-lying area is prone to flooding. The site survived as a grass-covered, horseshoe-shaped mound (Illus. 3.3), but most of it lay beyond the lands acquired for the new road, so only a small portion (the 'back' of the horseshoe) was excavated.

The mound comprised burnt, angular (limestone) stones and charcoal, and extended in a horseshoe shape, c. 10 m by 10 m and approximately 0.2 m thick. Washed-out material containing small stones and charcoal-flecked silt extended from the mound. Charcoals were recovered from the mound (Table 3.3), in addition to a single carbonised hazelnut shell. A radiocarbon date of 1601–1436 BC (UBA-12737) was returned for a fragment of the alder/hazel charcoal, indicating an Early to Middle Bronze Age date.

A linear feature, possibly a drain, extended downslope under the mound to the east, and continued beyond the limits of excavation. No other archaeological features were identified, but it is likely that any trough or pits associated with this mound survive outside the area of excavation, probably in the opening of the horseshoe-shaped mound. No artefacts were recovered from the site.

3.6—Gortavoher 1[5]

Two irregular deposits of heat-shattered stone and charcoal-rich peat (c. 35 m apart) were excavated at the base of a south-west-facing slope in Gortavoher, Co. Galway, c. 1.5 km south of Tubber crossroads. The site was situated at the interface between the firm, drift geology of the slope and an area of peat bog that had formed along the floodplain of the Scarriff Stream which flowed to the south. The eastern half of the site was on compact gravel strewn with earthfast boulders, while the western half overlay peat. The site was prone to flooding. No earth-cut features or artefacts were identified.

The eastern deposit measured 14.4 m by 12.4 m and survived to a thickness of 0.36 m (maximum). It comprised angular, heat-shattered stones (mainly sandstone) and charcoal, and represented the disturbed remnants of a burnt mound. A variety of charcoals were recovered (Table 3.3), in addition to carbonised seeds of mustard/cabbage, tufted vetch and water pepper. A fragment of hazel charcoal from the deposit returned a radiocarbon date of 2023–1887 BC (UBA-12753), placing the site in the Early Bronze Age.

The western deposit which had been heavily disturbed by modern land reclamation, was much smaller (4.2 m by 3.4 m and 0.22 m thick), and had a similar composition of stone and charcoal.

3.7—Monreagh 3[6]

Monreagh 3 consisted of the remains of two burnt mounds, located approximately 1.5 km SSW of Tubber, Co. Clare. The sites were on the edge of wetland, in an undulating, peat-covered area, within a low-lying north/south stream valley. The field boundary to the north was aligned on the Scarriff Stream. This is a townland, county and provincial boundary. The sites formed part of a 'cluster' of similar sites—two burnt mounds were identified c. 60 m north at Gortavoher 1 (above), and another two were located at Monreagh 1 and 2, c. 100 m south-east (below). The first site at Monreagh 3 was a spread of heat-shattered stone, and the other site consisted of a large rectangular pit or trough, surrounded by some small deposits of heat-shattered stone and charcoal.

The spread of heat-shattered sandstone and quartzite (9.6 m by 5.6 m and up to 0.3 m thick) was situated alongside the southern edge of the Scarriff Stream and occupied an irregular hollow. This hollow may represent a trough that had been cut in the bank of the stream. The mound and hollow contained charcoals and carbonised hazelnut shells (Tables 3.3 and 3.4). Hazel charcoal from the burnt mound deposit returned an Early Bronze Age radiocarbon date of 1871–1665 BC (UBA-12756).

Approximately 60 m south of the burnt mound was a large, rectangular trough, 2 m by 1.75 m wide and 0.25 m deep. A number of deposits of *in situ* heat-shattered stone surrounded the trough, which probably represent the vestigial remains of a burnt mound. The trough was regularly cut with vertical sides and a flat base. It was filled with silt and small amounts of heat-shattered stone (mainly limestone) and charcoal flecks. Alder/hazel charcoal recovered from this fill returned a Late Bronze Age radiocarbon date of 925–802 BC (UBA-12757). The trough also yielded charcoals of other tree species and unburnt seeds (Tables 3.3 and 3.4).

3.8—Monreagh 1 and 2[7]

Monreagh 1 and 2 were located in an undulating, peat-covered area running along the bottom of a low-lying, north/south stream valley, just within the border of County Clare. (The field boundary north of the site was aligned on the Scarriff Stream, being the provincial boundary.) The site had been heavily truncated by modern land improvements, but it contained evidence for a larger than average number of troughs at this burnt mound.

Monreagh 1 consisted of a series of non-archaeological features, the most notable being a natural hollow from which a large shale axehead was recovered during test excavations. A number of other natural depressions were noted in the area, apparently formed by spring water.

Monreagh 2 consisted of two spreads of burnt mound material (10 m by 5 m and 6 m by 3 m), six troughs, two wells or cisterns, and two further features which may also be the remains of troughs albeit heavily disturbed (Illus. 3.15). The two deposits of heat-fractured stones (predominantly limestone) and charcoal did not cover any of the earth-cut features, although three troughs and a well/cistern (C26) were situated between them. Six pits were interpreted as troughs (C28, C30, C35, C38, C46 and C24). They were all filled with heat-shattered stones and charcoal-rich material. One of the troughs (C46) was cut into the top of another trough (C35) and therefore post-dated it. Alder/hazel charcoal from one of the troughs (C35) returned a radiocarbon date of 1409–1269 BC (UBA-12755), indicating its use in the Middle Bronze Age.

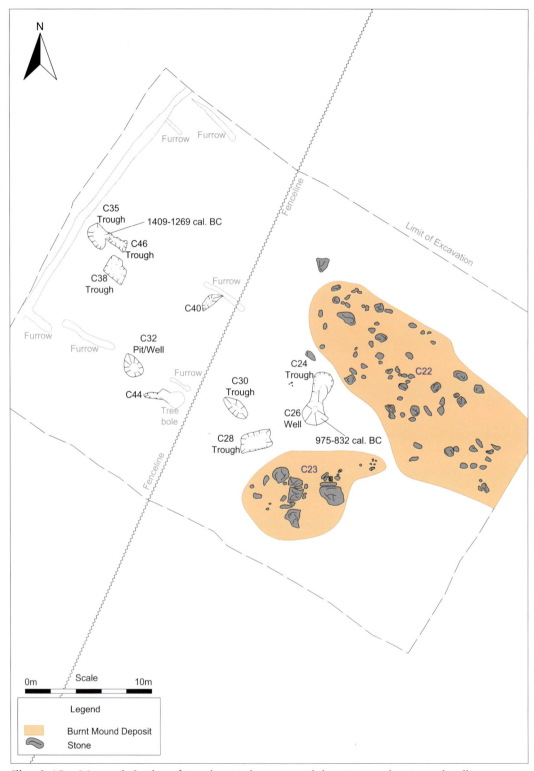

Illus. 3.15—Monreagh 2: plan of site, showing burnt mound deposits, troughs, pits and wells.

A sub-circular cut (C32) on slightly higher ground, south-west of the troughs, may have functioned as a well or a cistern. A linear cut with a V-shaped cross-section (C44) was recorded close to the possible cistern. Its fill was rich in burnt stone and the feature may represent the disturbed base of a seventh trough. A crescent-shaped pit (C40) with a single fill of heat-shattered stones towards the north of the site may represent the partial remains of an eighth trough. A fragment of sheep/goat tooth was recovered from its fill.

A figure-of-eight-shaped feature was formed by one shallow and one deep pit, conjoined. These were interpreted as a trough (C24) and a well/cistern (C26) respectively. The well/cistern could have been used to supply water for the trough, perhaps during the summer when the water table had receded. Both features were filled with the same material—dark, silty clay with unburnt limestone and some quartzite—suggesting that they were backfilled at the same time. Unidentified burnt and unburnt animal bone was recovered from both features (Table 3.6), and the trough contained a variety of charcoals (Table 3.3). Hazel charcoal from the cistern returned a Late Bronze Age radiocarbon date of 975–832 BC (UBA-12754).

No artefacts were recovered from any of the features at Monreagh 2, but a quartzite saddle quern (Illus. 3.10) was found on the surface of the peat that overlay this site and Monreagh 1.

3.9—Derrygarriff 1[8]

A deposit of burnt mound material and an associated pit were discovered at Derrygarriff, c. 3.5 km south of Tubber crossroads, Co. Clare. The site was located on the west-facing slope of a low gravel ridge that stood within an area of bog.

The site consisted of an irregular spread of compact, heat-fractured stones (mainly limestone) within a mixed charcoal and peat matrix (5 m by 4 m and 0.14 m thick). Beneath the heat-fractured stones was a single, small pit, 0.9 m by 0.86 m and 0.11 m deep. Charcoal (black/common alder) from the pit returned a radiocarbon date of AD 1326−1343 (UBA-12714), but a radiocarbon date of AD 1695−1955 (UBA-12713) was produced by hazel charcoal recovered from the burnt mound material. A variety of charcoals was recovered from the pit and the burnt mound (Table 3.3).

The pit and spread of heat-shattered stone had the appearance of a Bronze Age burnt mound, however, the pit yielded a radiocarbon date in the 14th century. While charcoal from the overlying mound provided a modern date, the deposit had clearly been disturbed—it included a modern gun cartridge—and appeared to have been the site of a camp fire in the relatively recent past. Consequently, neither date can be entirely trusted but the site possibly represents the remains of a medieval burnt mound. While something of a rarity, a small number of medieval burnt mounds have been excavated in Ireland, including examples at Peter Street, Waterford (Walsh 1990, 47) and Ballymount Great, Co. Dublin (Stout 1982, 217–8).

3.10—Derrygarriff 3[9]

A second burnt mound was discovered in Derrygarriff, Co. Clare, approximately 4 km south of Tubber. The site was situated on the west-facing slope of a low gravel ridge, within an area of bog and just south of the Derrygariff Stream. Derrygarriff 3 was found c. 550 m south of the possible medieval burnt mound at Derrygarriff 1 (above), and c. 550 m north of a Bronze Age burnt mound at Sranagalloon 1 (below). The Record of Monuments and Places shows an earthwork enclosure (CLO18-019) c. 440 m to the south.

Derrygarriff 3 comprised a horseshoe-shaped mound (11 m by 9 m and c. 0.77 m thick) of heat-shattered stone (limestone) and charcoal-rich soil, which sealed two troughs, a pit, and a possible drain. Most of the mound lay outside the corridor of the new road and only a portion of its western edge was excavated. Charcoals were recovered from the mound (Table 3.3), but no artefacts were recovered.

An oval trough, aligned north-east/south-west, was found beneath the southern arm of the horseshoe-shaped mound, but its full extent was not determined as it extended beyond the excavation limit. Its recorded dimensions were 1.6 m by 1.2 m and 0.4 m deep. It contained two fills, which comprised burnt mound material, suggesting that the trough and the overlying material were contemporary. The water table was high in this area and the trough was constantly filled with water during the excavation (between January and February). A fragment of alder/hazel charcoal from the trough returned a radiocarbon date of 1006–850 BC (UBA-12718), indicating its use in the Late Bronze Age. A range of other charcoals were recovered from the trough (Table 3.3).

An oval trough, aligned north/south, measured 2.85 m by 2 m and was 0.5 m deep. The trough contained three fills, which all included burnt mound material, suggesting that the two features were contemporary. The middle fill contained fragments of undiagnostic burnt animal bone. A fragment of alder/hazel charcoal from the basal fill returned a radiocarbon date of 829–793 BC (UBA-12717).

The pit was very shallow with an irregular cut. It was located between a possible drain and a trough. The function of the pit is unknown, but its fill comprised burnt mound material, suggesting that it was contemporary, and presumably associated, with the burnt mound and the troughs.

The possible drain was aligned NNE/SSW, and was located under the northern arm of the horseshoe-shaped mound. It was only identified in section, and extended beyond the limits of excavation. It was possibly designed to conduct water to the nearby trough.

3.11—Sranagalloon 1[10]

The burnt mound at Sranagalloon, Co. Clare, consisted of a spread of heat-affected limestone and charcoal-rich, silty clay, overlying the truncated remnants of a timber-lined trough. The site was c. 2.2 km north of Crusheen, in a flat pasture field prone to flooding. The natural geology consisted of limestone bedrock and gravel in the north-western part of the site, changing to a sandy till towards the south-east of the site. The exposed subsoil was waterlogged for the entire excavation (January to February). A modern, open drain was cut across the southern end of the site. A fragment of a polished, mudstone axehead or adzehead of Neolithic type was recovered from the base of the topsoil at its interface with the gravel subsoil.

The trough was oval in plan, 2.2 m by 1.15 m and 0.44 m deep, with steep irregular sides and a flat base. Part of the trough was truncated by a modern drain. The trough was lined with alder planks (Illus. 3.16). Three equally spaced, north/south aligned base timbers supported seven remaining east/west aligned planks. Two of the timbers were radially split but none included tool-marks. A fragment of hazel charcoal from the base of the trough returned a radiocarbon date of 1433–1313 BC (UBA-12759), in the Middle Bronze Age. Other tree species were also identified in the charcoal assemblage (Table 3.3). A large, flat stone was placed at the northern edge of the trough, and smaller slab-like stones on its eastern and western edges. It is possible that these functioned as retaining slabs to prevent discarded stone debris from tumbling into the trough.

After the trough was decommissioned, limestone rubble was dumped into it, to the same level as its surrounding burnt mound material. At a later phase, further burnt mound material sealed this earlier activity. This mound of heat-affected stones and charcoal-rich clay measured 9.3 m by 5.95 m and was 0.42 m thick. A sample of alder/hazel charcoal returned a radiocarbon date of 1260–1012 BC (UBA-12758), indicating reuse of the site.

Illus. 3.16—Sranagalloon 1: the trough under excavation, revealing the remnants of a timber lining.

3.12—Sranagalloon 3[11]

The burnt mound at Sranagalloon 3, Co. Clare, was a compact spread of heat-shattered stone (limestone) with three associated troughs and two pits (Illus. 3.17). Two distinct episodes of activity were identified, dating to the Middle Bronze Age and the Late Bronze/Early Iron Age. The site was c. 1.5 km north of Crusheen, in marginal land between pasture and wetland, at the bottom of a steeply sloping gravel ridge that formed part of a U-shaped valley. A canalised stream to the east of the site marked the field boundary. The subsoil was silty clay. Between this and the burnt mound was a dark layer of peat that formed a prehistoric surface. Two stone tools of Neolithic type were recovered from this layer, but were not associated with the burnt mound.

The Middle Bronze Age activity was represented by two troughs and a pit that were partly covered by a mound of heat-shattered stone and charcoal-rich soil. The largest, circular trough (C28) measured roughly 4 m by 3.5 m and was c. 1 m deep. It contained 12 alder timbers that may represent a dismantled or disturbed trough, though they formed no discernable pattern. The western, upper edge of the trough was lined with five stake-holes, which may have supported a structural element, such as fixing pegs for a trough lining or a windbreak. A carved yew club/handle was recovered from the basal fill of the trough and appeared to have been deliberately placed there (Illus. 3.8 and 3.9; see O Carroll, above). A cattle bone was retrieved from the trough, along with a variety of charcoals and a carbonised hazelnut shell (Tables 3.3 and 3.4). A sample of hazel charcoal returned a radiocarbon date of 1494–1399 BC (UBA-12729).

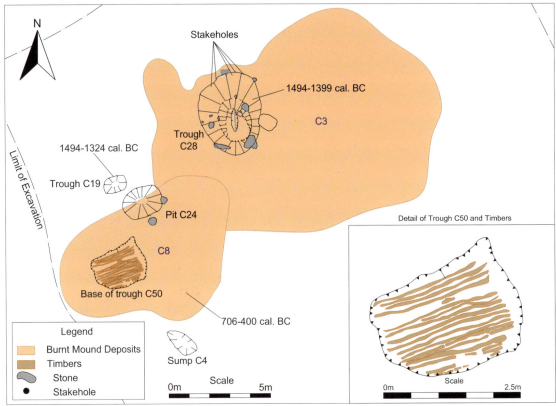

Illus. 3.17—*Sranagalloon 3: plan of the site, showing burnt mound deposits, troughs, pits and a possible sump. The trough (C50) contained a basal lining of 18 well-preserved, worked timbers, made of ash, alder and holly brushwood (inset).*

The second trough (C19) was much smaller (1.22 m by 1.08 m and 0.3 m deep) and did not contain timbers. Alder/hazel charcoal from this trough produced a radiocarbon date of 1494–1324 BC (UBA-12728), making it contemporary with the larger trough (C28). A nearby oval pit (C24) may also have been a trough, but it contained no charcoal and was not dated. The principal deposit of burnt mound material on the site (C3) sealed the large trough (C28) but did not extend as far west as the other earth-cut features (C19 and C24) (Illus. 3.17).

Following a period of abandonment, evidenced by a layer of peat (C13) that sealed the Middle Bronze Age features, a second phase of activity occurred on the site. This involved the construction of a shallow, rectangular, wood-lined trough (2.7 m by 1.8 m) and a small pit. The trough (C50) contained a basal lining of 18 well-preserved timbers, made of ash, alder and holly brushwood (Illus. 3.17 and 3.18). The adjacent pit (C4) was 1.2 m by 0.92 m and 0.5 m deep. It was constantly waterlogged and acted as a sump during the excavation, perhaps indicating its original function.

A deposit of burnt mound material (C8) sealed the trough (C50) and the peat deposit (C13). Hazel charcoal from the mound material returned a radiocarbon date of 706–400 BC (UBA-13022) that spans the Early Iron Age.

Illus. 3.18—Sranagalloon 3: the timber-lined trough.

3.13—Gortaficka 1[12]

The burnt mound at Gortaficka 1, Co. Clare, was c. 1.4 km north of Crusheen, on the margin of a peat-covered area running along the bottom of a long, north/south gravel ridge that formed the western slope of a classic, glacially formed, U-shaped valley. (Sranagalloon 3 to the north and Gortaficka 2 to the south occupied similar sites within this valley.) The site was situated at the interface between dry and wet land, with the steep slope of the valley to the west and a canalised stream and bog to the east. The subsoil was silty clay, and the canine tusk of a wild boar was recovered from an overlying layer of peat.

The site consisted of an irregular deposit of compact, heat-fractured stone (limestone and sandstone) within a charcoal/peat matrix. The deposit measured 8 m by 5 m and was 0.2 m thick. No trough or associated earth-cut features were identified, and no artefacts were recovered from the site. No radiocarbon dates were returned for the site, but it was only c. 50 m north-east of another burnt mound, Gortaficka 2 (below), and c. 250 m south-west of the mound at Sranagalloon 3 (above). Both of these sites were situated at the foot of the same gravel ridge as Gortaficka 1, and both produced Bronze Age radiocarbon dates.

3.14—Gortaficka 2[13]

The burnt mound at Gortaficka 2 shared the same topographical setting as Gortaficka 1, c. 50 m to the south-west (Illus. 3.19). The mound consisted of compact, heat-fractured stones (limestone and sandstone) within a charcoal/peat matrix. Three troughs, two pits, a gully and several stake-holes were identified beneath the burnt mound, belonging to two distinct Bronze Age horizons (Illus. 3.20).

The initial activity at Gortaficka 2 concentrated on a shallow trough, a pit and a single stake-hole. The oval trough (C3) was 2.13 m by 1.33 m and was 0.14 m deep. It had four, regularly spaced stake-holes in its base, which may have supported a timber lining. The trough was cut on its northern edge by an irregular, oval pit/trough (C21), 1.77 m by 0.92 m and 0.36 m deep. Charcoal (Maloideae) from this pit returned a radiocarbon date of 2287–2137 BC (UBA-12707) placing this activity in the Early Bronze Age. A single stake-hole was located just north-east of this pit. A burnt mound deposit (C20) comprising mainly sandstone was concentrated to the west, south-west and north of the trough and pit. The mound was then abandoned and sealed by a layer of naturally accumulating peat.

The second, Middle Bronze Age, phase of activity was concentrated on two troughs, one of which included the remnants of a timber lining. That trough (C39) measured 1.62 m by 1.26 m and 0.1 m deep. It contained 14 internal stake-holes (Illus. 3.4) and the remains of three oak planks, aligned east/west, that were pressed lengthways along its base. A fragment of alder/hazel charcoal from the basal fill returned a radiocarbon date of 1496–1409 BC (UBA-12706). Two stake-holes

Illus. 3.19—Gortaficka 2: the burnt mound after the topsoil had been stripped, looking south-west.

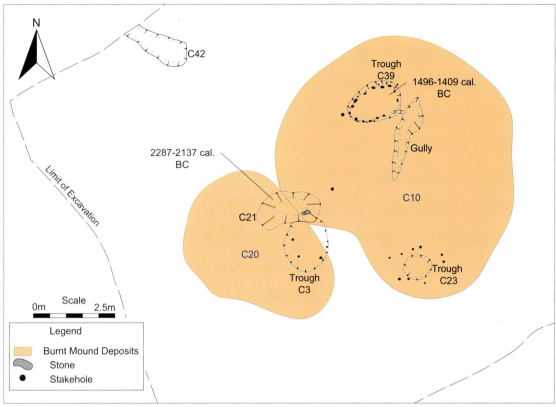

Illus. 3.20—Gortaficka 2: plan of the site, showing burnt mound deposits, troughs, pits and a gully (C53). Note the large number of stake-holes in and around the troughs. Stake-holes at the opposite edges of trough C39 may have supported a roasting rack or a spit.

were located at opposite edges of the trough (Illus. 3.20). These may have supported a roasting rack or spit. A gully extended from the eastern edge of the trough that may have managed the flow of water between trough C39 and another trough (C23).

The circular trough (C23) had a diameter of c. 0.9 m and was 0.32 m deep. It may originally have been leather or cloth-lined, as it was rounded and had a curved base. Nine, evenly spaced stake-holes encircled the trough, which may have held stakes used to peg a hide in place (Illus. 3.20). A cattle bone was recovered from the upper fill of this trough. A spread of burnt mound material (C8 and C10), comprising sandstone and some limestone, sealed all of the second phase features.

3.15—Clooneen[14]

A burnt mound with a timber-lined trough was found in Clooneen, Co. Clare, c. 750 m WNW of Crusheen. The mound was situated on relatively dry bogland within a peat basin, now used for pasture. The ground rose gently to the east and west of the site. The natural subsoil was not identified, as it lay beneath a deep peat deposit that extended across the site and below the water table beyond the limit of excavation. A large quantity of roots and a number of fallen oak trees were

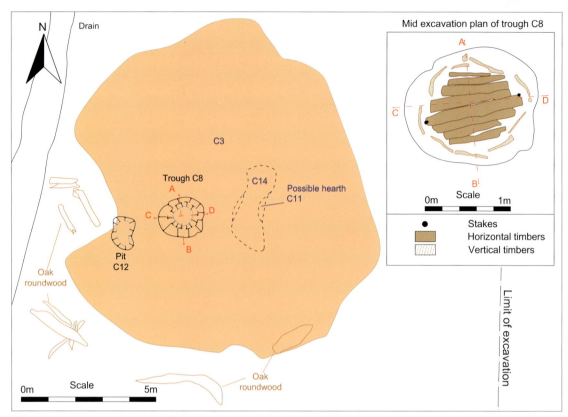

Illus. 3.21—Clooneen: plan of the site, showing the burnt mound deposit, trough, pit and a possible hearth (C14 and C11). Note the oak roundwood pieces preserved within the peat. None of these had tool-marks, but they possibly functioned as walkways across the peat.

preserved within the peat. None of these had tool-marks, but it is possible that they once functioned as walkways across the peat. A modern field-drain ran north/south to the west of the site.

The burnt mound (C3) was roughly horseshoe-shaped. It measured 12.1 m by 11.5 m and was c. 0.27 m thick (Illus. 3.21). It comprised heat-shattered, quartzite cobbles, ash and charcoal (Table 3.3). The cobbles were probably sourced in the local, glacial tills. Quartzite is a typical stone type used in burnt mounds, due to the manner in which it absorbs heat and can be reused a number of times before shattering or flaking. The mound sealed a trough (C8), a pit (C12) and a possible hearth (C11 and C14).

The circular trough measured 1.5 m in diameter and survived to a depth of 0.22 m. Nine vertical timbers (ash) were arranged, petal-like, around the sides of the trough (Illus. 3.22). These timbers were split tangentially, radially and half-split, and each plank was placed so that it partly overlapped that adjacent to it. Two ash stakes were then driven vertically into opposite sides of the trough-base and into the underlying peat (Illus. 3.23). These may have supported the vertical timbers in the trough or may have supported a spit. The base of the trough was lined with eight, split timbers (ash and alder), some of which overlapped. These basal planks rested on a thin layer of sandy ash. All the timbers were in a poor state of preservation, but traces of curved tool-marks on one of the planks indicates that a medium-sized, splayed, metal axe was used. Alder charcoal from the base of the trough returned a radiocarbon date of 2132–1909 BC (UBA-12730), placing the site in the Early Bronze Age.

Just west of the trough was a pit (C12), 1.15 m by 0.74 m and 0.15 m deep (maximum). It contained two charcoal-rich and stony fills and may have been a storage pit associated with the burnt mound. To the east of the trough was an area of scorching and ashy sand (C11 and C14) that may be the remnants of a hearth.

3.16—Caheraphuca 1[15]

The site at Caheraphuca 1, Co. Clare, was c. 750 m west of Crusheen, between two areas of reclaimed bog in Caheraphuca (to south) and

Illus. 3.22—Clooneen: the timber-lined trough with the base exposed following removal of the side-lining planks, which were all broken near the base (compare Illus. 3.5).

Clooneen (to north) townlands. The site was located on the west-facing slope of a low hill, in a slight hollow, within a strongly undulating landscape (Illus. 3.1). The land had recently been used for pasture. The site consisted of a Bronze Age burnt mound and three troughs, two of which may have been wood-lined (Illus. 3.24). Three large pits were located just north of the mound; and a

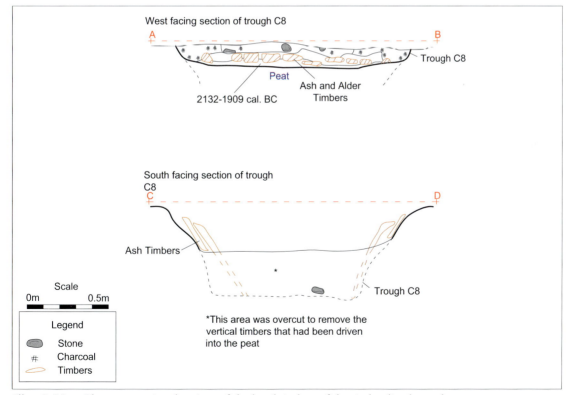

Illus. 3.23—Clooneen: section drawings of the basal timbers of the timber-lined trough.

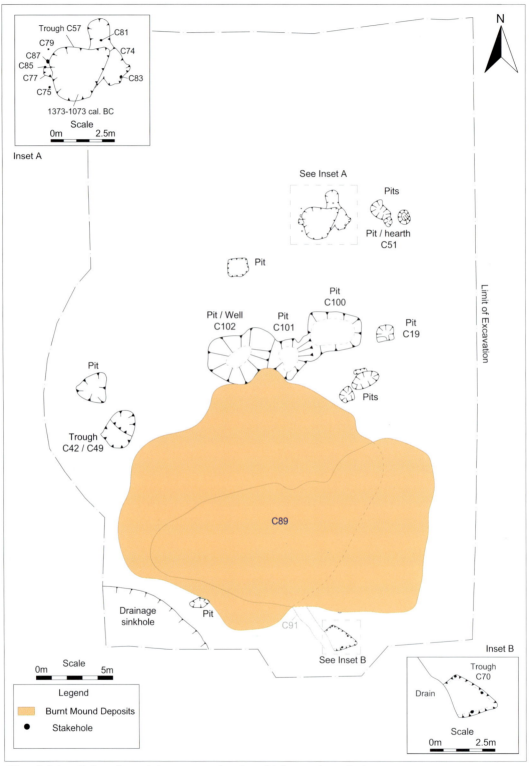

Illus. 3.24—Caheraphuca 1: burnt mound and multiple troughs and pits.

number of smaller pits were situated around the mound. Early modern/modern activity consisted of a linear drain, a drainage pit, agricultural furrows, and associated artefacts.

The main concentration of burnt mound material comprised silty clay with burnt limestone and charcoal, and was 16 m by 13 m and 0.4 m thick. This mound sealed a thin layer of peat that had accumulated in a former pond, and contained two stone axeheads of Neolithic type (Illus. 1.8 and 3.11). A chert, plano-convex knife and two chert flakes were recovered from the interface between the peat and the burnt mound deposit (see Sternke, above). An animal tooth was recovered from the burnt deposit, in addition to modern ceramics. The latter finds indicate that the mound was recently disturbed, but alder/hazel charcoal from the deposit returned an Early Bronze Age radiocarbon date of 1877–1620 BC (UBA-12745).

Three large pits (C100, C101 and C102) were located just beyond the north edge of the burnt mound (Illus. 3.24). Two of the pits (C100 and C101) are interpreted to have been broadly contemporary as they were inter-cutting and shared similar, charcoal-rich, silty fills, with heat-shattered chert and limestone stones. They also included unidentified animal bones and charcoal (Tables 3.3 and 3.6). The remaining pit (C102), while adjacent, contained different fills from the other two—the result of natural silting—and may have been cut at a later date. These pits are likely to have been the focus of the burnt mound activity and possibly had a water management function, perhaps acting as silt traps. Pit C102 was cut into the water table and may have functioned as a well. Seven smaller pits were situated around the burnt mound. Their function is unclear, but most of them contained charcoal and they are probably associated with activity on and around the burnt mound.

A trough, a pit, one post-hole and six stake-holes were identified to the north of the burnt mound deposit and the three large pits (Illus. 3.24). An irregular-shaped pit (C74) containing a single, silty fill, had been cut by a later trough with a concave base and sides (C57). The trough was 2.6 m by 2.4 m and 0.24 m deep, and was filled with charcoal-rich material and burnt stone. Four stake-holes (C75, C79, C81 and C83) were positioned in an approximately rectangular arrangement around the outer edges of the trough. Two stake-holes (C85 and C87) and a post-hole (C77) were cut into the western edge of the trough. Together these may have been supports for a trough lining. A radiocarbon date of 1373–1073 BC (UBA-12744) was returned for alder/hazel charcoal from the trough (C57), indicating its use in the Middle Bronze Age. A shallow pit (C51) located just east of the trough (C57) may have been a hearth.

A rectangular trough (C70) was located to the south-east of the burnt mound deposit, and had stake-holes in each of its corners suggesting it was timber lined. It was 1.8 m by 1.05 m and 0.15 m deep. The trough contained a charcoal-rich basal fill and an upper fill with small stones and occasional charcoal flecks. The trough was cut by a modern drain. A fragment of a rubbing stone was recovered from the trough.

A stepped trough (C42 and C49) was situated to the north-west of the burnt mound. The main cut (C42) was 1.7 m by 1.61 m and 0.22 m deep, and had been further cut (C49), creating a step. The trough contained charcoal-rich soil and heat-affected stones.

Four further deposits of charcoal-rich and heat-shattered stone were identified in the section of the mound . One of the spreads (C89) contained a large assemblage of unburnt animal bone, dominated by cattle remains (Table 3.6). Sheep/goat and horse bones were also recovered, in addition to a red deer antler. The majority of cattle bones were from meat-rich areas of the body, and butchery marks were identified on the caprovine scapula (see Geber, above).

3.17—Caheraphuca 3[16]

Caheraphuca 3 was one of 10 burnt mound sites situated around a peat basin in a steep-sided valley, north of Caheraphuca Lough, Co. Clare (Illus. 3.25; also see Caheraphuca 4–12, below). The sites were approximately 1 km south-west of Crusheen and c. 200 m west of the old N18 road. They were concentrated along a c. 500 m stretch of the new road corridor. A burnt mound (RMP: CLO2-143) was previously recorded in the area, and a wedge tomb (RMP: CLO26–015) survives c. 150 m east of the excavated sites. The small peat basin, which was the focus of activity, had been agriculturally improved to support grass pasture, and was crossed with large, water-filled drains.

Caheraphuca 3 comprised a disturbed spread of charcoal-rich material and heat-affected limestone, measuring 3.7 m by 4.5 m and 0.35 m thick. The burnt mound was truncated and disturbed by later agricultural activity, including land clearance and field drainage. No associated features were found, probably due to modern disturbance. A number of deliberately backfilled tree holes were also recorded, some of which included evidence of burning at their bases. This may represent land clearance by burning.

A bipolar flake and a flake produced from a platform core were recovered from modern field drains, and represent residual finds. Their presence suggests that stone tool production was carried out in the immediate area. No radiocarbon dates were returned for this site, but given its form and close proximity to other, similar sites, it probably dates to the Bronze Age.

Illus. 3.25—View to south-east over the peat basin at Caheraphuca, where a cluster of burnt mounds was discovered.

Illus. 3.26—Caheraphuca 4: the timber-lined trough consisted of 12 horizontally laid, alder timbers, with another plank running perpendicularly along the northern edge.

3.18—Caheraphuca 4[17]

Caheraphuca 4 comprised two spreads of burnt mound material, 1.4 m apart. The larger deposit sealed a timber-lined trough, and both mounds yielded animal bones. A deposit of peat containing fallen trees and tree roots was present, predominantly to the north and west of the site. This deposit is part of a large peat basin in Caheraphuca, which accumulated in a former lake bed. Oak, alder and pine were represented in the natural wood assemblage surrounding the sites and, although unworked, may have served as gangways associated with the burnt mound.

The largest mound was 13.3 m by 13 m and c. 0.4 m thick, and was situated on the peat deposit. It comprised heat-shattered stone (limestone with some quartzite) and charcoal-rich soil. It covered a wood-lined trough. The mound included a variety of charcoals (Table 3.3) and unbutchered animal bones (Table 3.6). Hazel charcoal returned a Middle Bronze Age radiocarbon date of 1299−1024 BC (UBA-12746). The trough measured 2.5 m by 1.26 m and was 0.06 m deep. It consisted of 12 horizontally laid, alder timbers, aligned north-east/south-west, with another plank running perpendicular along the northern edge (Illus. 3.26). The timbers were sealed by a layer of redeposited, ashy, fire debris. The wood was in poor condition with no noticeable tool-marks. The planks were half-, quarter- and radially split.

The smaller burnt mound was situated on the edge of the peat basin and consisted of charcoal-rich material and heat-affected stone (quartzite and sandstone). No associated features were found. A complete cow metatarsal was recovered from within the mound, but no butchery marks were apparent.

3.19—Caheraphuca 5[18]

Caheraphuca 5 consisted of a thin spread of charcoal-rich soil and heat-affected stones (quartzite) located on the eastern edge of a peat basin. The deposit measured 7.2 m by 6.6 m and was 0.16 m thick. A large piece of timber was identified to the south-west of the burnt mound deposit. No tool-marks were evident, but it may have had some function relating to the burnt mound, such as a small bench or part of a gangway. A variety of charcoals were recovered from the burnt mound deposit (Table 3.3). A Chalcolithic/Early Bronze Age radiocarbon date of 2340–2149 BC (UBA-12719) was returned for a fragment of hazel charcoal.

3.20—Caheraphuca 6[19]

Caheraphuca 6 was another of the group of 10 burnt mounds located in a steep-sided peat basin (Illus. 3.25). The site was excavated in two areas (A and B), which were 9.5 m apart and divided by a field boundary (Illus. 3.27). Area A consisted of a burnt mound, a timber trough and an associated stone platform. Area B contained a spread of burnt mound material with no associated features. The mounds were situated on a deep peat basin, which included stones, tree roots and unworked

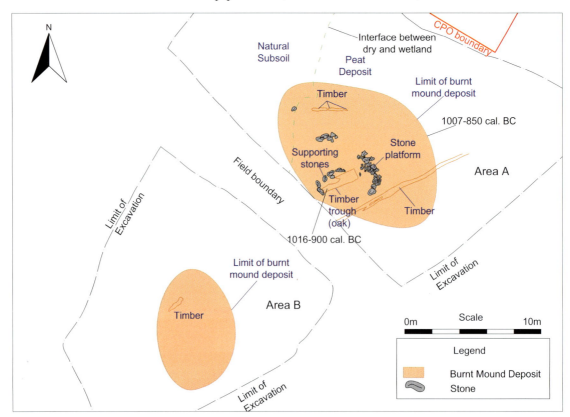

Illus. 3.27—Caheraphuca 6: plan of the site, showing burnt mound deposits and associated features in Area A and Area B. Note the timber trough and stone platform in Area A.

timbers. While no tool-marks were evident, it is possible that the timbers (oak and alder) functioned as gangways across the waterlogged peat.

The large mound in Area A was 14.5 m by 9 m and 0.44 m thick, and comprised two layers of charcoal-rich material and heat-affected stone (limestone with some quartzite). Alder charcoal from the basal layer returned a Late Bronze Age radiocarbon date of 1007–850 BC (UBA-12720). The mound sealed a roughly linear setting of 24 large, flat, limestone flags that had been laid adjacent to a wooden trough (Illus. 3.6). These stones covered an area of 3.4 m by 1 m, and may have functioned as a work surface or platform relating to activity at the trough. The trough survived as a single piece of oak (2.7 m by 0.8 m) that was surrounded by nine large stones. The stones are interpreted as having supported wooden sides which are no longer extant. A fragment of alder charcoal from the bedding layer of the timber returned a Late Bronze Age radiocarbon date of 1016–900 BC (UBA-12721).

The immediate area around the trough was waterlogged and included a spring. A number of fragmented sheep skull bones were found in the surrounding peat, but they included no evidence of butchery (Table 3.6). Another deposit of burnt material was recorded near the site (4.4 m by 4 m and 0.16 m thick), but it was sitting in topsoil and probably represents disturbed material from the burnt mound. The burnt mound in Area B comprised a thin layer of redeposited subsoil, peat, charcoal and heat-affected stone (quartzite and sandstone), roughly 8.3 m by 5 m. No associated features or artefacts were identified in Area B.

3.21—Caheraphuca 7[20]

Caheraphuca 7 consisted of a spread of burnt stone, a trough/pit, and two large pits. The large deposit of heat-affected limestone was c. 10 m by 9 m and 0.4 m thick, but contained very little charcoal. The stones sealed a trough/pit (2.45 m by 1.4 m and 0.25 m deep) and a small deposit of burnt stone and charcoal. Two natural chunks of chert were recovered from the stone spread and the small deposit. The trough was oval in plan with a flat base. Its basal fill comprised dark, silty clay with charcoals from a number of tree species (Table 3.3) and heat-affected stones. The remainder of the trough was filled with material from the covering mound.

A radiocarbon date of 766–420 BC (UBA-12722) was obtained from hazel charcoal in a separate—but probably associated—deposit of heat-affected material, near the main stone spread. That date spans the Late Bronze Age and the Early Iron Age.

The main stone spread was cut by two, large oval pits 0.9 m apart and may represent a second phase of activity on the site. Both pits were filled with charcoal-rich silt and heat-affected stones. Although the function of the pits is unknown, they possibly represent single-use cooking pits. A radiocarbon date of 813–554 BC (UBA-12723) was returned for alder/hazel charcoal in one of the pits, again indicating Late Bronze Age, or more probably Early Iron Age activity.

3.22—Caheraphuca 8[21]

Caheraphuca 8 was another of the 10 burnt mounds situated around a peat basin. Two areas of prehistoric activity were identified: Area A was on the interface between the peat basin and the drier land to its east (a former lake shore), and Area B was just west of Area A, within the peat bog (Illus. 3.28). Four spreads of burnt mound material and two possible timber platforms were identified, in addition to a number of pits and small deposits of charcoal-rich clay and burnt stone. Two modern drains crossed the site.

Two distinct peat types were evident at Caheraphuca 8: the earlier was rich, orange-coloured sphagnum peat, and the later deposit was damp, dark, peat containing roots and stones. A number of unworked timbers of oak, alder and pine were discovered within both deposits. The depth of the peat was not ascertained but a nearby field-drain revealed that it exceeded 1.5 m. The depth of the peat indicates a gradual build up of material over a long period of time, while the presence of two different layers of peat suggests a change in vegetation caused, perhaps, by climatic conditions and a change in hydrology (i.e. a higher or lower water table). Artefacts recovered from the peat included a mudstone axehead (Illus. 3.12), a chert convex end scraper and a chert flake of Neolithic type, in addition to the leather sole of an early modern/modern shoe.

Area A—Neolithic/Chalcolithic period

A series of timbers on the western side of site appeared to form some kind of rectangular structure or platform (Illus. 3.28). The timbers were deliberately positioned as a platform/structure on the former lake shore between the thick, waterlogged peat and the dry, natural subsoil. The feature was constructed of oak and alder, radial and tangential split planks. A number of similar, unworked timbers, 1.5 m to the south-west, may have been related to the structure but became displaced over time.

Approximately 10 m north-east of the 'platform', on the edge of the drier land, were two deposits of burnt mound material (Illus. 3.28). The larger of these (C829) was 5.15 m by 5 m and 0.15 m thick, and comprised heat-affected stones (limestone, sandstone and quartz). The deposit contained charcoals of alder and oak and a fragment of a carbonised hazelnut shell. It covered, and filled, two oval pits/troughs, but no finds were recovered to establish their specific function. The second burnt mound deposit (C830) overlay the larger deposit (C829) and consisted of charcoal-rich clay and heat-affected stones. It contained a chert blade and a flint, hollow scraper fragment, characteristic of the Neolithic period and Early Bronze Age.

Another spread of heat-affected stone (limestone, quartzite and chert) and charcoal was located to the south of the site (C835). A fragment of charcoal (Maloideae) returned a radiocarbon date of 2480–2300 BC (UBA-12725). This date range places the activity in the Chalcolithic period.

Area B—Early Bronze Age

The main group of features at Caheraphuca 8 included a timber feature, a root system, a number of burnt mound deposits and a pit (Illus.3.29). The timber feature (C814) consisted of a series of longitudinally placed alder planks, which was truncated by a modern field drain. The planks were mostly half-split with one radial and one quarter-split timber. The feature may have been more extensive, perhaps extending towards an adjacent root system (C809). The planks were located just 0.8 m from the root system and, although there was no physical relationship between the two, it is possible that they combined to form a surface, or platform, on the peat. The system of intertwining

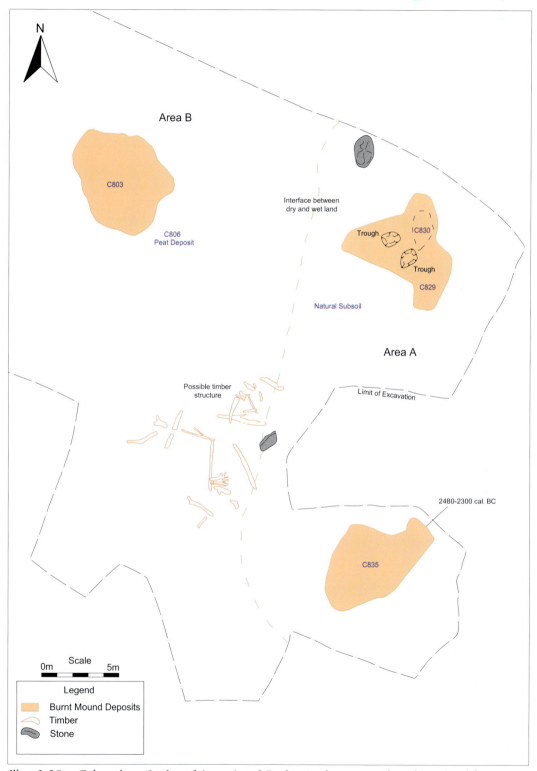

Illus. 3.28—Caheraphuca 8: plan of Areas A and B, showing burnt mounds and associated features.

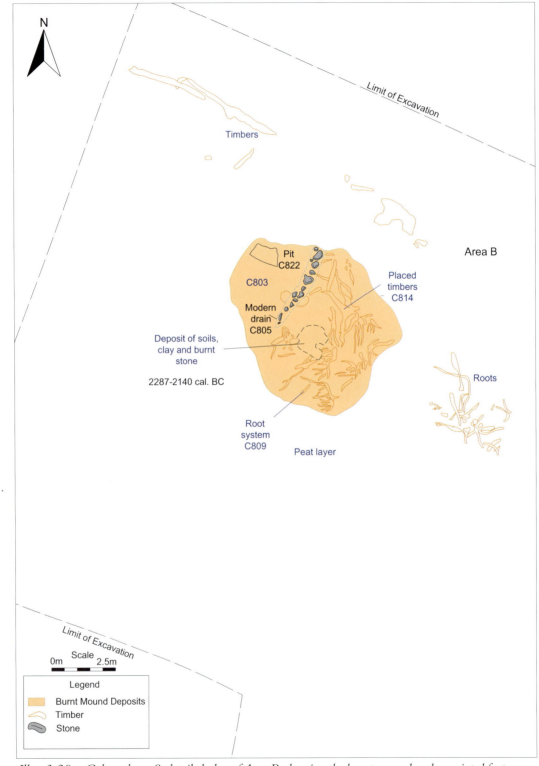

N

Limit of Excavation

Timbers

Area B

Pit
C822

Placed
timbers
C814

C803

Modern
drain
C805

Deposit of soils,
clay and burnt
stone

Roots

2287-2140 cal. BC

Root
system
C809

Peat layer

Limit of Excavation

Scale
0m   2.5m

Limit of Excavation

Legend

Burnt Mound Deposits
Timber
Stone

Illus. 3.29—Caheraphuca 8: detailed plan of Area B, showing the burnt mound and associated features.

roots (C809), while ostensibly a natural formation, appeared to have been held in place by at least one wooden peg (Illus. 3.7).

A rectangular pit (C822) (1.7 m by 1 m by 0.37 m) was just north-west of the timber feature (C814). It contained heat-affected stones and may have been a trough connected to activities on and around the platform(s), though no direct relationship was established.

Beside the root system, in a natural depression in the peat, was a series of four small deposits, comprising a mix of redeposited soil, charcoal-rich clay and burnt stone. A piece of burnt wood was found in one of the deposits, and alder charcoal from another returned an Early Bronze Age radiocarbon date of 2287–2140 BC (UBA-12724).

A shallow spread of charcoal-rich soil and heat-affected stone represented the final phase of prehistoric activity in Area B. The spread (C803) (approximately 10 m by 7 m) sealed a thin layer of peat, that itself covered the timber feature, the root system, the rectangular pit and the small deposits of burnt stone. No associated trough or other features were identified.

3.23—Caheraphuca 9[22]

One archaeological feature was identified at Caheraphuca 9—a pit dating to the Chalcolithic period. The site was on the western edge of a peat basin that included 10 other burnt mounds.

The pit was roughly circular in plan, had steep sides and an uneven base. It measured 1.05 m by 1 m and was 0.4 m deep (maximum). The pit had four fills, one of which was charcoal rich (the remainder had accumulated naturally and were sterile). A fragment of alder charcoal returned a radiocarbon date of 2465–2299 BC (UBA-12726). Charcoal (ash wood) was also identified, but no artefacts were recovered. The pit may have been used over a short period, perhaps as a single-use cooking pit or hearth.

3.24—Caheraphuca 10[23]

Caheraphuca 10 comprised two spreads of heat-affected material, situated on dry land on the eastern edge of a peat basin. The more substantial of the two spreads measuring 9 m by 7 m and 0.4 m thick (maximum), comprised loose, sandy gravel and contained heat-shattered stones and small amounts of charcoal. The stones consisted mainly of limestone and chert, with some sandstone and quartzite. The limited quantity of charcoal may be due to the seasonal flooding of the area, which possibly washed out charcoal from the spread. Alternatively, other types of fuel may have been used, such as peat. No associated features or artefacts were identified, but alder/hazel charcoal from the spread returned a radiocarbon date of 2204–1974 BC (UBA-12747) placing it in the Early Bronze Age.

Approximately 10 m to the north-east of the larger spread was another spread of unburnt stone (limestone, chert and quartzite) with moderate amounts of charcoal. It was 7.2 m by 4.5 m and 0.13 m thick. No other features or finds were associated with the spread, and given that none of the stones appeared to have been burnt, it possibly just represents a pile of stones gathered with the intention of future use. Alternatively, it may have accumulated through land clearance or modern agricultural practices.

3.25—Caheraphuca 11[24]

This site consisted of a thin deposit of burnt mound material, an associated trough and a pit, and was situated on the south-eastern edge of a large peat basin. A chert flake was recovered from the surrounding peat and probably represents Neolithic activity in the vicinity.

The roughly circular deposit was 4.95 m by 3.4 m and 0.12 m thick, and comprised charcoal-rich soil and heat-affected stones. It partly covered a pit/trough and another pit. The pit/trough was circular in plan, with a diameter of 1.5 m and a depth of 0.34 m (maximum). The basal fill was relatively sterile and may represent a phase of natural silting before the pit was backfilled. The upper fill appeared to have derived from the overlying burnt mound. A fragment of alder/hazel charcoal from this fill returned a radiocarbon date of 2458–2143 BC (UBA-12748). This date spans the period between the Chalcolithic and the Early Bronze Age. A chert flake of Neolithic type was also recovered from this fill.

The pit was irregular in shape and had a concave base. It was c. 1.25 m by 0.75 m and 0.28 m deep, and contained two, naturally accumulated fills. The form of the pit and nature of its fills suggested that it was a natural feature, perhaps a tree hole. However, three chert artefacts were found near its base. Two of the pieces were debitage and, while undiagnostic, suggest that stone tool manufacturing occurred in the immediate area. The retouched artefact (Illus. 3.12) probably dates to the Middle Neolithic period. It is unclear how the artefacts found their way into the pit. It is possible that they (a) were thrown into the pit and abandoned there; (b) were randomly discarded and washed into the feature; or (c) they were pushed in through bioturbation (i.e. by the action of roots, worms and other fauna). It is unknown what, if any, relationship the pit had with the burnt mound and the pit/trough.

3.26—Caheraphuca 12[25]

A burnt mound and an associated pit/trough were investigated at Caheraphuca 12, at the northern end of a peat basin. A natural spring was identified immediately to the south-west of the burnt mound. One piece of worked chert and two natural, chert chunks were recovered from the topsoil. Radiocarbon dates from the site place the activity in the Middle Bronze Age.

The roughly circular mound was 12.5 m by 12.25 m and c. 0.64 m thick, and comprised heat-shattered stones (quartzite) and charcoals from a variety of tree species (Table 3.3). A sample of this charcoal (hazel) returned a radiocarbon date of 1108–922 BC (UBA-12749). The mound sealed a rectangular pit/trough that measured 2.85 m by 2.1 m and 0.22 m deep (maximum). A radiocarbon date of 1730–1510 BC (UBA-12750) was returned for hazel charcoal from the pit/trough.

3.27—Ballyline 1[26]

Ballyline 1 was the more northerly of two burnt mounds located on flat land at the base of a hill in Ballyline, c. 2 km south of Crusheen, Co. Clare. The site was in pasture prone to flooding, and had been cut by modern drains to the north and south. The area sloped southwards to the Millbrook River, and was flanked to the east by the existing N18 road and to the west by a hedge. The area

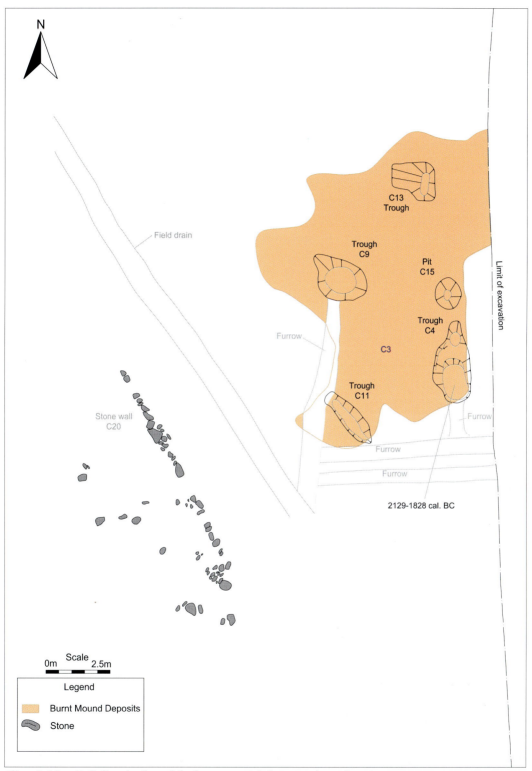

N

Field drain

C13
Trough

Trough
C9

Pit
C15

Trough
C4

C3

Trough
C11

Furrow

Stone wall
C20

Furrow

Furrow

Furrow

2129-1828 cal. BC

Limit of excavation

Scale
0m   2.5m

Legend

Burnt Mound Deposits

Stone

Illus. 3.30—Ballyline 1: plan of the burnt mound, four troughs and a pit.

had been altered in the 20th century during land improvements associated with the demesne of Ballyline House. Ballyline 1 comprised five troughs/pits, filled and covered with a spread of heat-shattered stone and charcoal-rich soil (Illus. 3.30).

The area was heavily disturbed, and of the five troughs/pits identified (C4, C6, C9, C11 and C13), trough C4 was the largest, measuring 2.5 m by 1.5 m and 0.3 m deep. It truncated another trough (C6), which itself was cut by a modern furrow. A thin spread of heat-shattered stone and burnt material sealed the troughs. Alder/hazel charcoal from one of the troughs (C4) returned a radiocarbon date of 2129–1828 BC (UBA-12742), indicating Early Bronze Age use. A variety of tree species were represented in the charcoal assemblage recovered from the trough, including oak, ash and alder/hazel (Table 3.3). The stone comprised quartzite, sandstone, limestone and chert (Table 3.2). An oval pit (C15) was located centrally to the troughs, and contained a single fill of silt with stone and charcoal inclusions.

The earth-cut features were, for the most part, covered by a spread of burnt material. This had been disturbed, and as a result survived only in several concentrations/patches across the site. The main concentration measured 10 m by 9 m and was 0.15 m thick.

3.28—Ballyline 2[27]

This site was situated about 80 m south of the burnt mound at Ballyline 1, and shared the same topographical setting. Both of these sites were located in an area that contained a high concentration of burnt mounds, including the cluster at Caheraphuca, c. 800 m to the north. Ballyline 2 consisted of two spreads of fire-cracked stone and charcoal-rich, silty clay, which were associated with three troughs and a pit. Modern artefacts (mainly tableware sherds) were recovered from the topsoil, a field boundary, and furrows and drains that crossed the site. The butt of a possible stone axehead was also retrieved from the peaty topsoil.

The largest, most southerly, burnt spread comprised 50% limestone and 50% sandstone, and measured 6.95 m by 5.6 m and 0.15 m thick. It sealed an oval trough with a flat base (1.95 m by 1.25 m and 0.63 m deep). The trough yielded a variety of charcoals—ash, Maloideae species and alder/hazel (Table 3.3)—among which was a fragment of alder/hazel charcoal that returned an Early Bronze Age radiocarbon date of 1897–1692 BC (UBA-12740). A round, straight-sided, flat-bottomed pit was just south of the trough. It contained similar material of sandy silt and fire-cracked sandstone.

The northern burnt mound deposit was 5.2 m by 3.5 m and 0.15 m thick. It sealed an oval trough (2.7 m by 1.9 m and 0.42 m deep), that included an internal step or shelf. This trough was filled with burnt stones and charcoal. Another, possible trough was identified to the north of the burnt mound, measuring 2.4 m by 0.85 m and 0.36 m deep. This trough/pit was not sealed by the burnt mound, but contained a single fill of charcoal-rich, sandy silt.

3.29—Ballyline 3[28]

This site was located approximately 500 m south of the burnt mounds at Ballyline 1 and 2, on the margins of wetland at the base of a hill. It consisted of a rectangular pit (1.75 m by 1.68 m and

0.14 m deep) which contained a single fill of heat-affected stones and charcoal (alder/hazel, birch, oak, ash, and Maloideae species). An Early Bronze Age radiocarbon date of 2286–2035 BC (UBA-12743) was returned for alder/hazel charcoal from the pit. Beside the pit was a small deposit/dump of heat-affected stone and charcoal-rich soil. A modern field-drain truncated the site. The site was not a burnt mound, but probably an isolated cooking pit. It was, however, broadly contemporary with the burnt mound at Ballyline 1.

Notes

2   Excavation No. E3720; Director Siobhán McNamara; NGR 144104 201641; height 24 m OD; parish of Kilmacduagh; barony of Kiltartan; County Galway.

3   Excavation No. E3721; Director Shane Delaney; Curtaun 1: NGR 142125 195440; Curtaun 2: NGR 142070 195370; height 25 m OD; parish of Beagh; barony of Kiltartan; County Galway.

4   Excavation No. E3655; Director Ed Lyne; NGR 141150 193931; height 26 m OD; parish of Beagh; barony of Kiltartan; County Galway.

5   Excavation No. E3984; Director Shane Delaney; NGR 140657 193043; height 24 m OD; parish of Beagh; barony of Kiltartan; County Galway

6   Excavation No. E4037; Director Shane Delaney; NGR 140607 193039 and 140570 192971; height 24–25 m OD; parish of Kilkeedy; barony of Inchiquin; County Clare.

7   Excavation No. E3712; Director Siobhán McNamara; Monreagh 1: NGR 140584 192871; height 24 m OD; Monreagh 2: NGR 140512 192804; 25 m OD; parish of Kilkeedy; barony of Inchiquin; County Clare.

8   Excavation No. E3710; Director Joe Nunan; NGR 140463 191046; height 24 m OD; parish of Inchicronan; barony of Bunratty Upper; County Clare.

9   Excavation No. E3716; Director Joe Nunan; NGR 140399 190444; height 26 m OD; parish of Inchicronan; barony of Bunratty Upper; County Clare.

10   Excavation No. E3713; Director Joe Nunan; NGR 140187 190023; height 28 m OD; parish of Inchicronan; barony of Bunratty Upper; County Clare.

11   Excavation No. E3897; Director Joe Nunan; NGR 129751 189290; height 34 m OD; parish of Inchicronan; barony of Bunratty Upper; County Clare.

12   Excavation No. E3898; Director Joe Nunan; NGR 139592 189162; height 33 m OD; parish of Inchicronan; barony of Bunratty Upper; County Clare.

13   Excavation No. E3898; Director Joe Nunan; NGR 139549 189124; height 33 m OD; parish of Inchicronan; barony of Bunratty Upper; County Clare.

14   Excavation No. E3722; Director David Bayley; NGR 139186 188268; height 32 m OD; parish of Inchicronan; barony of Bunratty Upper; County Clare.

15   Excavation No. E3654; Director David Bayley; NGR 139206 188029; height 34 m OD; parish of Inchicronan; barony of Bunratty Upper; County Clare.

16   Excavation No. E3653; Director David Bayley; NGR 139078 187630; height 29–34 m OD; parish of Inchicronan; barony of Bunratty Upper; County Clare.

17   Excavation No. E3653; Director David Bayley; NGR 138994 187460; height 29–34 m OD; parish of Inchicronan; barony of Bunratty Upper; County Clare.

18   Excavation No. E3653; Director David Bayley; NGR 138943 187441; height 29–34 m OD; parish of Inchicronan; barony of Bunratty Upper; County Clare.

19   Excavation No. E3653; Director David Bayley; NGR 138874 187424; height 29–34 m OD; parish of Inchicronan; barony of Bunratty Upper; County Clare.

20   Excavation No. E3653; Director David Bayley; NGR 138957 187367; height 29–34 m OD; parish of Inchicronan; barony of Bunratty Upper; County Clare.

21   Excavation No. E3653; Director David Bayley; NGR 138903 187351; height 29–34 m OD; parish of Inchicronan; barony of Bunratty Upper; County Clare.

22   Excavation No. E3653; Director David Bayley; NGR 138855 187335; height 29–34 m OD; parish of Inchicronan; barony of Bunratty Upper; County Clare.

23 Excavation No. E3653; Director David Bayley; NGR 138894 187242; height 29–34 m OD; parish of Inchicronan; barony of Bunratty Upper; County Clare.

24 Excavation No. E3653; Director David Bayley; NGR 138854 187190; height 29–34 m OD; parish of Inchicronan; barony of Bunratty Upper; County Clare.

25 Excavation No. E3653; Director David Bayley; NGR 138009 187503; height 29–34 m OD; parish of Inchicronan; barony of Bunratty Upper; County Clare.

26 Excavation No. E3717; Director Siobhán McNamara; NGR 138473 186446; height 26 m OD; parish of Kilraghtis; barony of Bunratty Upper; County Clare.

27 Excavation No. E3717; Director Siobhán McNamara; NGR 138473 186446; height 26 m OD; parish of Kilraghtis; barony of Bunratty Upper; County Clare.

28 Excavation No. E3715; Director Joe Nunan; NGR 138183 185987; height 27 m OD; parish of Kilraghtis; barony of Bunratty Upper; County Clare.

4

PREHISTORIC FARMING IN WESTERN IRELAND: POLLEN ANALYSIS AT CAHERAPHUCA, CO. CLARE

by Karen Molloy and Michael O'Connell

The impact of prehistoric farmers on the local environment is considered here, in the light of detailed palaeoecological investigations of a lake-sediment core from Caheraphuca Lough, Co. Clare. The study area lies to the south-west of Crusheen, in hummocky terrain with drumlins and depressions partly filled with peat and the occasional lake (Illus. 4.1). Here, and further to the south, a dense concentration of burnt mounds (*fulachtaí fia*) points towards this part of north Clare being a focus for Bronze Age activity (see Chapter 3). While the focus in this contribution is on the Bronze Age, insights are also provided into woodland change and farming activity during much of the post-glacial period.

4.1—Methods

The peat basin, referred to as Caheraphuca Bog, was investigated using a gouge corer. In this basin, 10 burnt mounds were recorded and excavated (Caheraphuca 3–12; see Chapter 3). In the deeper parts of the basin, peat deposits of 3–4 m thickness were recorded. At several points, a Late-glacial (c. 13000–9500 BC) sequence consisting of silt/clay, marl and organic-rich silt/clay, corresponding to the late Pleni-glacial, Bølling/Allerød and Younger Dryas, respectively, was recorded. This was typically followed by a short marl sequence, indicating the presence of a lake during the early post-glacial period. Peat, in which small pieces of wood and *Phragmites* (the common reed) remains were common, lay above the marl. This suggests that the peat was formed mainly by fen/reed-swamp/carr (woody species on fen peat) rather than bog plants such as sphagnum moss. Several oak trunks and smaller pieces of pine wood were noted in a drainage cutting that ran north/south through the bog, or had been removed from the peat and lay on the reclaimed surface. This indicates that, like most peatlands in Ireland, oak and pine trees grew on Caheraphuca Bog in the past.

Cores were taken with an Usinger piston corer (Illus. 4.2 and 4.3) where the deepest deposits were recorded, i.e. approximately midway between the burnt mounds at Caheraphuca 9 and 10.[29] A pollen diagram, spanning the interval 22–254 cm (depths are with respect to the surface that now carries grassland; 20 samples analysed), was constructed. Pollen spectra from the peat below 112 cm recorded early Holocene (Boreal) woodlands that consisted mainly of pine, oak and hazel. Evidence for human impact (probably Neolithic) was first recorded at a depth of 80 cm. This, and the pollen data from the uppermost samples—*Taxus* attained 13% at 40 cm; this is indicative of an expansion of yew, a feature datable to the Late Neolithic and recorded in several recent pollen profiles from western Ireland—suggest that most of the upper peat was cut away or removed during reclamation. It

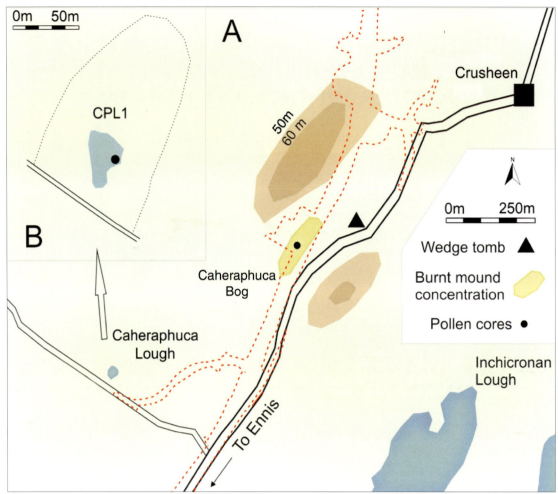

Illus. 4.1—The main map (A) shows the location of the sampling site at Caheraphuca Bog, i.e. the area with the main concentration of burnt mounds. The inset (B) shows Caheraphuca Lough (after early 20th-century, 25-inch Ordnance Survey map), the surrounding peat-filled basin (broken line) and the location of pollen core CPL1. The footprint of the new road is shown in red.

was therefore decided to concentrate on nearby Caheraphuca Lough as a source of suitable sediments and a record of past environmental change.

Caheraphuca Lough is a small lake (<0.1 ha) largely hidden by trees growing on peat. It is located c. 750 m south-west of Caheraphuca Bog and lies in a peat-filled basin (c. 250 m by 150 m) surrounded by a low, glacial ridge with much shrub, including juniper. The lake is fringed by tall reedswamp (mainly *Cladium mariscus*, or saw sedge) and appears to be in the final stages of infilling. Parallel cores (CPL1 and CPL2), c. 9 m long, were taken at the eastern edge of the lake where the thickest sediments were noted (Illus. 4.3).[30] Pollen analysis and radiocarbon dating were carried out on core CPL1 following standard procedures (see Molloy & O'Connell 2004). Pollen samples were 1 cm thick. The sampling interval was mainly 4 cm, but closer interval sampling—including continuous sampling—was used where large changes in pollen representation were suspected. In

Illus. 4.2—Coring at the edge of Caheraphuca Lough with an Usinger piston corer, held by Ingo Feeser and Pat O'Rafferty.

addition to the usual pollen and spores, non-pollen palynomorphs (NPP; this includes fungal spores) and also micro-charcoal (charcoal particles ≥37 μm) were routinely counted during the analyses. In most samples, at least 1,000 pollen were counted.

4.2—Results

Near the base of the core, between 852 cm and 860 cm (Illus. 4.4), there was a distinctive, dark minerogenic layer that represents the Younger Dryas period. This was a cold period of about 1,000 years that immediately pre-dated the beginning of the post-glacial period (c. 9500 BC). Marl deposition resumed as temperatures increased at the beginning of the post-glacial. The upper part of the sequence (starting at c. 485 cm) was darker (with more organics/less marl and more shell) until about 173 cm from the surface, when the sediment became

Illus. 4.3—Lake sediment (marl) from Caheraphuca Lough partly extruded from the core tube.

Illus. 4.4—Core segment sequence CPL1. The core was retrieved using 1 m (segments I–III) and 2 m-long drives (segments IV–VI).

more organic rich and shell became less frequent. These changes probably reflect a variety of factors, including increased in-wash, which normally stimulates lake productivity, and general lowering of lake levels as infilling progressed and the lake became smaller.

Radiocarbon dates, from macrofossils and other material such as fine charcoal, are presented in Table 4.1, and an age/depth pollen curve is presented in Illus. 4.5. This curve is derived from a third order polynomial fitted to the radiocarbon dates, and the top of the core and the Elm Decline, which are regarded as dating to AD 2000 and 3850 BC, respectively (dates cited as BC or AD are derived from calibrated radiocarbon dates; radiometric dates as returned by the radiocarbon laboratory are

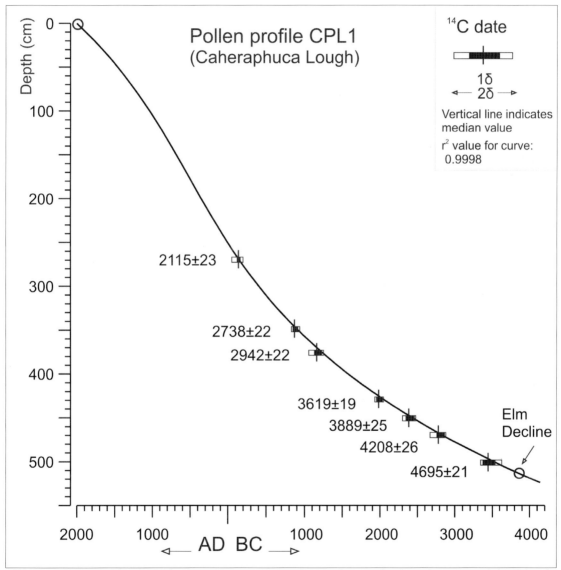

Illus. 4.5—Age/depth relationship in core CPL1. A polynomial curve fitted to the points defined by the radiocarbon dates (median probability values of the calibrated dates were used), the top of the profile, and the Elm Decline. The radiocarbon dates, from which the calibrated ages are derived, are also shown (in years BP).

cited as BP—before present, where 'present' is c. 1950). The resulting curve provides a chronology for the profile. The pollen diagram (Illus. 4.6) shows percentage composite and individual pollen curves, as well as concentration curves for the main taxa. The percentage values are based on a total terrestrial pollen sum (TTP); the lower cut-off size for cereal-type pollen was 40 μm (see Molloy & O'Connell 2004). The pollen diagram is divided into pollen assemblage zones (PAZs) based on major changes in the pollen curves. Four phases, during which there are substantial changes probably caused by human impact, are also highlighted (labelled Neol., and BA1, BA2 and BA3 which relate to the Neolithic and Bronze Age, respectively).

Given the small size of the lake and its sheltered location, it is assumed that the pollen profile is local rather than regional in character. In other words, it is assumed that most of the pollen derives from, at most, a kilometre radius of the lake.

4.3—Reconstruction of long-term environmental change

Early post-glacial woodlands (zone 1: 604–514 cm: c. 6000–3850 BC)

The lowermost part of the pollen profile indicates full woodland cover (trees and shrubs account for c. 97% of the total pollen). The dominant trees were oak and elm, and hazel was also abundant, probably mainly as an understorey shrub. Pine was present but it may not have been a major contributor to the local woodland. Note the macrofossil records for pine (Illus. 4.6) that consist mainly of pine periderm (bark) and bud scales noted in the sieving from the pollen samples. These provide firm evidence for the presence of pine near the lake.

The Elm Decline, datable to 3850 BC, defines the upper boundary of this zone. An *Alnus* (alder) curve is already established as the zone opens, and so zone 1 represents probably most of the so-called Atlantic period. The approximate age of the base of the profile is c. 6000 BC, based on the assumption that sedimentation rates do not deviate greatly from the expected and that the *Alnus* curve would have commenced shortly before the profile opens. The pollen data suggest a stable environment with no evidence of human impact. The presence of Mesolithic peoples in the vicinity of the lake is unlikely, at least on the basis of the evidence provided by the pollen data.

The Elm Decline (zone 2: 512–502 cm: c. 3850–3550 BC)

The mid post-glacial Elm Decline—a feature of most north-west European and particularly Irish pollen diagrams—is particularly well expressed in the pollen profile from Caheraphuca Lough (Illus. 4.6). Every other centimetre of sediment was analysed so that the record in this part of the profile is close to being continuous. *Ulmus* (elm) decreases from values generally in excess of 10% to almost 1% and, at the same time, *Corylus* (hazel) values increase. The concentration curves show a similar pattern (Illus. 4.6). This suggests a severe reduction in the elm population that enabled hazel to expand and flower more freely as a result of opening-up of the woodland canopy. *Quercus* (oak) percentage values decline somewhat, but the concentration values remain rather steady. In other words, it seems that elm was the main tree to be adversely affected at this time.

It is generally agreed that the Elm Decline phenomenon is best explained by the disease hypothesis (a disease such as the Dutch Elm Disease; see Molloy & O'Connell 1987; Peglar & Birks 1993; Parker et al. 2002). Human activity, in the form of Neolithic farming, may also have had a role—stone tools of Neolithic type were recovered from the burnt mound sites Caheraphuca 1, 3, 8, 11 and 12 (see Chapter 3). The impact of farming, if any, at Caheraphuca, is difficult to quantify. *P. lanceolata* (ribwort plantain; Illus. 4.7), the classic indicator of farming activity, shows only a relatively minor increase (<2% in all but one spectrum), and cereal-type pollen were not recorded. There is probably a human-impact factor operating, at least at a regional level, as well as a disease of elm. It is also clear that there was no major Neolithic Landnam (woodland clearance in the context of farming) at Caheraphuca, comparable to that at Céide Fields, north Mayo (Molloy & O'Connell 1995) or Ballinphuill, east Galway (Molloy et al. in press a & b).

Woodland change in the aftermath of the Elm Decline (zone 3: 500–452 cm: c. 3550–2400 BC)

Following the Elm Decline, elm recovers and attains its previous status in the local woodlands. Later (c. 3100 BC), ash, which was probably present in the region since prior to the Elm Decline (Atlantic period), established locally but failed to expand. Subsequently, yew, which seemed to have been present for a time (occasional pollen consistently recorded), expanded to become the dominant tree (*Taxus* maximum value: 34%), mainly at the expense of elm and, to a lesser extent, pine. This resulted in a high-shade, yew-dominated woodland with a poorly developed understorey.

Macro-remains of pine and also a stoma (from a leaf of pine) show that pine was important near the lake (Illus. 4.6; see also macro-remains in Table 4.1).

The causes of the above changes in woodland composition are uncertain. A perturbation, involving some opening up of the woodland cover, is suggested by the short *Juniperus* (juniper) curve that extends over the sub-zone boundary. This perturbation may be climate-induced rather than the result of human impact. Similar expansions of *Taxus* are recorded in several other pollen profiles from western Ireland at about this time. This would suggest that a regional factor such as climate may have been the main catalyst for change (O'Connell & Molloy 2001).

Land-use and woodland dynamics from the Neolithic/Bronze Age transition (Chalcolithic) to the Middle Bronze Age (zone 4: 448–376 cm: c. 2400–1200 BC)

Through this long interval of c. 1,200 years, the pollen data suggest human activity involving mainly pastoral farming but with a minor arable component (occasional cereal-type pollen were recorded in several spectra). More intensive farming phases are recorded at the beginning of the zone (c. 2400–2300 BC) and again in the middle (c. 1800–1600 BC; phases BA1 and BA2; Illus. 4.6). In each instance, elevated levels of human impact were followed by reduced farming and woodland regeneration that involved mainly elm. Yew was present but unimportant throughout the period under consideration. The slender pine curve may derive mainly from long-distance-transported pollen (pine pollen is noted for such) but macro-remains, and also pine wood from the archaeological excavations, indicate local survival of pine until quite late (pine bud scales recorded in the radiocarbon-dated sample from 348–350 cm point to a local presence until at least 1100 BC; see also section 4.4 'Conclusions').

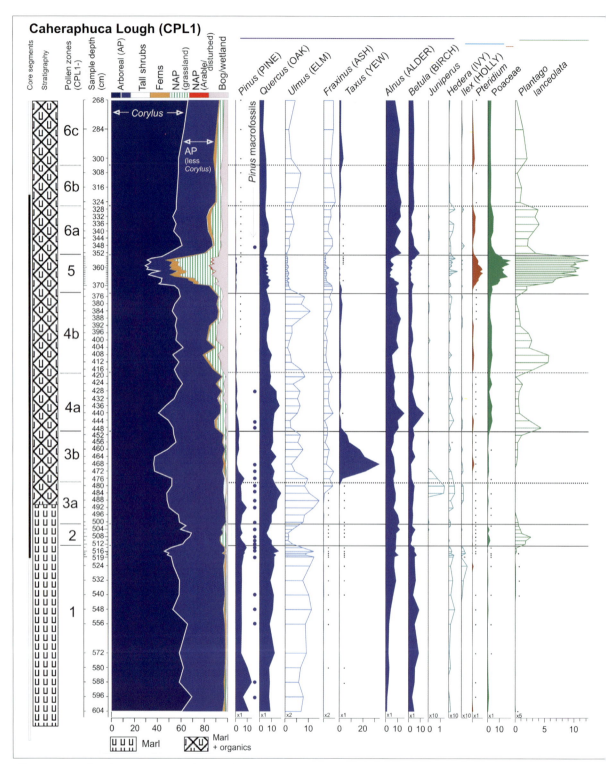

Illus. 4.6—Pollen diagram, CPL1, from Caheraphuca Lough. Percentage composite and individual curves (main taxa), and concentration curves for selected taxa are shown. Conventions used are as follows. Curves without infill

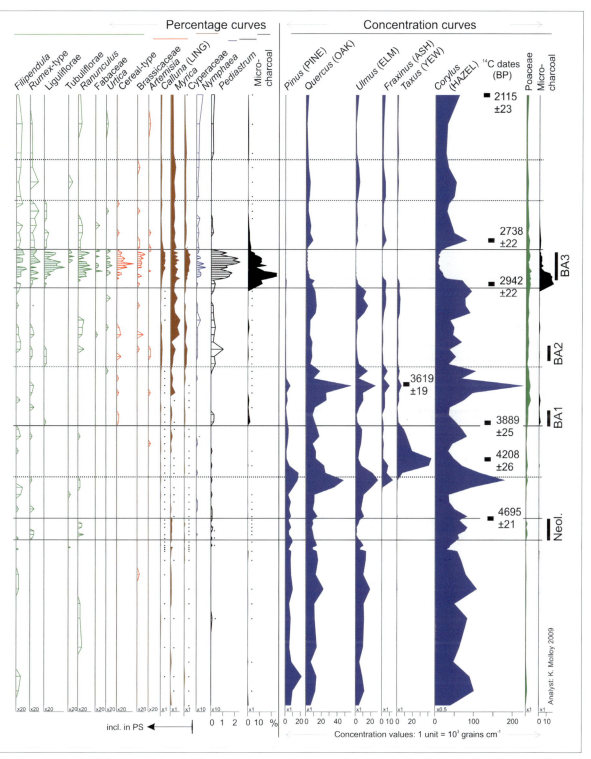

are magnified (to improve readability); the exaggeration factor is indicated above the x-scale. Large dots indicate macro-remains of pine. Small dots are used to emphasise low values that may otherwise not be obvious.

*Illus. 4.7—Top: Yew twigs showing pollen producing specimen (left) and with berries (right). Yew pollen is illustrated in the inset. Bottom: flowering heads of ribwort plantain (*Plantago lanceolata*) with buttercups in the background. Ribwort plantain pollen is illustrated in the inset.*

Landnam in the Middle–Late Bronze Age (zone 5: 372–354 cm: c. 1200–950 BC)

The most pronounced changes, in terms of human impact, are recorded in this zone. Large-scale woodland clearance, in the context of substantial farming, is signalled by the decline in arboreal pollen (AP) from an average of 89% in zone 4 to 52% over the 11 pollen spectra with the lowest AP values. The concentration diagram shows an even more pronounced decline (Illus. 4.6). There is a correspondingly large expansion of indicators of open habitat and especially pasture, including *Pteridium* (bracken) and a suite of NAP taxa including *P. lanceolata* (ribwort plantain), *Filipendula* (meadowsweet), *Rumex*-type (dock), *Ranunculus* (buttercup) and Liguliflorae (dandelion and hawkweed). There is a large increase in micro-charcoal, without a corresponding increase in macro-charcoal (as recorded in the sievings from the pollen samples), which suggests frequent fires but at some distance from the lake. It is likely that fires connected with the burnt mounds are reflected in the micro-charcoal curve. *Pediastrum* (alga) expands which suggests increased soil erosion in the lake catchment. Soil erosion is expected following the loss of tree cover and increased farming, especially arable farming which is reflected in the consistent records for cereal-type pollen.

The age/depth model suggests that zone 5, i.e. the Landnam phase, spanned roughly 250 years (Illus. 4.5). Interestingly, during the initial c. 50 years, while micro-charcoal values are high, there is no major expansion of pollen indicative of grassland. This suggests that farming was not particularly intensive in the vicinity of the lake (also no cereal-type pollen recorded) and population levels were probably also low.

Woodland and farming dynamics during the Final Bronze Age to the Middle Iron Age (zone 6: 352–268 cm: c. 950–130 BC)

As zone 5 ends (c. 950 BC), woodland regeneration was already well underway, mainly due to the expansion of hazel, birch and alder. Human impact continued to be relatively strong, and this was presumably the main factor limiting tree expansion—especially elm—until the end of sub-zone 6a (c. 650 BC). A short interval of approximately two centuries with greatly reduced farming activity followed. This facilitated a short-lived expansion of elm (sub-zone 6b). The uppermost spectra (sub-zone 6c) suggest a substantial clearance of the rather small elm population. There is also the possibility that elm was affected by disease, a view that is supported by the subdued increase in NAP curves and the regeneration of yew (though the latter is modest). A small increase in *Pediastrum* suggests some disturbance in the catchment of the lake.

4.4—Conclusions

The pollen profile from Caheraphuca Lough shows that the early post-glacial woodlands at Caheraphuca were dominated by oak, elm and, to a lesser extent, pine. The woodlands were also rich in hazel. At Caheraphuca Bog, c. 750 m to the north-west, pine and alder were more important, presumably favouring the extensive, local wet environment.

At the Elm Decline (c. 3850 BC), the elm population collapses. It is suggested that this is attributable to disease, the spread of which may have been facilitated by modest woodland clearances by Neolithic farmers. Elm subsequently recovered strongly and tall canopy woodland was fully restored by c. 3300 BC. Shortly after this, the initiation of a short *Juniperus* pollen curve suggests a perturbation that led to disruption of the woodland cover that, in turn, gave rise to conditions favourable to juniper. As there is no evidence for human activity, this perturbation may have been climatically induced. The initiation of a slender *Fraxinus* curve reflects the expansion of ash, and this is quickly followed by a major expansion of yew, which became the dominant tree by c. 2800 BC. The dominance of yew, however, is short lived. This may be due to natural causes (yew regenerates poorly under its own canopy; see Perrin et al. 2006), as the evidence for human activity continues to be weak.

In contrast to the Neolithic period, the Bronze Age is characterised by substantial human activity. Between c. 2400 and 2300 BC (i.e. at approximately the Neolithic/Bronze Age transition, or Chalcolithic period) elm declined, grasses and ribwort plantain expanded, and there was an increase in micro-charcoal. This suggests increased farming impact (phase BA1). A farming phase with greater impact and longer duration is recorded in the Early Bronze Age (c. 1800–1600 BC). By far the greatest impact, in terms of woodland clearance and farming activity (pastoral but also with cereal growing), occurred towards the end of the Bronze Age (c. 1200–950 BC). The radiocarbon dates from the burnt mounds at Caheraphuca and adjoining townlands extend over a long period of time—some relate to the Neolithic/Bronze Age transition, but most relate to the Middle and Late Bronze Age (c. 1600–850 BC) (Appendix 1). The pollen record suggests more or less continuous human activity throughout the Bronze Age, and thus supports the archaeological evidence, which points in the same direction (see Chapter 3). On the other hand, the pollen evidence shows that the most intense farming activity, at least in the vicinity of Caheraphuca Lough, relates to the final two centuries of the second millennium BC and extended into the early years of the first millennium BC. A reduced, but nevertheless substantial, level of farming, but with very little cereal production, continued into the Iron Age (c. 650 BC). From that point until the profile ends in the second century BC, human impact remained rather low, and the landscape was largely dominated by hazel scrub, with some oak, ash, elm and yew. Pine was probably extinct by then, at least locally and probably in the wider region.

The charcoal and wood analyses carried out in the context of the excavations of the burnt mounds provide additional insights into the local woodland and the use of its timbers for construction and fires (see Cobain & O Carroll, Chapter 3). In the Early Bronze Age, ash, oak, alder and yew were the most frequent charcoals recorded, while in the Late Bronze Age, oak and ash, and also yew, are much less frequent in the charcoal assemblages. Not surprisingly, hazel and hazel/alder (this category is used where more specific identification was not possible) were always important. On the other hand, birch and elm were infrequent. The infrequency of elm is somewhat surprising given its relative importance in the pollen record. Elm, as a source of charcoal, may have been differentially selected against. On the other hand, elm prefers fertile, well-drained soils and so it may have been growing at a distance from the burnt mounds.

In the unburnt wood samples recovered from the burnt mounds, alder and oak dominate, and alder was the main timber used for trough construction (Chapter 3). There are also records for pine, including some from burnt mound Caheraphuca 6 where alder wood gave the radiocarbon date 2806 ± 24 BP (UBA-12721). There is also a rather late record for pine wood from Caheraphuca 4, a burnt mound that yielded the radiocarbon date 2950 ± 41 BP (hazel charcoal; UBA-12746). These records point to pine, though mainly <0.5% in the pollen samples, persisting in the landscape until at least the Late Bronze Age. O'Carroll (2010, lxxii), referring to pine, indicates that she recorded it 'at numerous prehistoric and early medieval sites throughout Ireland'. Surprisingly, it has not been recorded in charcoal material from the Caheraphuca burnt mounds, so it was probably already rare in the locality at the beginning of the Bronze Age as suggested by the pollen record.

Finally, it is worth noting the strong similarity between the pollen profile from Caheraphuca and that from Mooghaun Lough, Co. Clare (Molloy 2005), in terms of both woodland dynamics—especially the role of yew—and also the impact of farming (see also Molloy & O'Connell 2011). Not surprisingly, given the location of Mooghaun Lough near a large hillfort dating to the Late Bronze

Table 4.1—Radiocarbon dates from palaeoecological investigations at Caheraphuca

Radiocarbon Lab code★	Material dated	Depth (cm)	Yrs BP	Range (2σ) Yrs cal. BC	Median Yrs cal. BC
Caheraphuca Lough					
UBA-11710	*Calluna* seeds; leaf fragments; charcoal fragments; plant stems	268–270	2115 ± 23	200–54 BC	138 BC
UBA-11714	*Pinus* bud scales; *Betula* bract; *Cladium* fruit; charcoal fragments	348–350	2738 ± 22	924–827 BC	874 BC
UBA-11716	Charcoal and leaf fragments	372–374	2942 ± 22	1258–1055 BC	1164 BC
UBA-10624	*Pinus* periderm and bud scales; *Betula* bud scale and fruit†	427–429	3619 ± 19	2032–1921 BC	1979 BC
UBA-11717	*Pinus* periderm and bud scales; *Betula* fruit and bud scale	448–450	3889 ± 25	2464–2298 BC	2387 BC
UBA-11718	*Pinus* periderm and bud scales; small bits of wood	468–470	4208 ± 26	2897–2680 BC	2794 BC
UBA-10625	*Pinus* periderm and bud scales; charcoal	500–502	4695 ± 21	3624–3374 BC	3435 BC
Caheraphuca Bog					
GrN-31603	*Alnus* wood	117–119	6500 ± 40	5534–5370 BC	5470 BC

★ Lab codes prefixed UBA are AMS dates from Chrono, Belfast (QUB). The lab code GrN indicates a date from the Centre for Isotope Research (CIO), University of Gronigen. Calibrations are based on CALIB ver. 6 (Stuiver et al. 2006) and IntCal09 (Reimer et al. 2009).

† Also *Calluna* fragments and charcoal fragments.

Age, and the presence of burnt mounds in its catchment area (three in all; the nearest to the lake core was dated to c. 1200 BC), the main Landnam phase in the pollen diagram, which dated to the Late Bronze Age, was exceptionally strong (Molloy 2005). The new pollen data from Caheraphuca Lough serve to emphasise the regional importance of the Late Bronze Age in terms of human activity and impact on the natural environment in central and south-east Clare (Plunkett 2009). Furthermore, it shows that high levels of human activity need not necessarily be connected with high-status sites such as hillforts. In the pollen profile from Caheraphuca Lough, human impact registers most strongly in the period 1200–950 BC, while the dates from the burnt mounds span the Bronze Age. This too is noteworthy in that it indicates that it may not be advisable to make a direct link between the frequency of burnt mounds and levels of human impact.

Notes

29 N52° 55.990', W8° 54.589'; 32 m above sea level (asl); Irish Grid ref. 131097, 187383

30 N52° 55.744', W8° 55.194'; 26 m asl; Irish Grid ref. 138187, 186831.

5

IRON AGE RING-DITCHES AND CREMATION BURIALS AT BALLYBOY

by Siobhán McNamara and Shane Delaney
with contributions by J Geber, F Sternke, J Carroll, I Riddler, N Trzaska-Nartowski
and J MacDermott

The Iron Age is one of the least archaeologically represented periods in Irish prehistory, and 'our understanding of settlement, economy and social structure in the period from 600 BC to the early centuries AD is meagre in the extreme'(Waddell 2000, 319). Consequently, the discovery of two previously unrecorded Iron Age funerary monuments in the townland of Ballyboy, Co. Galway is a significant and welcome addition to our knowledge of the period in the western region.

A long, whale-backed, gravel ridge rises above the surrounding bogs, about 5 km south of the town of Gort, in the townland of Ballyboy. The raised ridge of well-drained, good arable land is exactly the type of topographical feature where one might expect to find evidence of prehistoric activity, and Ballyboy did not disappoint. Two ring-ditches were found but were not located together, being at 1 km apart, on opposite ends of the ridge, at north and south. They both contained cremation burials and a large assemblage of artefacts, dominated by glass and amber beads. Radiocarbon dating of the human remains, in addition to comparable burial practices and artefactual assemblages, indicate that the two ring-ditches were broadly contemporary, and in use between the final century BC and the first century AD. Given the potential for additional prehistoric sites on the ridge a supplementary geophysical survey was carried out, but none were identified.

5.1—Site typology: ring-ditches

Ring-ditches are one of the monument types classified under the general 'barrow' label. Newman (1997, 155–70) identified five main types of barrow in the Tara area based mainly on morphological differences between monuments. They include the ring-ditch, the embanked ring-ditch, the ring-barrow, the bowl-barrow and the bowl-barrow lacking an external bank. Two additional barrow types—the stepped barrow and the enclosure barrow—have also been identified (Farrelly & Keane 2002). Ring-ditches generally consist of a single ditch enclosing a roughly circular area, however, examples with two and even three enclosing ditches have been noted, such as at Tankardstown, Co. Limerick (Gowen & Tarbett 1988), and Creevy, Co. Donegal (Waddell 2000, 366, fig. 182.3). The incorporation of an entrance into the enclosed area, generally a simple undug causeway, appears to be more common in later monuments.

Ring-ditches and barrows became common burial monuments in the Middle to Late Bronze Age. They may contain central cremation pits or cremated bone/funeral pyre debris, either in or beneath a mound, or in the fill of the enclosing ditch. Sometimes there is no direct funerary evidence associated with the ring-ditch, but in such examples the monuments are commonly located within a prehistoric cemetery complex (Daly & Grogan 1993). It is often unclear whether ring-ditches formed stand-alone funerary monuments or whether they are the remnants of flattened barrows. It is also possible that those examples lacking associated burials represent cemetery markers or even non-funerary structures.

The manner in which human remains were deposited in the ring-ditch varies from site to site. Both inhumation and cremation burials have been noted, but the latter appears to have been the dominant rite. Human remains were most commonly buried in simple unlined pits, but were also interred in cists and stone-lined pits. The interior burial space was usually defined by the ring-ditch, but in some cases burials can be found outside this enclosed area. It is also common to find cremated deposits in simple spreads within the interior or in the enclosing ditch. In many cases a variety of burial forms are found in one ring-ditch. In general the burials represent only a small proportion of the population and, given the type of artefacts that often accompany the remains, they probably represent the treatment of high-ranking individuals.

Ring-ditches are generally located on higher ground and are often found in close proximity to streams or rivers. Sites may be clustered, along with other barrow types, to form barrow cemeteries. In general, ring-ditches date to the Bronze Age, with the earlier examples being simpler in form and later examples incorporating entrances and a wider range of burials practices. Ring-ditches continued to be built, or earlier monuments reused, during the Iron Age and early medieval period. Iron Age ring-ditches were excavated at Ardsallagh, Co. Meath (Clarke & Carlin 2009), Cherrywood, Co. Dublin (O'Neill 2000, 54; 2006, 66–86), and Knockcommane, Co. Limerick (McQuade et al. 2009, 163–5), while two early medieval examples were excavated in Cross, Co. Galway (McKeon & O'Sullivan in press).

5.2—Ballyboy 1: ring-ditch and cremation burials[31]

This ring-ditch was discovered in the townland of Ballyboy, c. 4.5 km south of Gort and approximately 200 m east of the Gort to Tubber road. The ring-ditch was situated in an elevated, hedge-bound pasture field just below the crest of a long east-facing ridge, with good views to east and west (Illus. 5.1). Three human cremations were identified within the ring-ditch, bone from which produced Iron Age radiocarbon dates (Appendix 1). The earth-cut remains of a later structure were also found, and artefacts included decorated beads and an antler die.

The ring-ditch enclosed a space 6.4 m by 6.2 m with an external diameter of 8.6 m (maximum) (Illus. 5.2). The ditch was 1.65 m wide and 0.46 m deep (maximum). The primary fill of the ditch comprised silty clay with occasional charcoal (birch, crab apple, ash) and cremated bone. A cremation pit (C34), measuring 0.29 m in diameter by 0.14 m deep, was cut into this fill in the western arc of the ring-ditch. Cremated human remains of a single adult recovered from the pit returned a radiocarbon date of 90 BC–AD 47 (UBA-13026). A decorated antler gaming piece (Illus. 5.5) and six water-rolled stones were included in the deposit, along with charcoal fragments of ash and Maloideae species (hawthorn, rowan, and crab apple).

The ditch had been recut above the cremation pit. The shallow recut was deliberately filled (C4) with black, silty clay, rich in charcoal (hazel, birch, oak, ash, Maloideae) and cremated human bone from at least one adult. A sample of the bone returned a radiocarbon date of 89 BC–AD 48 (UBA-

Illus. 5.1—Ballyboy 1: elevated view of the ring-ditch looking north-east (AirShots Ltd).

13024). Seven glass beads and one of amber (Illus. 5.4) were recovered from the top of this fill, and two pieces of corroded iron.

Another small cremation pit (C11) was situated in the north-west quadrant of the ring-ditch interior—towards the centre—which measured 0.34 m by 0.3 m and was 0.27 m deep (Illus. 5.2). The position of this pit suggests that it was the primary burial and the focus of the ring-ditch. The cremated remains of an adult female were recovered and returned a radiocarbon date of 89 BC–AD 52 (UBA-13025). Charcoal from the pit included hazel, ash, crab apple and hawthorn. A post-hole (C13) was identified c. 1 m to the east.

Some possible structural features were cut into the top of the ring-ditch, at its southern extent (Illus. 5.2). The remains consisted principally of three L-shaped trenches (C7, C9 and C36) with well-defined cuts and V-shaped cross-sections. There were fragmentary remains of two other possible slot-trenches (C41 and C38), but these were heavily disturbed by a series of east/west cultivation furrows of later date. Together the slot-trenches defined an area 6 m north–south by 4.8 m east–west. No datable material was recovered from the trenches, but these features post-dated the ring-ditch and pre-dated the furrows. There is no positive evidence that they had any relationship to the ring-ditch or that they were of early date.

5.3—Ballyboy 2: ring-ditch and cremation burials[32]

The site of this previously unknown ring-ditch was approximately 5.5 km south of Gort, on the lower eastern flank of the same ridge as the ring-ditch at Ballyboy 1, but c. 1 km to the SSW.

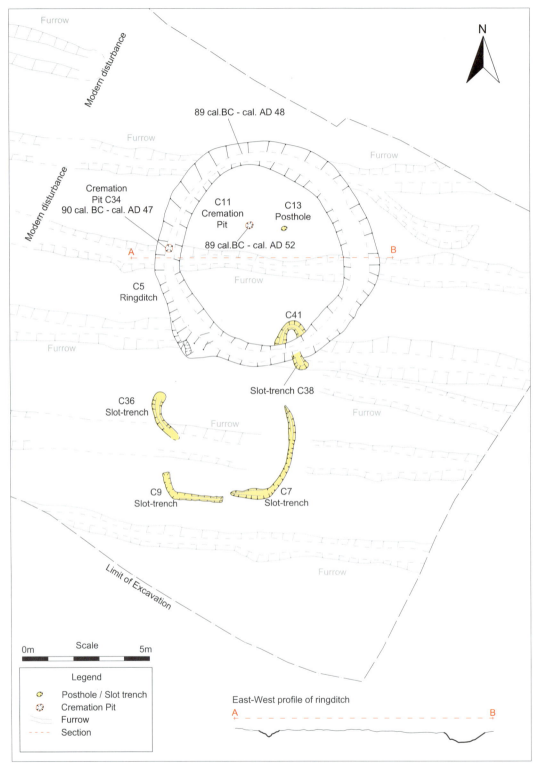

Illus. 5.2—Ballyboy 1: plan of the ring-ditch and associated features.

Ballyboy 2 lay in a pasture field that was enclosed by hedgerows on stony embanked field dykes, with a low-lying bog to the south. Unlike Ballyboy 1, the views from the site were restricted due to its low-lying aspect. The site included a number of cremation burials and a rich artefactual assemblage, including 69 glass and 24 amber beads (Illus. 5.4), and pieces of copper alloy (Illus. 5.6). The surface of the ring-ditch was crossed by later cultivation furrows.

The ring-ditch at Ballyboy 2 (C38) had an average diameter of 6.2 m (Illus. 5.3). The ditch measuring 1.27 m wide by 0.55 m deep (maximum) defined an area of roughly 4.15 m by 4.2 m. Four cremation pits were identified in the interior of the ring-ditch (C19, C24, C26 and C28); all of similar size (c. 0.49 m by 0.42 m and 0.2 m deep) and fills. The pits were arranged along a roughly west/east line, just south of the middle of the interior, and may have been the primary focus of activity on the site (Illus. 5.3). Charcoals from the pits included birch, oak and ash, and cremated human bone provided radiocarbon date ranges of 163 BC–AD 24 (UBA-13030) and 44 BC–AD 53 (UBA-13031) (Appendix 1).

The primary fill of the ditch (C30) contained bone fragments and charcoals of alder/hazel, birch, oak, ash, elm and poplar. A large cremation pit (C22) (1 m by 0.7 m and 0.28 m deep) was cut into the primary fill of the ditch, and contained charcoal and adult human (35–64 years) bone. The cremation pit was substantially larger than the others identified in the ring-ditch and was marked with stones. Cremated bone from the pit returned a radiocarbon date of 164 BC–AD 4 (UBA-13032).

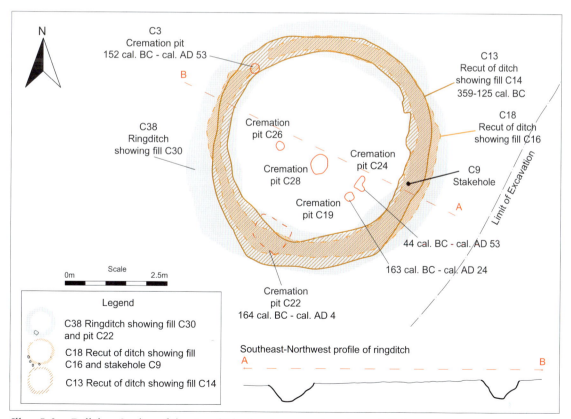

Illus. 5.3—Ballyboy 2: plan of the ring-ditch, showing cremation pits and ditch re-cuts.

The ditch was recut (C18) (cutting cremation pit C22) and deliberately filled with sandy silt containing charcoal, bone and stones. This fill (C16) contained the largest deposit of cremated bone (189 g), and while it was recovered from the entire ditch, it was identified as belonging to one adult individual (18–44 years). Charcoals from the fill included hazel/alder, birch, oak, ash, hawthorn and some carbonised hazelnut shell. The fill was homogenous apart from one lens of sandy silt that contained stones, charcoal and the skeletal remains of a juvenile (12–17 years). The fill of the recut, and the cremation pit (C22), were covered by a layer of stones; one of these stones was positioned directly over the cremation pit. A sealing layer, including charcoal and bone, was then deposited on top of the ring-ditch. A stake-hole within this layer may have held a site marker.

At a later stage the ditch was recut again (C13) and refilled with dark, sandy silt with charcoal, bone and stone inclusions (C14). A fragment of cremated human bone yielded a radiocarbon date of 359–125 BC (UBA-13028), which pre-dates the stratigraphically earlier cremation (C22). This most likely indicates that the later deposit was contaminated with earlier material. An area of oxidisation, or heat-scorching, was noted at the base of the second recut ditch. A charcoal-rich layer with cremated human bone on this scorched area may represent an *in situ* cremation, possibly performed immediately prior to the backfilling of the recut ditch. A small cremation pit (C3) was cut into the top fill of the recut. Burnt human bone from the pit returned a radiocarbon date of 152 BC–AD 53 (UBA-13027), and came from a juvenile aged 12–18 years.

5.4—Radiocarbon dates

The radiocarbon dates from the Ballyboy ring-ditches indicate that they were broadly contemporary, though the earliest activity may have occurred at Ballyboy 2. The three cremations at Ballyboy 1 produced dates between 90 BC and AD 52, while four of the radiocarbon dates recorded at Ballyboy 2 spanned the years between 164 BC and AD 53 (Appendix 1). However, bone from the cremation pit (C22) that cut the primary ditch fill of Ballyboy 2 returned a radiocarbon date of 164 BC–AD 4 (UBA-13032), providing a *terminus ante quem* of AD 4 for the initial construction of the ring-ditch. While cremated bone in the second recut ditch at Ballyboy 2 returned an earlier radiocarbon date, 359–125 BC (UBA-13028), this was at odds with the stratigraphical evidence, and must represent residual material. It does, however, reveal earlier Iron Age funerary activity in the immediate vicinity.

At both sites it is argued that the cremation pits within the ring-ditch interiors represented the primary focus of activity. At Ballyboy 1 this consisted of a single burial while at Ballyboy 2 four cremations were identified. However, no real chronological distinction was revealed in the radiocarbon dates returned for the burials in the interiors and those in the enclosing ditches, suggesting that little time separated those funerary events.

5.5—Human remains
by Jonny Geber

Three cremation burials were interred in the ring-ditch at Ballyboy 1. These contained the remains of at least three adult individuals, of which at least one is likely to have been a female and one a male. One burial was located in a cremation pit (C11) almost in the centre of the ring-ditch interior (Illus. 5.2). It contained approximately 500 g of well-cremated, but fragmented, clean bones, comprising over 2,200 fragments. About 33% of the weight could be identified to skeletal elements, and these included bones from all four anatomical regions (skull, axial, upper and lower limbs). Age at death was estimated to have been 18–44 years, and the sex was determined as probable female, based on a fragment of a mastoid process of a temporal bone (this anatomical landmark is smaller and less marked in females than in males). A second burial (in secondary fill C4) contained nearly 900 fragments of cremated bone, weighing almost 80 g. It was deposited within the cut of the ring-ditch. The bones were well preserved, but had suffered considerable fragmentation. A minimum of one individual was identified, of indeterminate sex. Bones from all anatomical regions of the body were present, indicating that a complete body was cremated. The final burial was interred within a pit (C34), which in turn cut the principal fill of the ring-ditch. Almost 564 g of cremated bone was found in this feature, comprising about 2,400 fragments. Again, bones from all four anatomical body regions were identified. The age at death was estimated at 18–44 years. The sex of the individual is likely to have been male, based on an assessment of the mastoid process of a temporal bone.

A total of 18 samples of cremated bone were analysed from Ballyboy 2. Six cremation pit burials were identified (Illus. 5.3), all of which contained adult remains, except for one possible exception (C28), which might constitute the remains of an adolescent. A total of 12 depositions of cremated human bone were found within the ring-ditch. The largest deposit (189 g) derived from an adult individual aged 18–44 years at the time of death. The remaining deposits were very small, ranging from only 0.07 g to 18.24 g. Unfortunately, severe fragmentation of the bones hindered much of the age and sex estimation of the cremated individuals. There is no evidence therefore suggesting that the difference in choice between burial contexts could have been related to social factors such as age and sex.

5.6—Artefacts

The artefactual assemblage from the Ballyboy ring-ditches is dominated by glass and amber beads. Other significant finds comprise Neolithic worked stone tools, a decorated antler/bone die, and copper-alloy fragments that probably represent clothes-fasteners or jewellery.

Worked stone
by Farina Sternke

Nine pieces of worked chert (not illustrated) were recovered from topsoil and from the fills of later cultivation furrows at Ballyboy 1, comprising one bifacial blade core, four flakes, one piece of debitage and two convex end scrapers. The worked lithics are typologically and technologically diagnostic and date to the Middle Neolithic period. There is evidence of *in situ* flint-knapping/tool resharpening at this site in the form of cores and debitage. The artefacts recovered are most likely associated with domestic tasks carried out in and around the environs of a possible nearby Neolithic settlement. Six natural, small water-rolled pebbles (manuports) of sandstone, limestone and chert were recovered from the fill of a cremation pit (C34). The inclusion of small water-rolled pebbles, often made of quartz, with cremation and inhumation burials occurs frequently throughout prehistory and the early historic period.

Beads
by Judith Carroll

A minimum of 105 beads made from glass (>77) and amber (>28) were recovered from cremation deposits in the ring-ditch (ditch and interior) at Ballyboy 2, while nine glass and one amber bead were recovered from the upper fills of the ditch at Ballyboy 1 (Illus. 5.4). The glass beads comprised two main types. Type A was a very small, light blue-green, translucent annular glass bead (though some were opaque). There were 38 of these from Ballyboy 2 and five from Ballyboy 1, which were almost all 1.75 mm to 2.5 mm in diameter and 1 mm thick (Illus. 5.4a). The chalky, opaque surface of some of these beads would appear to be due to heat damage or deterioration of the antimonite (tin or lead) components of the glass. Type B was a plain, dark-blue, annular glass bead, mainly of translucent glass, and is the most common type of bead found on Iron Age burial sites. At Ballyboy 2 there were 28 examples 2–3.5 mm in diameter and a further eight 3.6–9 mm in diameter (Illus. 5.4b). Three (fused together) examples were found at Ballyboy 1 measuring 2–3.4 mm.

There were three further glass beads at Ballyboy 2. One was roughly circular in shape, dark red/red-brown in colour, with a marvered (glass-blowing technique of shaping vessels by rolling or pressing the hot glass on a flat polished surface) brown and white twisted cable decoration in the form of an elongated S-shape placed laterally around its outer surface (Illus. 5.4c). A toggle/dumb-bell bead was also found, composed of two translucent pale blue-green spheres with a heavily pitted surface (Illus. 5.4d). Finally, four small sherds of opaque blue glass with marvered red linear decoration probably represent parts of one large decorated annular bead, which split in the heat of the cremation pyre (Illus. 5.4e). At Ballyboy 1 there was one almost spherical bead that measured 12.75 mm by 12 mm and had slightly flattened ends. It was pale blue-green in colour and clear to translucent with bubbles visible in its interior (Illus. 5.4f).

There were at least 28 amber beads recovered from Ballyboy 2—one small group (one to three beads) had melted due to exposure to intense heat and the number of beads was unclear. Most of the amber beads were of the same shape as, but larger than, the glass beads. They were 5–6.5 mm in diameter and roughly 3.5 mm thick (Illus. 5.4g). The single amber example from Ballyboy 1 was a large toggle/dumb-bell bead, 14 mm in length and 9–10 mm thick (Illus. 5.4h). It was dark yellow-brown in colour and had been heat damaged/distorted.

In summary, the beads were mostly small, annular and monochrome. There were only three beads (including four glass fragments making up one bead) decorated with a second colour or motif, and only one bead from each site (toggle beads) that deviated from the annular, spherical or tub-shaped varieties. A large number of the beads were heat affected, and in several cases, were fused together. The melting and carbonisation of the beads, as well as the linear fusing of groups of beads—which retain the shape of the perforation for the string throughout—indicate that the beads were lying horizontally in some cases as they were exposed to heat, probably as a consequence of being strung together and worn on the corpse in a pyre.

a) Glass bead fragment
E3718:8:6

b) Glass bead
E3718:14:9

c) Decorated glass bead
E3718:16:2

d) Glass toggle bead
E3718:23:2

e) Glass bead fragment
E3718:17:21

f) Large clear glass bead
E3719:4:3

g) Amber bead
E3718:33:33

h) Amber toggle bead
E3719:4:10

0   10mm

Illus. 5.4—Ballyboy 1 and 2: selected glass and amber beads.

Antler/bone die
by Ian Riddler and Nicola Trzaska-Nartowski

An antler/bone gaming piece was recovered from the cremation pit (C34) at Ballyboy 1, and has been identified as a parallelopiped die of flat rectangular form (Illus. 5.5). It measured 26.3 mm long by 15.1 mm wide and was 5.4 mm thick. It weighed 1.9 g. The incomplete antler/bone die lacks a part of both of its broad faces and less than half of one of those faces now survives. It has been intensely burnt to a light grey colour and most of the inner tissue no longer survives. The extent of the burning can be clearly seen on the broader faces, where the triple ring-and-dot motifs are now oval, although they were originally inscribed as circular patterns. The die has been reduced in size by heat along its length and to a greater extent across its width. The original parallelopiped form of the die is evident however, despite its subsequent history, and it was originally rectangular and noticeably flat, the narrow sides being scarcely wide enough to accommodate the ring-and-dot patterning.

The sequence of ring-and-dot designs allows the numbering of the die to be reconstructed. The broad faces were originally incised with five and six motifs. One of the longer sides is complete and has three motifs, while both of the short sides have two motifs. On a six-sided die, the number 4 would be expected to fill the remaining space, but this is less likely than a repetition of the number 5. The other long side has three motifs surviving, crowded towards one end, and could have accommodated four awkwardly spaced motifs originally, or as many as five in a more orderly arrangement, as noted below. The numbering sequence was almost certainly 3-5-5-6-2-2.

The antler/bone parallelopiped die from Ballyboy 1 conforms to a small group of similar gaming pieces known from Iron Age contexts in Ireland, including examples from Mentrim Lough *crannóg* and Lough Crew, in Co. Meath, and Cush, Co. Limerick (Raftery 1984, 248–50). The majority of Irish rectangular dice (both this flat type and those of square section) are dated to the first few centuries AD based on parallels from Britain. The flat series, to which the Ballyboy example belongs, is thought to be a little earlier, dating between the late first century BC and the first century AD (Raftery 1997, 95).

Metal objects
by Jacqueline MacDermott

A total of 15 fragments of copper alloy were recovered from Ballyboy 2. These were mostly unidentified pieces from the ring-ditch and a cremation pit (C22). Seven of the copper-alloy objects are thin curved fragments of wire. One is bent in a ring shape with overlapping ends and a sub-rectangular section. Other pieces are thin, curved, wire fragments with an oval/rectangular section, possibly from a single spiral-ringed object. This suggests a parallel with small spiral rings from early medieval pins (Fanning 1994, 13–15). Two pieces are similar flat, curved fragments, possibly from small copper-alloy washers or flat beads. A small rivet is still encased in a fragment of folded sheet metal. Two items (Illus 5.6) are roughly L-shaped with protrusions and are possibly terminals or feet from the same unidentified object. The remaining copper-alloy objects remain unidentified. The metal artefacts were found in association with the glass/amber beads and it is probable that, collectively, the objects are fragments of jewellery or clothes fasteners that were on the body when it was cremated.

Illus. 5.5—Ballyboy 1: parallelopiped antler/bone die (E3719:35:7), front and reverse.

Illus. 5.6—Ballyboy 2: conserved copper-alloy artefacts: terminals E3718:33:38 (top left) and E3718:33:41, a possible washer or bead E3718:17:32 (bottom left), and a rod or bar fragment E3718: 33:39.

5.7—Discussion

The ring-ditches at Ballyboy can be added to a number of Iron Age funerary monuments identified in the south Galway/north Clare region, many of which have been excavated in advance of recent infrastructural/road projects. A concentration of funerary barrows is known to the north of the Gort–Crusheen scheme (to the east and north-east of Ardrahan) that may date to the Iron Age. One excavated example at Grannagh, Co. Galway, consisted of a ring-ditch containing pockets of cremated bone and a variety of finds, including glass and dumb-bell-shaped beads and bone pins (Waddell 2000, 367). Another ring-ditch, complete with cremation deposits, was excavated at Oran Beg, near Oranmore, Co. Galway (Rynne 1970). Over 80 glass beads were recovered during the excavation and, like many of those from Ballyboy, some appeared to have been fused in the cremation pyre. South of the Gort–Crusheen road scheme there was evidence for Iron Age funerary activity identified during excavations along the N18 Ennis Bypass and the N85 Western Relief Road (Bermingham et al. in press). At Manusmore, Co. Clare, 27 burial pits returned radiocarbon dates spanning the Neolithic to the Iron Age, although the later pits contained burnt animal bone that may not be specifically related to the cremations. Another Iron Age pit burial was located nearby. At Killow, Co. Clare, cremation pits returned Iron Age radiocarbon dates of 750–390 BC

(Beta-211589) and 390–180 BC (Beta-211592), and a wooden (ash) bowl found in nearby peat returned a radiocarbon date of 777–407 BC (UB-6287). An Iron Age ring-ditch was also excavated on the Ennis Bypass scheme, at Claureen, Co. Clare. The ring-ditch measured 6 m in diameter and, although it had been disturbed, yielded cremated bone deposits and finds, including glass beads and fragments of quartz. Most of the Iron Age sites identified within close proximity to the new road relate to the funerary deposition of cremated bone, either in ring-ditches or in pits.

The bones in the cremation burials at Ballyboy 1 and 2 were all well incinerated, indicating that the cremations were successful and reached temperatures exceeding 650°C. All the bones were clean, which suggests that they were collected and sorted immediately after burning, as soot staining on the bones would have indicated that they were left in a smouldering pyre for some time before collection (Gevjall 1948, 155; Lisowski 1968, 78). The cremation of an average adult individual would generate around 1,000–2,400 g of bone (McKinley 1993, 285). At Ballyboy 1 the largest deposit of cremated bone amounted to 563.22 g (C34) while at Ballyboy 2 the largest deposit contained only 189 g (C17). The obvious absence of bone is indicative of token burial practice, and since the act of collecting the bones from the spent pyre would have been a time-consuming task, it may be an indicator of the high social status of the deceased (McKinley 1997, 142). Like the ring-ditches at Ballyboy, evidence from most of the excavated Iron Age funerary sites in the region reveals that the bones recovered from human cremation burials commonly do not represent complete individuals. This indicates that the practice of placing token deposits within pits and monuments was a common characteristic of Iron Age burials in the region.

The successful cremation of an average human requires about one ton of fuel and, in common with other prehistoric cremation sites in Ireland, the local community of Ballyboy appear to have specifically selected wood—such as oak, hazel and ash—which burns slowly at high temperatures, in order to optimise the cremation process and minimise the amount of fuel required (Grogan et al. 2007, 48–9). Again as noted elsewhere, the presence of charcoal from the Maloideae family, particularly crab apple (which has an aromatic scent when burnt) may indicate a conscious decision to also select fuels which would help to mask the smell of burning human remains (ibid., 112).

The Ballyboy beads add to our knowledge of Iron Age bead assemblages and of Iron Age burial practices. Glass and amber bead assemblages from this period are increasingly found in cremation burial sites between the latter centuries BC and the first century AD, and it is possible that in the future we will be able to refine their dates and identify the trade and importation of particular bead types. It is of great interest that bead assemblages are closely comparable and that a number of different bead types constantly recur between Iron Age burial sites producing beads. Strings of very small, coloured beads seem to have been particularly popular in opaque yellow, translucent and opaque dark blue, and a translucent blue-green, almost turquoise colour. Larger, coloured beads seem to have been common in ones and twos. A string of beads may have typically held a small number of decorated beads, interspaced by small monochrome beads which formed most of the necklace (or bracelet).

The origin of many of the beads of this period is likely to have been Britain rather than the European mainland, and the beads may have been sourced from factories such as that at Meare, in Somerset (Guido 1978, 65–75). There is no evidence for similar bead production factories in Ireland and the fact that the majority of sites at which beads are found are coastal, or fairly close to main rivers, increases the likelihood that they were traded from abroad by water. The Ballyboy beads can be closely paralleled with Iron Age bead assemblages along the east coast of Ireland such as Donacarney, Co. Meath (Carroll 2010), Balrothery, Co. Dublin (Ryan 2008, 134, pls. 14–17), Loughey, Co. Down (Jope & Wilson 1957, 84) and Ferns and Ask in Co. Wexford (Carroll 2000; 2007). A similar assemblage was also found with Iron Age inhumation burials at Knowth, Co. Meath (Eogan 1974, 81–2; pl. 26a and 26b), and small, blue glass beads akin to those from Ballyboy were found within a burial mound ('Carnfanny') at Pollacorragune, near Tuam, Co. Galway (Riley 1936, 48). Ballyboy is not far from the mouth of the Shannon and the west coast of Ireland, and is close to Grannagh and Derrybrien, Co. Galway. A toggle-bead comparable to the Ballyboy 2 example was found at Grannagh (Raftery 1984, 202), while a spectacular amber necklace of 500 strung beads was recovered from an Iron Age context in a bog at Derrybrien (O'Kelly 2005). Trade links between these and several other sites producing similar beads at a similar time may very well be worth exploring in the future.

The fragmented copper-alloy objects from Ballyboy 2 were mostly unidentified pieces found in association with the glass and amber beads in the ring-ditch and a cremation pit (C22). They included curved pieces of wire, possible washers and rivets, folded sheet metal and L-shaped terminals or feet (Illus. 5.6). Their material, form and provenance would suggest that, along with the decorative beads, they represent fragments of jewellery or clothes fasteners that were on the body when it was cremated.

The antler/bone gaming piece found at Ballyboy 1 has been interpreted as a parallelopiped die of flat rectangular form by Riddler and Trzaska-Nartowski and it is part of a small group of these gaming pieces known from Iron Age contexts in Ireland. Raftery (1984, 248–50) has drawn attention to similar 'rectangular plaques' from Mentrim Lough *crannóg*, Co. Meath, and Cush, Co. Limerick, and an unfinished strip of bone from Lough Crew, Co. Meath, can also be added to this group. The Cush die, although more elaborate in its decoration, nonetheless includes five triple ring-and-dot motifs on one broad face and six on the other, as is the case with the Ballyboy example. One of the long sides has three motifs and two survive on the other, fragmentary long side, where there may have originally been four or five (Ó Ríordáin 1940, fig. 38; Raftery 1984, fig. 122.2). The identification of the Cush implement as a die was confirmed with the publication of a comparable die of Iron Age date from Navan Fort, Co. Armagh (Raftery 1997). This is a rectangular antler or bone strip of a simple type, without any elaboration of its single ring-and-dot markings. Both this die and another of the flat die series from Kilcurrivard, Co. Galway, include the numbers 5 and 6 on the broad faces, with 3 and 5 on the long sides.

There appears to be some consistency in the numbering arrangements across all of the dice of this flat die series. They have five and six motifs on the broad faces, and three and five motifs on the long narrow sides. Interestingly, however, the short narrow faces are different. The Navan die has one motif at either end, while Ballyboy 1 has two; Cush has no motifs on these sides. The Mentrim Lough strip is more problematic, being considerably larger than the other members of this class, with three and four motifs on the long narrow sides, six on one broad face but only two apparent on the other (Raftery 1984, fig 122.1). The dice from Cush, Navan and Ballyboy 1 are all less than 30 mm in length and 12–16 mm in width, whilst the Mentrim Lough strip is 64 mm by 27 mm.

Raftery (1997, 95) argued that the majority of Irish rectangular dice (both the flat type and those of square section) should be dated to the first few centuries AD, on the basis of parallels from Scotland and England. The flat series, to which the Ballyboy die belongs, is thought to be a little earlier, belonging to the period of the late first century BC to the first century AD. The Scottish series of parallelopiped dice were catalogued by D V Clarke (1970), and subsequent discoveries have been noted by Hall (2007, 9, fig. 18). The earliest Scottish dice go back to the late first century BC and extend well into the first millennium AD, a dating scheme that matches the Irish evidence. The English series also consists of both flat rectangular dice and those of square section. The former group includes examples from Cadbury Castle and Maiden Castle, of Late Iron Age to early Roman date (St George Gray 1966, 296; Wheeler 1943, 310–11, fig. 106.5-6). While there can be some differences in numbering arrangements, flat rectangular dice from England generally come from contexts of the late first century BC to the first century AD. This is the same dating that Raftery has proposed for the Irish series.

5.8—Summary

The ring-ditches at Ballyboy represent small funerary monuments that were used for a period between the first century BC and the first century AD. The radiocarbon dates returned for both sites, in addition to the comparable burial practices and artefactual assemblages, indicate that Ballyboy 1 and 2 were contemporary, or near contemporary, with one another. The sites were used for multiple burials, comprising token cremations, over a relatively short period of time. Due to the fragmented nature of the burnt bone the diagnostic traits for sexing and aging the remains were mostly absent; however, most age groups were noted in those remains that could be identified. The funerary activity at the sites was represented by pit burials and also by the deposition of cremated material in the enclosing ditches, perhaps as a ritual clearing of the non-specific pyre material. The recovery of a large assemblage of imported glass and amber beads (often heat-affected) and the remnants of possible copper-alloy dress fasteners at Ballyboy 2, indicates that at least some of the bodies were cremated clothed and presumably in their finery. The artefacts recovered from the sites, and the funerary rites revealed, combined with the specific dating of the burials, has furthered our knowledge of Iron Age funerary monuments and practices both locally and on a national level.

The ring-ditches at Ballyboy compare well with a number of other Iron Age funerary monuments identified in the south Connacht/north Munster area and beyond, with regard to their form, date, use and artefactual assemblages. The antler/bone die, in particular, represents a significant find, as it joins only a small group of similar objects recorded in the country.

On a final note, the anomalous radiocarbon date of 359–125 BC returned for cremated human bone at Ballyboy 2, reveals earlier, Iron Age funerary activity in the immediate vicinity, and the diagnostically Neolithic chert tools and debitage from Ballyboy 1 push the human story of the townland even further back in prehistory.

Notes

31 Excavation No. E3719; Director Siobhán McNamara; NGR 143125 197976; height 39 m OD; parish of Beagh; barony of Kiltartan; County Galway.

32 Excavation No. E3718; Director Siobhán McNamara; NGR 142802 197359; height 33 m OD; parish of Beagh; barony of Kiltartan; County Galway.

6
CROPS, IRON AND WATER

by Shane Delaney, Ed Lyne and Joe Nunan
with contributions by S Cobain, J Geber and J Carroll

This chapter focuses on the evidence for industrial and agricultural activities carried out at four distinct sites along the route of the new M18 motorway. Three cereal-drying kilns dating to the early and later medieval periods were discovered in Curtaun townland, Co. Galway, in the shadow of a bivallate ringfort (GA128-043) that stood in immediate proximity to the road scheme. At Rathwilladoon, Co. Galway, and Derrygarriff, Co. Clare, iron-working furnace pits and charcoal-production kilns indicated Iron Age and later metal-working activities at those sites. Finally, agricultural features dating to the later medieval and post-medieval periods were excavated at a previously recorded enclosure (CLO18-017) in Sranagalloon, Co. Clare. This was also the site of a Bronze Age cremation burial.

6.1—Curtaun 1: medieval corn-drying kilns[33]

A series of three corn-drying kilns, spanning the early and later medieval periods, was excavated at Curtaun, Co. Galway, c. 1.8 km north-east of Tubber crossroads. The kilns were located on the east-facing slope of a long, whale-backed ridge, in a strip of land between an existing railway line and an upstanding bivallate ringfort (GA128-043; Illus. 6.1). The land was well-drained but overlooked bog to the east and south-east. The corn-drying kilns are a significant discovery, as their close proximity to a ringfort hints at the continuous occupation, or reoccupation, of that site from the early to the later medieval period. No artefacts were recovered from the kilns, but two glass beads were found in the surrounding topsoil, that are likely to be associated with activity either at the kilns or the ringfort (see below). The bank of the ringfort was a simple dump-constructed earthwork. The ditch-fills were sterile mineral soils.

Post-medieval/modern activity was also evident, in the form of six, wide, hand-dug cultivation furrows, some isolated features of unknown function, and a limited number of artefacts. These included a copper-alloy, James II halfpenny, dating to 1691 and minted in Limerick, recovered from the topsoil.

Cereal-drying kilns

Kiln 1 was the earliest of the three kilns (Illus. 6.2 and 6.3), and survived as an oblong pit with remnants of a stone lining. It was orientated roughly north/south, and appeared to widen at the drying chamber end (north). That end was truncated by the later kilns but the cut appeared to have

Illus. 6.1—Curtaun 1: the kilns were situated downslope and south-east of a bivallate ringfort (GA128-043), now covered with trees (AirShots Ltd).

originally been keyhole-shaped in plan, comprising a drying chamber and a flue. The flue was 1.5 m wide and 0.62 m deep, and the overall length of the kiln would have been approximately 5 m. A layer of sandy silt lay along the base of the cut. This fill appears to have supported the stone lining of the kiln wall, which was set onto it. Not much of the stone lining remained, and it is likely that much of this drystone wall was robbed out and used for the construction of the later kiln(s). A number of charcoal- and ash-rich 'use-fills' indicative of *in situ* burning were found within the chamber and along the flue. The kiln was later backfilled with sterile soils, which probably included stones from the kiln wall. Charcoal (wild/bird cherry) recovered from a use-fill within the chamber returned a radiocarbon date of AD 674–870 (UBA-12710). Kiln 1 also yielded charcoals of sessile oak, hawthorn, rowan, sloe, blackthorn and yew. Cattle and sheep/goat bones were recovered from the backfill material, and caprovine bones were identified in one of the use-fills, along with the remains of field mice.

Kiln 2 was the second kiln constructed. It survived as a long, narrow, oblong pit (1.1 m wide by 0.5 m deep), again with some remnants of the stone lining *in situ* (Illus. 6.2 and 6.3). The pit widened and deepened at the northern, drying chamber end (1.5 m wide by 1 m deep) to form a keyhole shape in plan. The overall length of the kiln was 7 m, and it was aligned north-west/south-east. The flue and chamber were lined with drystone walls but, as with Kiln 1, most of the stones were missing

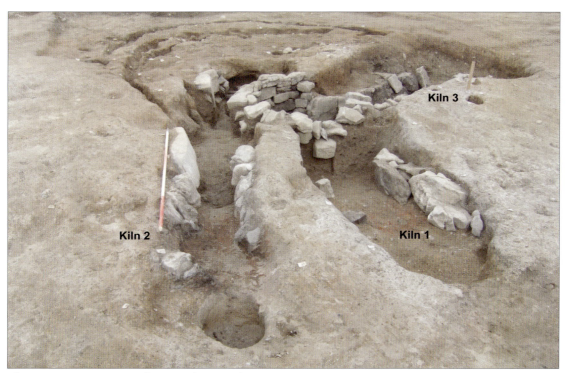

Illus. 6.2—Curtaun 1: Kilns 1–3, from south.

Illus. 6.3—Curtaun 1: Kilns 1–3, from west.

Illus. 6.4—Curtaun 1: Kiln 3, from north-east. Note the large, unlined fire-bowl and the lintel stone across the flue.

and may have been reused in the construction of Kiln 3. The chamber of the kiln contained evidence of *in situ* burning, in the form of heat-affected clay and a charcoal-rich fill. A sterile layer above these 'use-fills' may indicate a period of inactivity. A layer of charcoal and burnt clay overlay this sterile fill within the flue. It contained fragments of barley (*Hordeum vulgare*), emmer wheat (*Triticum dicoccum*) and indeterminate grain (*Poaceae*). An irregular cut (C192) at the southern end of the flue may represent a recessed fire setting for the kiln, which would have helped to prevent burning fuel from entering the flue. Above this, a layer of charcoal (C72) and ash constituted the final stages of use. This context contained charcoals of alder, hazel, oak, ash and crab apple, in addition to barley, emmer wheat, free-threshing wheat (*Triticum aestivum/durum*), indeterminate grain and hazelnut shell. The kiln then appeared to have been backfilled through a series of deliberate depositions and natural silting. A radiocarbon date of AD 779–947 (UBA-12712) was returned for a fragment of charred, hulled barley recovered from the final use-fill (C72). Cattle bone was recovered from lower fills of the flue, sheep/goat bones came from the uppermost fill, and a fragment of pig mandible and a bone fragment from an adult horse were recovered from backfill material in the chamber.

Kiln 3 was the final kiln to be constructed. It was aligned north-east/south-west—a completely opposite alignment to the previous two kilns. It was a more substantial and better preserved construction than Kilns 1 and 2, and comprised a large, unlined, bowl-shaped fire pit (C29) and a stone-lined flue leading to a stone-lined chamber (C31) (Illus. 6.4 and 6.5). The chamber walls were of drystone construction, and the lining of the flue consisted of edge-set, un-mortared stones topped

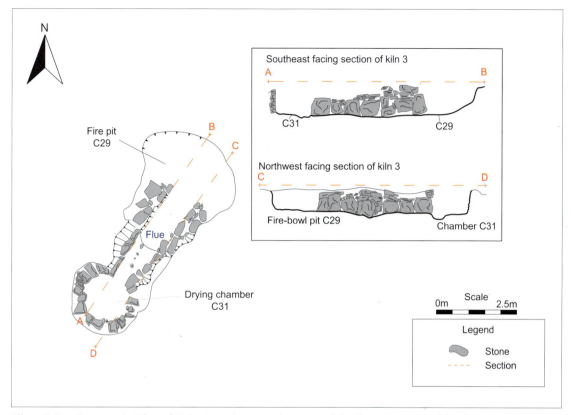

Illus. 6.5—Curtaun 1: Plan of Kiln 3, and section drawings of the drystone walls of the flue.

with lintels. Although the cut for the kiln was an oblong pit, c. 7 m by 2 m and c. 1 m deep, the stone structure within it was of the classic keyhole-shape in plan. The fire-bowl contained five layers with evidence of burning—three of ash and two of charcoal. The flue also contained three layers of ash and charcoal and some probable trample layers. It was then partly backfilled with charcoal-rich, silty clay, which included some collapsed lintels. Finally, it was filled by layers of silt.

Hazel charcoal from the basal layer of the Kiln 3 chamber yielded a radiocarbon date of AD 1218–1270 (UBA-12709). This context also produced charcoals of alder, birch, oak, ash, crab apple, wild/bird cherry and yew, and produced seed and grain fragments of stinking chamomile (*Anthemis cotula*), oats (*Avena* spp), wheat and free-threshing wheat. Another fill contained oats, barley, naked barley (*Hordeum vulgare*), wheat, einkorn wheat (*Triticum monococcum*) and indeterminate grain. Animal bones recovered from the kiln came from cattle and sheep/goats. A large number of fox bones were also recovered, in addition to hare and field mice bones, and the fragmented remains of the common frog. Early modern/modern pottery sherds (pearlware) and broken clay pipes found in two of the upper fills represent intrusive finds.

Four curvilinear slot-trenches were located on a level area to the immediate north-west, and upslope, of the kilns (Illus. 6.6 and 6.7). For the effective drying of grain a superstructure was sometimes constructed over or around the drying chamber, and this is sometimes represented by the presence of post-holes, stake-holes or foundation gullies (Monk & Kelleher 2006, 84). It is

Illus. 6.6—Curtaun 1: excavation in progress of the three corn-drying kilns. Note the curvilinear foundation trenches to north, and the pit at the southern end of Kiln 2 (bottom left). This is probably a recessed fire pit (AirShots Ltd).

possible that the curvilinear slot-trenches at Curtaun supported the structural walls of a C-shaped building, or buildings, that shielded the drying chamber(s) from the elements. It is unclear whether this structure was roofed and covered the drying chamber, or whether it formed an open-topped, curvilinear windbreak.

The earliest of the foundation trenches (C173) was truncated by Kiln 2 at its southern end, and was probably contemporary with Kiln 1, which was at the centre of its arc. Another foundation trench (C52) may represent a later repair/reinforcement for this trench. The outermost foundation trench (C44) may have supported a shelter for Kiln 2. It is possible that a shallow, sub-oval pit (C169) on the south-east side of Kiln 3 was a continuation of this trench, and that Kiln 3 truncated it. A short trench (C42) was truncated by Kiln 3 at its east extent and may have been related to activity in Kiln 1 or 2. Eight post-/stake-holes to the south of that foundation trench may have supported an associated superstructure, or an independent structure, which was partly truncated by the kilns. In purely spatial terms, the foundation trenches appear to be aligned on Kilns 1 and 2, rather than on Kiln 3. Hazel charcoal from the fill of slot-trench C52 returned a radiocarbon date of AD 717–888 (UBA-12711). This early medieval date range overlaps the dates of both Kilns 1 and 2. Oak charcoal was also recovered from this context, in addition to the carbonised seeds of oats, barley, free-threshing wheat and indeterminate cereal grains.

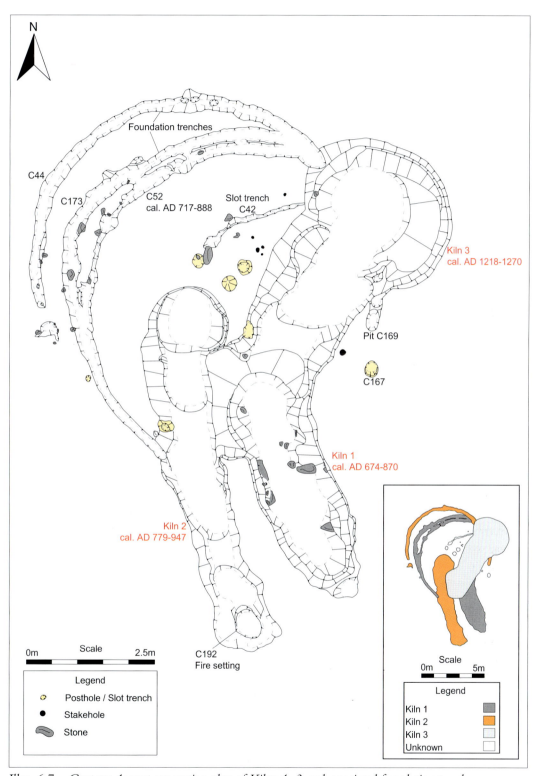

N

Foundation trenches

C44

C173

C52
cal. AD 717-888

Slot trench
C42

Kiln 3
cal. AD 1218-1270

Pit C169

C167

Kiln 1
cal. AD 674-870

Kiln 2
cal. AD 779-947

C192
Fire setting

Scale	
0m	2.5m

Legend	
⚬	Posthole / Slot trench
●	Stakehole
▬	Stone

Scale	
0m	5m

Legend	
Kiln 1	
Kiln 2	
Kiln 3	
Unknown	

Illus. 6.7—Curtaun 1: post-excavation plan of Kilns 1–3 and associated foundation trenches.

Charcoal and plant remains
by Sarah Cobain

Oats, barley and wheat were identified in all three phases of kiln activity. Crop husbandry was important in early and later medieval society, with regard both to consumption within the local community and as an economic resource for trade. Oats, barley and wheat would have been made into bread, porridge, soups, stews, cakes, tarts and beer; but oats and barley may have also been used as fodder, and wheat straw makes useful thatching material. The damp climate of the west meant that grain would have been moist when harvested, and needed to be dried before further processing could take place. This drying halted any possible germination of the grain, prevented decay, and hardened the grain, making it easier to mill (Gibson 1989, 219; Monk & Kelleher 2006, 77–8). Cereal-drying kilns would therefore have been essential to arable farmers.

The charcoal remains included ash, oak, hazel, alder, poplar/willow, wild/bird cherry, blackthorn/sloe, Maloideae (hawthorn, rowan, crab apple) and yew. Oak and ash were identified as the main fuel used in the kilns, supplemented with other species. While some of the ash and oak may have been acquired through trade, the remaining species were probably obtained from the local environment. This would indicate an oak-ash woodland on drier land and an alder-carr fen in the wetland areas towards the south and south-east of the site.

Animal bone
by Jonny Geber

Nine cattle bones were recovered, one of which bore knife marks indicative of butchery. The kilns also yielded 16 sheep/goat bones, one pig bone, one horse bone, 124 fox bones (from a minimum of three animals), 16 hare bones, 32 bones from field mice and three from the common frog. None of these had been butchered. The majority of animal bones are a reflection of wild nature rather than human activity. Kiln 3 appears to have been used as fox den some time following its abandonment, and foxes are probably responsible for most of the other animal bones found at the site. Additionally, bones from burrowing animals such as field mice and the common frog are indicative of relatively recent disturbances.

Glass beads
by Judith Carroll

Other than some unstratified and intrusive post-medieval/modern finds, the only artefacts recovered from the site were two glass beads found in the topsoil (Illus. 6.8). One example was a complete, though lopsided, opaque annular bead. It had a black base colour with a band of red glass fused over the outer surface. It was 7.5 mm in diameter, 2–4 mm in height, and had a 2 mm diameter perforation. While no direct comparisons could be found, it is similar to a bead found with a burial in Balrothery, Co. Dublin, dated between the second and fourth centuries AD (Ryan 2008, 115, 127). The second bead was made of turquoise blue, opaque glass, but had been broken in half (along the line of the perforation). It was 9 mm in diameter with a height of 5–6.5 mm, and a perforation of 4 mm in diameter. The bead is unusual: in shape, it is typical of beads found in Iron Age and early medieval contexts (and later ones), but the colour and type of glass are not. Most early medieval glasswork found in Ireland was made in Ireland (e.g. Henderson 1988) and differs somewhat from earlier imports. The manufacture of the glass colour of this particular bead would have necessitated the use of antimony—e.g. lead or tin—in the glass mix. Antimonite usually results in some (even slight) deterioration, but this bead shows no sign of decay and there is no pitting evident. Although this bead could belong to an Irish, early medieval context, its glass has a very industrial look. A turquoise

Illus. 6.8—Curtaun 1: glass beads (E3721:1:2 and E3721:1:1) recovered from topsoil at the kiln site.

glass bead was found in an Iron Age context at Navan Fort, Phase III (Waterman 1997, 87), but it was much smaller than the example from Curtaun. The bead could date to the early centuries AD, and be an import from the more industrialised factories of the Roman world. It is also possible that it represents an early modern period (or even later) import. Coloured beads were extensively produced from the late 16th century, particularly in Dutch factories, and were exported widely. The beads were usually multi-coloured but some plain turquoise examples are known (Sher Dubin 1987, 238).

In conclusion, no direct comparisons have been found for either of the beads. The closest parallel to the complete bead was found in a Late Iron Age context, while the broken, turquoise example could be Irish made and date to the Iron Age or early medieval period, or could equally be an import from the Roman Empire or from a post-medieval/early modern Dutch factory. Although both beads were recovered from unstratified contexts, their discovery in close proximity to the kilns and the ringfort would suggest that they are broadly medieval in date.

Discussion

All three of the kilns shared a similar form of construction—earth-cut, stone-lined and keyhole-shaped in plan—but returned different radiocarbon dates. Kiln 1 was in use between the late seventh and late ninth centuries, Kiln 2 between the late eighth and mid 10th centuries, and Kiln 3 during the 13th century. The overlap in dates between Kiln 1 and 2 suggests the continuous use of the site for cereal drying throughout the later first millennium, while the temporal break between Kiln 2 and Kiln 3—indicated by the later date for Kiln 3—may reflect a physical break in activities towards the end of that period. Despite this possible break, it is clear from the form and spatial arrangement of the kilns that each episode of construction was influenced by what preceded it (whether or not the kiln was still in use). Indeed, it is likely that many of the stones used to build Kiln 2 came from Kiln 1, and were subsequently recycled once more to construct Kiln 3. Apart from their various states of preservation, the only notable difference in the kilns was the orientation of Kiln 3. While Kilns 1 and 2 were aligned north/south (drying chamber to north and fire-bowl to south), Kiln 3 was constructed on an almost opposite alignment (drying chamber to south-west and fire-bowl to north-east).

Based on the dating evidence and their spatial arrangement, the curvilinear slot-trenches probably supported structures associated with Kiln 1 and/or Kiln 2. The earth-cut remains suggest that they formed semi-circular, or C-shaped, structures that sheltered the drying chambers of the kilns. These may have been roofed, open-fronted buildings that covered the drying chambers. Alternatively, they may have been uncovered windbreaks. Based on experiments at Lisnagun 1, Co. Cork (Monk & Kelleher 2006, 101), they may even have had detachable roofs that were used according to weather conditions. Structural evidence associated with corn-drying kilns has been identified at a number of Irish sites. Based on the arrangement of post-holes, it was postulated that kilns excavated at Ballynaraha, Co. Tipperary, and Carnalway, Co. Kildare, had roofed structures, while the kiln at Rathbane South, Co. Limerick, was enclosed by a curvilinear feature that may have represented a barn wall (ibid., 84). Another kiln, at Haynestown, Co. Meath, was described as being 'attached to a storage shed' (O'Sullivan 1994, 57). Other excavated kiln structures are best interpreted as screens or windbreaks, such as examples from Kiltenan South, Co. Limerick, and Jordanstown, Co. Dublin, the latter comprising a linear trench (Monk & Kelleher 2006, 84).

Corn-drying kilns were of great importance to the Irish economy throughout the medieval period, and are mentioned in early medieval texts (Kelly 1998, 241). According to one such text, *Críth Gablach*, a wealthy farmer of *bóaire* rank was expected to own a corn-drying kiln, while farmers of a lower social order, *ócaire*, would have only owned a share (ibid.). The early Irish law texts say little about corn-drying kilns, but one reference states that 'if somebody dries corn without permission in another's kiln, he must pay a milch cow and a yearling heifer, and must restore any damage' (ibid., 144). It was not, however, considered an offence for a person to 'forage among the kiln-scrapings belonging to another'—kiln scrapings were the ashes scraped from the base and sides of the kiln after use, and could contain grain (ibid., 242).

The location of the kilns at Curtaun, downslope and to the south-east of the ringfort, meant that the prevailing westerly winds would have blown smoke and any potential fire hazards away from the settlement site. Given the location and chronology of the kilns it can be assumed that they were constructed and used by the inhabitants of the ringfort. The repeated use of the site for cereal processing suggests that the ringfort was occupied between the late seventh and the mid 10th century at least and, while a temporary break in the sequence may have occurred in the 11th and 12th centuries, it would appear that the ringfort was reoccupied in the 13th century. It is, however, possible that cereal drying occurred elsewhere during this apparent hiatus—perhaps beyond the narrow corridor investigated in advance of the new road—and that the ringfort enjoyed continuous occupation from the late seventh to at least the mid 13th century.

6.2—Charcoal production and metal-working at Rathwilladoon 5[34] and Derrygarriff 2[35]

Rathwilladoon 5

Two sites produced evidence of both charcoal production and iron-working. At Rathwilladoon 5, Co. Galway, an Iron Age radiocarbon date was returned for a metal-working furnace, and while the adjacent charcoal-production kiln was not dated, this feature may be contemporary. This may not, however, be the case as illustrated at Derrygarriff 2, Co. Clare where an Iron Age date was also returned for a metal-working furnace, but despite the close proximity of a charcoal-production kiln, the latter feature yielded a date range spanning the 17th to the mid 20th centuries AD.

A charcoal-production kiln and a small metal-working furnace were discovered in Rathwilladoon, Co. Galway, c. 750 m south of Tubber crossroads. The site was located in a slightly elevated pasture, on the edge of wetland to the east. It was overlooked to the west by a steep slope leading to a north/south ridge.

The main feature was a shallow oblong pit (C3), 2.82 m by 1.22 m and 0.14 m deep (Illus. 6.9). The primary fill of the pit comprised densely packed pieces of oak charcoal, and the clay sides of the cut were scorched red from burning *in situ* (Illus. 6.10 and 6.11). Some hazel charcoal was identified in the upper fill, which probably constituted deadwood used as kindling. The evidence of *in situ* burning and the sheer quantity of charcoal suggest that this was a charcoal-production kiln/clamp. It is unclear why the charcoal was left in the base of the clamp after its abandonment. Perhaps it was not needed or, alternatively, it may have become damp and lost its usefulness.

Just west of the kiln/clamp was a small pit (C7), measuring 0.19 m by 0.15 m and 0.13 m deep (Illus. 6.9). It contained charcoal (mainly hazel) and ferrous fragments (slag), and probably represents a furnace pit. It is possible that this was a trial furnace used to test small amounts of bog ore, perhaps to ensure that it was of good quality before transporting it elsewhere. Alternatively, limited quantities of metal may have been produced at the site. Hazel charcoal from the fill of the furnace pit returned an Iron Age radiocarbon date of 155 BC−AD 67 (UBA-12739). No further finds were recovered.

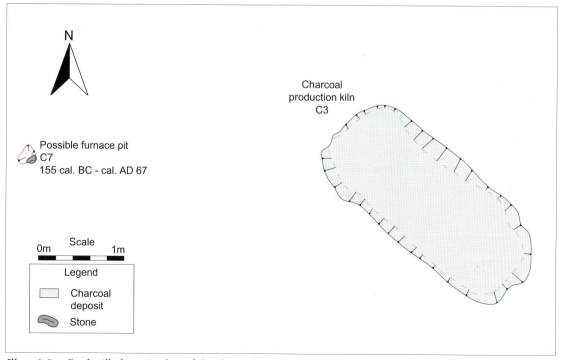

Illus. 6.9—Rathwilladoon 5: plan of the charcoal-production kiln (C3) and metal-working furnace (C7).

Illus. 6.10—Rathwilladoon 5: the charcoal kiln, from south-east, with its fill of charcoal-rich soil unexcavated.

Illus. 6.11—Rathwilladoon 5: Excavation Director Ed Lyne with the emptied charcoal kiln and a piece of the charcoal that was its intended product.

Derrygarriff 2

Further evidence of metal-working and a charcoal-production kiln were identified in Derrygarriff, Co. Clare, c. 3.5 km south of Tubber crossroads, and roughly 6 km south of Rathwilladoon 5. The features were situated on the south-facing slope of a low, limestone ridge that rose above an area of bog. The Derrygarriff Stream was located to the south of the site.

Metal-working was indicated by three earth-cut features: a furnace, a possible hearth, and a pit (Illus. 6.12). The furnace (C5) consisted of a linear pit, 2.45 m by 0.68 m and 0.48 m deep, and included evidence of intense *in situ* burning (Illus. 6.13). The hearth-pit was lined with gravel, possibly to create a working surface. The primary fill consisted of orange-black, silty clay with occasional burnt stone, charcoal and approximately 10 kg of ferrous/slag residue. The material is indicative of iron-smelting in a shaft furnace, and analysis of the residues suggests that the primary fill of the pit may represent the collapsed superstructure of the furnace. The assemblage also contained two fragments of smithing-hearth cakes and some hammerscale indicative of smithing. Oak charcoal appears to have been the dominant fuel used in the furnace, while probable kindling was represented by charcoals of hazel, alder, holly and Maloideae species (hawthorn, rowan, crab apple). Oak charcoal would have produced the high temperatures required for iron-working. A fragment of alder/hazel charcoal from this feature returned an Iron Age radiocarbon date of 350–100 BC (UBA-12716).

The possible hearth (C12) was an oval pit, 0.6 m by 0.52 m and 0.46 m deep. It contained two fills, the primary one being burnt clay, the result of *in situ* burning, and the secondary fill being charcoal-rich silt. The pit is likely to have been a hearth, and was probably used in association with the other metal-working features on the site. A shallow, oval pit (C11) was adjacent to the hearth, and measured 0.32 m by 0.3 m and 0.1 m deep. Its function is unclear, but it included limited amounts of charcoal, and may be related to the other features.

Just north of the metal-working features was an elongated, oval pit (C10), c. 4 m by 1 m and 0.5 m deep (Illus. 6.12). The pit contained large amounts of charcoal and was interpreted as a charcoal-production kiln or clamp. The charcoal assemblage indicates that ash was the main wood type undergoing the combustion process to produce charcoal, while additional species—hazel, alder and Maloideae species (hawthorn, rowan, crab apple)—were probably used as kindling to ignite and maintain the fire. It was assumed that the kiln would be contemporary with the metal-working features. However, hazel charcoal from the middle fill of the kiln returned a radiocarbon date of AD 1683–1953 (UBA-12715).

Discussion

Significant evidence for iron-working has been discovered during recent road projects in Ireland, and has given rise to a number of publications that have greatly increased our understanding of the processes and morphological characteristics of iron metallurgy (e.g. Carlin 2008; Kenny 2010; Wallace & Anguilano 2010). Features such as metal-working furnaces, charcoal-production kilns, and smithing hearths have returned radiocarbon dates from the Late Bronze Age to the post-medieval period (e.g. Carlin 2008, 101–04; Kenny 2010, 109). Prehistoric and early historic examples are rare, however, and the majority date to the latter part of the early medieval period and the early years of the later medieval period (between the ninth and 13th centuries). Iron-working

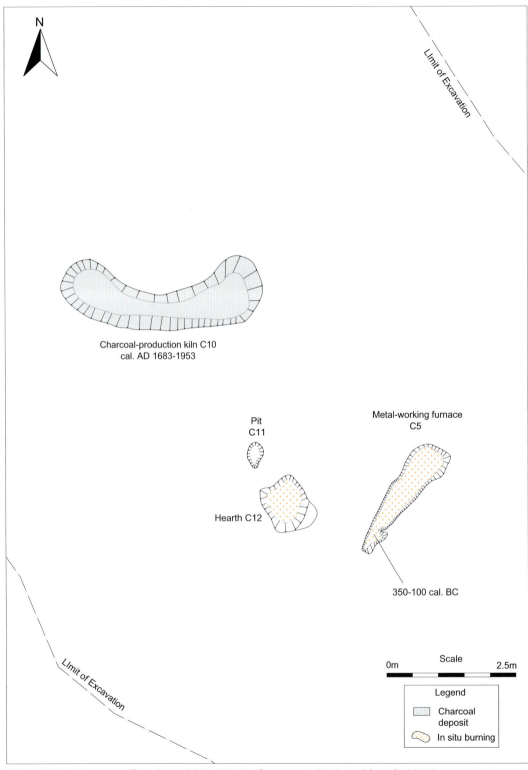

Illus. 6.12—Derrygarriff 2: charcoal kiln (C10), furnace pit (C5), and hearth (C12).

Illus. 6.13—Derrygarriff 2: iron-working furnace pit, from north-east. Note the fill of charcoal and fire-reddened clay.

technology essentially remained static until the introduction of the blast furnace in the 17th century, when it changed dramatically (Carlin 2008, 89). The surviving features of earlier iron-working are therefore similar in form and, because these sites are typically artefact poor, radiocarbon dating is vital for determining their age.

Most iron-working sites were located away from settlements and close to resources required for the industry. Large numbers of trees were required for charcoal production, and large quantities of iron ore—available as bog iron from surrounding bogs—were needed during the smelting process (Mytum 1992, 230; Raftery 2000, 147). Therefore, it made sense, logistically and for safety reasons, for furnaces and kilns to be situated at a distance from habitation sites and close to available raw materials. Furnaces have, however, been identified within enclosed, early medieval settlements, such as Killickaweeny, Co. Kildare (Walsh 2008, 40–2). It appears then, that iron-smelting was sometimes practised within enclosures, possibly in controlled environments away from the dwellings.

Charcoal-production kilns were essential to the iron-working process. Charcoal is produced when wood is burned under conditions where a restricted air supply prevents the complete combustion of the wood (Kenny 2010, 100). It was used as an effective fuel—more so than wood or turf—during the smelting and forging stages of iron-working (O'Sullivan & Downey 2009, 23). It was produced by piling wood, mainly oak, against a vertical post in earth-cut pits that were covered by layers of straw or bracken and were then sealed by a layer of earth or turf (Kenny 2010, 101–2; Illus. 6.14 and 6.15). The post was removed and the kiln was subsequently ignited as the wood was roasted over a number of days to produce charcoal (Carlin 2008, 89–91). This was a labour-intensive and skilled

Illus. 6.14—Experimental reconstruction of a charcoal-production 'mound kiln', based on an early medieval example excavated at Russagh, Co. Offaly, by IAC Ltd (Niall Kenny).

Illus. 6.15—Experimental reproduction of a charcoal-production 'pit-kiln', similar to the feature recorded at Rathwilladoon 5 (Niall Kenny).

process that required plentiful raw materials and careful supervision, to maintain the stoke-holes and cladding of the kiln and to monitor and regulate the oxygen supply. Recent research (Kenny 2010, 110) has shown that most kilns were located on sloping and agriculturally unproductive ground. Good drainage was important because it was crucial to keep the charcoal dry.

Charcoal-production kilns in Ireland range in plan from rectangular to oval/circular, but current evidence suggests that the classic type is a large, rectangular pit, such as at Hardwood 3, Co. Meath, where long carbonised pieces of oak were found lying lengthwise in the bottom of the kiln (Carlin 2008, 101–2, illus. 5.8b). The rectangular kiln-pits tend to be larger than oval and circular examples, with an average length of c. 2.4 m. Smaller kilns are known, but if the pit is less than 0.7 m in diameter or length, it is unlikely to have performed that function (Kenny 2010, 106–9). The kilns are identified archaeologically as earth-cut pits, with charcoal-rich fills and evidence for extensive *in situ* burning along the base and sides (Carlin 2008, 101; Kenny 2010, 99). However, these sites are often only recognised because carbonised wood has survived *in situ* (Carlin 2008, 101; Hull & Taylor 2006, 29–30). This may occur when kilns were abandoned due to the charcoal becoming wet, leaving it useless as a fuel. Successful kilns would not have abundant charcoal within their fills, so would appear archaeologically as heat-scorched pits containing only moderate amounts of charcoal. In this condition, with the majority of charcoal removed, positive identification becomes problematic.

Iron-working furnaces were used for smelting ores into an iron bloom prior to the smithing stages (Wallace & Anguilano 2010, 70–1). They survive as small, shallow, heat-scorched pits, usually oval or hemispherical in shape, containing fills of iron slag, charcoal and, in many cases, oxidised clay (Carlin 2008, 91–3). Dense blocks of slag commonly formed at the bottom of the furnace, and these have been termed plano-convex or 'furnace-bottoms' (Scott 1990, 155–6). A total of 30 furnaces were identified during excavations in advance of the M4 motorway route in Meath/Westmeath, and survived as bowl-shaped pits, with heat-reddened sides and bases, which contained slag and, in many examples, vitrified clay fragments (Carlin 2008, 94). Similar morphological characteristics were revealed at a number of furnaces associated with ringforts (Comber 2008, 115–7).

There is some disagreement over exactly what type of furnace was primarily used in Ireland. Some authorities (Carlin 2008, 91–3; Crew & Rehren 2002, 96; Mytum 1992, 231) argue for the existence of the low-shaft furnace, as used in Britain, while others (Pleiner 2000; Scott 1990; Raftery 2000, 148) favour the bowl furnace. Bowl furnaces consisted of small, open-air, bowl-shaped pits, occasionally with a domed clay roof, where the flames were fanned with bellows and the separated ore pooled at the base of the pit (Scott 1990, 159). Low-shaft furnaces differed, in that they were clay-lined, with a clay superstructure built above ground in the shape of a conical or cylindrical-shaped chimney (Carlin 2008, 92). They also differed to the bowl furnace because the charcoal and ore were placed in alternating layers (Mytum 1992, 231). Experimental work by O'Kelly (1961) and Tylecote (1986) found that bowl furnaces were inefficient, which suggests that the low-shaft furnace was a more viable option. Archaeologically, however, it is difficult to distinguish between the two furnace types, because both survive as heat-scorched pits containing charcoal and slag and, in many cases, vitrified clay fragments. The presence of the latter cannot be used as evidence for the existence of the low-shaft furnace because bowl furnaces may also have been clay-lined or roofed.

Regardless of which type was used, the increasing numbers of iron-working furnaces, charcoal-production kilns, and other metallurgical features found during development-led excavations across the country, demonstrate that the industry was widespread. While this industry appears to have peaked between the ninth and 13th centuries AD, the technology appears to have remained essentially the same from prehistory until the early modern period. Iron Age metal-working sites are rare, but a charcoal-production kiln dating to this period was identified at Barnasallagh, Co. Laois (Lennon 2008), and four furnaces were excavated during pre-construction archaeological investigations on the M4 motorway (Carlin 2008, 104). A possible stone-lined smelting furnace excavated at Tonybaun, Co. Mayo, returned a radiocarbon date of 477–210 BC (UB-6765), making it one of the earliest examples from the West of Ireland (Nolan 2006, 98–9).

While no radiocarbon dates were returned for the kiln at Rathwilladoon 5, its close proximity to an iron-working furnace suggests that the two features were contemporary. Charcoal-production kilns are often found associated with furnaces—which require charcoal for fuel—and the two features probably represent a small-scale, Iron Age, industrial site. Perhaps significantly, this activity was located c. 300 m from a possible Iron Age settlement site at Rathwilladoon 3 (Chapter 2). While that site was heavily disturbed, it consisted of the partial foundation gully of a circular structure, and produced a radiocarbon date of 186–52 BC (UBA-12731). This date overlaps with that returned for the Rathwilladoon furnace pit of 155 BC–AD 67 (UBA-12739), so it is possible that the two sites were contemporary, and may even have been used by the same community.

The two main features identified at Derrygarriff 2—an iron-working furnace and a charcoal-production kiln—were securely dated and represent industrial activity from two different periods. The radiocarbon date returned for the furnace was 350–100 BC (UBA-12716), which, again, overlaps with the Iron Age dates from Rathwilladoon 5 and 3, so the sites may be contemporary. The early modern/modern date returned for the kiln at Derrygarriff 2 was unexpected. The kiln appeared to form part of an Iron Age metal-working industry, but instead revealed that similar industrial activities shared a location but were separated by millennia. The site was probably chosen on both occasions as it was sheltered and dry, located on the south-facing slope of a ridge running through an area of bog, close to a source of bog iron.

As discussed, the technology and morphology of iron-working appears to have remained essentially the same from prehistory until the early modern period. The evidence from Derrygarriff 2 highlights the importance of producing secure radiocarbon dates for individual features at these sites, and raises doubts over the perceived association between the metal-working furnace and the kiln at Rathwilladoon 5. Despite this, both Derrygarriff 2 and Rathwilladoon 5 revealed evidence of metal production in the Iron Age. Given the paucity of metal-working (and other) sites dating to that period, they represent significant discoveries for the region.

6.3—Sranagalloon 2: cattle enclosure and Bronze Age cremation[36]

Approximately half of a previously recorded, upstanding earth and stone enclosure (CLO18-017) lay within the footprint of the new M18 road in Sranagalloon, Co. Clare, c. 1.7 km north of Crusheen. The portion affected by the road was excavated by hand. The enclosure was located on elevated, well-drained pasture land, on the saddle of a north-east/south-west ridge between the crests of two hills, and had extensive views to the east and west (Illus. 6.16).

The oval enclosure measured 32 m north–south by 16 m, externally, and 23 m by 12 m internally (Illus. 6.17). It was formed by a bank (3.5–6 m wide) that included large, *in situ* natural boulders, and was later augmented by field-clearance stones and redeposited subsoil.

The earliest feature was a rectangular pit in the interior of the enclosure, which contained charcoal and 13 fragments (8.03 g) of cremated human bone. The pit measured 0.86 m by 0.18 m and 0.2 m in depth, but had been disturbed by later agricultural activities. Two of the bones were identified as skull fragments (cranial vault), four as lower limb fragments (femur diaphysis), and the remainder were unidentifiable. A cross-section of the vault fragments suggests an age at death of 18–44 years, but the sex could not be determined. A fragment of cremated human bone returned a Late Bronze Age radiocarbon date of 908–821 BC (UBA-13023).

The western half of a large, sub-oval pit/trough was excavated within the enclosure (the eastern half lay outside the limit of excavation). The pit (C11) had steep sides and an uneven base, and measured c. 10.4 m by 4.6 m and had a depth of 1.4 m (maximum). An earthen ramp was incorporated into the north side of the feature to allow safer access along that side. The lower two thirds of the pit were filled with silty clay with large limestone boulders at the base, and the upper fill was the same sterile, silty clay that covered the interior of the enclosure. Alder/hazel charcoal from

Illus. 6.16—Sranagalloon 2: aerial view of the excavated enclosure looking south-east. The site was located on a hilltop in pasture land (AirShots Ltd).

the base of the pit returned a radiocarbon date of AD 1432–1481 (UBA-12727). The charcoal in the pit probably derived from a hearth/fire located outside the excavated area, which had washed/silted into the feature, and thereby provides a *terminus ante quem* for the pit. The fuel used appears to have been exploited from an oak-ash woodland, consisting of poplar/willow, alder/hazel, oak, ash and blackthorn/sloe. The pit appears to have been sited to take advantage of the high water table, in order to ensure a continuous supply of water. It probably functioned as a self-filling watering hole for livestock, before it was deliberately backfilled.

Early modern/modern features within the enclosure comprised two small, shallow pits, a group of evenly spaced (1 m) cultivation furrows, a drystone field-wall aligned north-west/south-east, and the field-clearance stones incorporated into the bank of the enclosure. Topsoil covered the interior of the enclosure and partly filled the trough. It contained modern artefacts, including glass, ceramics, clay pipe fragments, and an Irish silver 10-pence piece minted in 1805–06, during the reign of George III. Also recovered from the topsoil was a chert, single platform flake, diagnostic of the Early Neolithic period. A sherd of glazed (exterior) pottery, suggestive of a later 14th- to 16th-century date was recovered from the lower topsoil layer in the water trough. No archaeological features were identified outside of the enclosure.

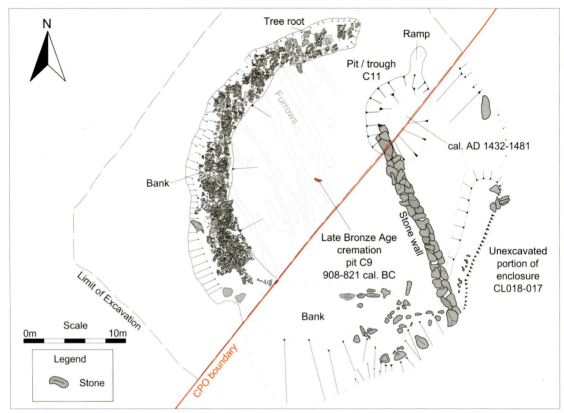

Illus. 6.17—Sranagalloon 2: plan of the site, showing the Bronze Age cremation pit (C9), the medieval watering hole (C11), redeposited stones on the bank of the enclosure and cultivation furrows across the interior.

Discussion

Prior to excavation, the enclosure at Sranagalloon 2 had the appearance of a denuded ringfort or cashel. However, it was found to be a partly natural feature made up of earthfast boulders that had been augmented with field stones and redeposited subsoil to form a bank. The only medieval feature within the interior was a large watering hole, suggesting that the enclosure functioned as a stock corral. The 15th-century date returned from the trough is later than the early medieval date range usually ascribed to these 'ringfort-type' monuments (e.g. Stout 1997, 22–31). It is possible that an early medieval enclosure was reused in the later medieval period, and that evidence of this earlier use survives within the unexcavated, eastern half of the site. Alternatively, the monument was first used in the late medieval period. Perhaps significantly, other than a prehistoric flake, none of the artefacts recovered from the topsoil pre-date the late 14th century. The apparent pastoral use of the site in the late medieval period appears to have changed to arable farming by the post-medieval/modern period, at which time the trough was filled in and cultivation furrows were dug across the interior of the enclosure.

The Late Bronze Age cremation pit appears to represent an isolated burial that was deposited on the crest of the ridge prior to its use as an enclosure. The small quantity of bone (8.03 g) contained within the pit suggests a token burial. Modern crematoria generally produce between 1,000 g and 2,400 g of bone from an adult individual (McKinley 1993, 285), while prehistoric cremation burials appear often to have been token or ritual deposits, with only the partial remains of an individual being interred. A number of cremation burials have been investigated in the region during recent infrastructural projects (see Chapter 1 'Bronze Age'), and multiple cremation pits containing token burials were found in two ring-ditches at Ballyboy, Co. Galway (see Chapter 5), although these dated to the Iron Age. Burnt mounds were located downslope of the site, at Sranagalloon 1, to the north-east, and Sranagalloon 3, to the south, both of which included a Late Bronze Age horizon (see Chapter 3). Neither site, however, was contemporary with the cremation pit—Sranagalloon 1 was earlier and Sranagalloon 3 later.

6.4—Conclusion

The sites discussed in this chapter produced unexpected, but significant, results. While occupying the same space, the corn-drying kilns at Curtaun enjoyed three separate episodes of use. This hints at either the continuous occupation of the adjacent ringfort from the early to the later medieval period, or its reoccupation in the 13th century. The industrial sites at Rathwilladoon and Derrygarriff included rare evidence of Iron Age metal-working, in the form of two furnace pits. The late date returned for the charcoal-production kiln at Derrygarriff was unexpected, as it first appeared to be associated with the other iron-working features on the site. This highlights the dangers of presuming that metal-working features are contemporaneous on the basis of their form and close proximity. The enclosure at Sranagalloon yielded no evidence of early medieval activity, although prior to excavation it would have been considered a likely monument of that period. While only half of the site was excavated, the evidence suggests that the enclosure was a partly natural feature that was adapted between the late medieval and modern periods, and used first as a livestock corral/watering hole, and later as an area of crop cultivation. The discovery of a Bronze Age cremation within the enclosure was a further surprise. Only one burial was found, suggesting that it was an isolated feature, however, it is possible that more burials lie beneath the unexcavated portion of the enclosure, and that the site had a more significant prehistoric horizon than our excavations have discovered.

Notes

33 Excavation No. E3721; Director Shane Delaney; NGR 142125 195440; height 25 m OD; parish of Beagh; barony of Kiltartan; County Galway.
34 Excavation No. E3657; Director Ed Lyne; NGR 141099 193900; height 29 m OD; parish of Beagh; barony of Kiltartan; County Galway.
35 Excavation No. E3711; Director Joe Nunan; NGR 140356 190940; height 26 m OD; parish of Inchicronan; barony of Bunratty Upper; County Clare.
36 Excavation No. E3714; Director Joe Nunan; NGR 139899 189520; height 37 m OD; parish of Inchicronan; barony of Bunratty Upper; County Clare.

APPENDIX 1
Radiocarbon dates from excavated archaeological sites

Dates were obtained from Queen's University, Belfast (UB and UBA lab codes) and were calibrated using the IntCal09 dataset (Reimer et al. 2009) and the CALIB REV5.0.2 calibration programme (Stuiver et al. 2005).

Chapter 2—Multiphase prehistoric settlement at Rathwilladoon

Site	Lab Code	Context	Years BP	$\delta^{13}C$	Calibrated date ranges
Rathwilladoon 2	UBA-12732	Charcoal from Phase 3, Pit F, within rectangular structure	2695 ± 25	-26.8 ‰	893–810 BC (1 sigma) 898–807 BC (2 sigma)
Rathwilladoon 2	UBA-12733	Charcoal from Phase 3, post-hole (C188) defining rectangular structure	2710 ± 32	-30.1 ‰	895–823 BC (1 sigma) 913–807 BC (2 sigma)
Rathwilladoon 2	UBA-12734	Charcoal from Phase 3, post-hole (C126) defining rectangular structure	2740 ± 23	-24.9 ‰	904–842 BC (1 sigma) 928–825 BC (2 sigma)
Rathwilladoon 2	UBA-12736	Charred hazelnut shell from Phase 2, Pit A	3753 ± 26	-28.6 ‰	2204–2064 BC (1 sigma) 2280–2042 BC (2 sigma)
Rathwilladoon 3	UBA-12731	Charcoal from Phase 4 curvilinear cut	2103 ± 22	-27.2 ‰	171–93 BC (1 sigma) 186–52 BC (2 sigma)

Chapter 3—Burnt mounds: kitchen sinks of the Bronze Age?

Site	Lab Code	Context	Years BP	$\delta^{13}C$	Calibrated date ranges
Drumminacloghaun 1	UBA-12751	European ash charcoal from base of trough	2580 ± 38	-29.3 ‰	806–671 BC (1 sigma) 817–551 BC (2 sigma)

Site	Lab Code	Context	Years BP	δ¹³C	Calibrated date ranges
Drumminacloghaun 1	UBA-12752	Alder/hazel charcoal from burnt mound	3779 ± 39	-25.6 ‰	2282–2141 BC (1 sigma) 2339–2042 BC (2 sigma)
Curtaun 1 and 2	UBA-12708	Hazel charcoal from base of pit (C9)	3256 ± 21	-28.6 ‰	1604–1495 BC (1 sigma) 1608–1459 BC (2 sigma)
Rathwilladoon 4	UBA-12737	Alder/hazel charcoal from burnt mound	3231 ± 22	-29.6 ‰	1520–1457 BC (1 sigma) 1601–1436 BC (2 sigma)
Gortavoher 1	UBA-12753	Hazel charcoal from eastern burnt spread	3591 ± 25	-27.4 ‰	2007–1905 BC (1 sigma) 2023–1887 BC (2 sigma)
Monreagh 3	UBA-12756	Hazel charcoal from burnt spread	3427 ± 23	-29.8 ‰	1749–1691 BC (1 sigma) 1871–1665 BC (2 sigma)
Monreagh 3	UBA-12757	Alder/hazel charcoal from trough	2708 ± 39	-23.8 ‰	896–820 BC (1 sigma) 925–802 BC (2 sigma)
Monreagh 1 and 2	UBA-12755	Alder/hazel charcoal from trough (C35)	3067 ± 23	-27.8 ‰	1390–1313 BC (1 sigma) 1409–1269 BC (2 sigma)
Monreagh 1 and 2	UBA-12754	Hazel charcoal from cistern (C26)	2758 ± 25	-30.3 ‰	925–844 BC (1 sigma) 975–832 BC (2 sigma)
Derrygarriff 1	UBA-12713	Hazel charcoal from burnt spread	69 ± 21	-30.0 ‰	AD 1706–1954 (1 sigma) AD 1695–1955 (2 sigma)
Derrygarriff 1	UBA-12714	Charcoal (black/common alder) from pit	534 ± 21	-28.4 ‰	AD 1402–1425 (1 sigma) AD 1326–1343 (2 sigma)
Derrygarriff 3	UBA-12718	Alder/hazel charcoal from trough (C6)	2788 ± 24	-28.2 ‰	976–904 BC (1 sigma) 1006–850 BC (2 sigma)
Derrygarriff 3	UBA-12717	Alder/hazel charcoal from trough (C4)	2640 ± 21	-30.0 ‰	813–798 BC (1 sigma) 829–793 BC (2 sigma)
Sranagalloon 1	UBA-12759	Hazel charcoal from base of timber-lined trough	3106 ± 26	-29.4 ‰	1420–1322 BC (1 sigma) 1433–1313 BC (2 sigma)
Sranagalloon 1	UBA-12758	Alder/hazel charcoal from base of burnt mound	2925 ± 38	-29.2 ‰	1207–1052 BC (1 sigma) 1260–1012 BC (2 sigma)

Site	Lab Code	Context	Years BP	δ¹³C	Calibrated date ranges
Sranagalloon 3	UBA–12729	Hazel charcoal from trough (C28)	3157 ± 22	–29.2 ‰	1450–1471 BC (1 sigma) 1494–1399 BC (2 sigma)
Sranagalloon 3	UBA–12728	Alder/hazel charcoal from trough (C19)	3144 ± 27	–31.4 ‰	1446–1401 BC (1 sigma) 1494–1324 BC (2 sigma)
Sranagalloon 3	UBA–13022	Hazel charcoal from burnt mound (C8)	2403 ± 22	–27.5 ‰	508–406 BC (1 sigma) 706–400 BC (2 sigma)
Gortaficka 2	UBA–12707	Maloideae charcoal from pit/trough (C21)	3776 ± 24	–26.6 ‰	2275–2142 BC (1 sigma) 2287–2137 BC (2 sigma)
Gortaficka 2	UBA–12706	Alder/hazel charcoal from base of trough (C39)	3168 ± 25	–27.1 ‰	1490–1417 BC (1 sigma) 1496–1409 BC (2 sigma)
Clooneen	UBA–12730	Alder charcoal from base of trough (C8)	3637 ± 33	–34.8 ‰	2108–1947 BC (1 sigma) 2132–1909 BC (2 sigma)
Caheraphuca 1	UBA–12745	Alder/hazel charcoal from main burnt spread	3418 ± 40	–23.8 ‰	1769–1643 BC (1 sigma) 1877–1620 BC (2 sigma)
Caheraphuca 1	UBA–12744	Alder/hazel charcoal from trough (C57)	2979 ± 39	–24.8 ‰	1267–1129 BC (1 sigma) 1373–1073 BC (2 sigma)
Caheraphuca 4	UBA–12746	Hazel charcoal from largest burnt mound	2950 ± 41	–28.7 ‰	1260–1115 BC (1 sigma) 1299–1024 BC (2 sigma)
Caheraphuca 5	UBA–12719	Hazel charcoal from burnt spread	3814 ± 23	–29.5 ‰	2288–2206 BC (1 sigma) 2340–2149 BC (2 sigma)
Caheraphuca 6	UBA–12720	Alder charcoal from base of burnt mound (C604) in Area A	2789 ± 24	–29.7 ‰	976–905 BC (1 sigma) 1007–850 BC (2 sigma)
Caheraphuca 6	UBA–12721	Alder charcoal from bedding layer of timber trough in Area A	2806 ± 24	–29.6 ‰	994–923 BC (1 sigma) 1016–900 BC (2 sigma)
Caheraphuca 7	UBA–12722	Hazel charcoal from deposit of heat-affected material	2478 ± 23	–29.1 ‰	753–540 BC (1 sigma) 766–420 BC (2 sigma)

Site	Lab Code	Context	Years BP	δ¹³C	Calibrated date ranges
Caheraphuca 7	UBA-12723	Alder/hazel charcoal from oval pit	2577 ± 35	−22.7 ‰	803–672 BC (1 sigma) 813–554 BC (2 sigma)
Caheraphuca 8	UBA-12725	Maloideae charcoal from burnt spread (C835)	3923 ± 27	−25.8 ‰	2471–2349 BC (1 sigma) 2480–2300 BC (2 sigma)
Caheraphuca 8	UBA-12724	Alder charcoal from small deposit near root system	3783 ± 22	−30.4 ‰	2278–2145 BC (1 sigma) 2287–2140 BC (2 sigma)
Caheraphuca 9	UBA-12726	Alder charcoal from pit	3892 ± 22	−27.7 ‰	2459–2346 BC (1 sigma) 2465–2299 BC (2 sigma)
Caheraphuca 10	UBA-12747	Alder/hazel charcoal from main burnt spread	3705 ± 40	−27.1 ‰	2189–2034 BC (1 sigma) 2204–1974 BC (2 sigma)
Caheraphuca 11	UBA-12748	Alder/hazel charcoal from upper fill of pit/trough	3823 ± 39	−23.0 ‰	2340–2201 BC (1 sigma) 2458–2143 BC (2 sigma)
Caheraphuca 12	UBA-12749	Hazel charcoal from burnt mound	2844 ± 21	−27.6 ‰	1039–942 BC (1 sigma) 1108–922 BC (2 sigma)
Caheraphuca 12	UBA-12750	Hazel charcoal from pit/ trough	3325 ± 39	−25.7 ‰	1663–1532 BC (1 sigma) 1730–1510 BC (2 sigma)
Ballyline 1	UBA-12742	Alder/hazel charcoal from trough (C6)	3604 ± 40	−24.2 ‰	2023–1913 BC (1 sigma) 2129–1828 BC (2 sigma)
Ballyline 2	UBA-12740	Alder/hazel charcoal from trough beneath southern burnt mound	3481 ± 38	−25.4 ‰	1878–1750 BC (1 sigma) 1897–1692 BC (2 sigma)
Ballyline 3	UBA-12743	Alder/hazel charcoal from fill of pit (C3)	3751 ± 40	−24.4 ‰	2271−2050 BC (1 sigma) 2286−2035 BC (2 sigma)

Chapter 5—Iron Age ring-ditches at Ballyboy

Site	Lab Code	Context	Years BP	δ¹³C	Calibrated date ranges
Ballyboy 1	UBA-13024	Cremated human adult bone from recut ditch (C4)	2024 ± 19	-24.6 ‰	45 BC–AD 1 (1 sigma) 89 BC–AD 48 (2 sigma)
Ballyboy 1	UBA-13025	Cremated human (female) bone from cremation pit (C11)	2019 ± 23	-23.5 ‰	46 BC–AD 16 (1 sigma) 89 BC–AD 52 (2 sigma)
Ballyboy 1	UBA-13026	Cremated human adult bone from cremation pit (C34)	2026 ± 19	-27.6 ‰	46 BC–AD 1 (1 sigma) 90 BC–AD 47 (2 sigma)
Ballyboy 2	UBA-13027	Cremated human bone from pit in fill of second recut ditch (C3)	2027 ± 28	-23.4 ‰	52 BC–AD 18 (1 sigma) 152 BC–AD 53 (2 sigma)
Ballyboy 2	UBA-13028	Cremated human bone from second recut ditch (C14)	2171 ± 24	-21.0 ‰	350–180 BC (1 sigma) 359–125 BC (2 sigma)
Ballyboy 2	UBA-13030	Cremated human (adult) bone from cremation pit (C19)	2043 ± 29	-25.3 ‰	92 BC–AD 1 (1 sigma) 163 BC–AD 24 (2 sigma)
Ballyboy 2	UBA-13031	Cremated human (adult) bone from cremation pit (C24)	2000 ± 20	-25.8 ‰	38 BC–AD 23 (1 sigma) 44 BC–AD 53 (2 sigma)
Ballyboy 2	UBA-13032	Cremated human (adult) bone from cremation pit (C22)	2052 ± 24	-22.0 ‰	104–3 BC (1 sigma) 164 BC–AD 4 (2 sigma)

Chapter 6—Crops, iron and water

Site	Lab Code	Context	Years BP	δ¹³C	Calibrated date ranges
Curtaun 1 cereal kilns	UBA-12710	Charcoal (wild/bird cherry) from chamber of Kiln 1	1252 ± 37	-24.0 ‰	AD 685–803 (1 sigma) AD 674–870 (2 sigma)
Curtaun 1	UBA-12711	Charcoal (hazel) from curvilinear slot trench (C52)	1211 ± 24	-30.3 ‰	AD 776–867 (1 sigma) AD 717–888 (2 sigma)
Curtaun 1	UBA-12712	Charred, hulled barley from final fill of Kiln 2	1165 ± 18	-30.2 ‰	AD 783–935 (1 sigma) AD 779–947 (2 sigma)
Curtaun 1	UBA-12709	Charcoal (hazel) from basal layer of Kiln 3	790 ± 20	-30.1 ‰	AD 1225–1261 (1 sigma) AD 1218–1270 (2 sigma)
Rathwilladoon 5	UBA-12739	Charcoal (hazel) from fill of furnace pit (C7)	2018 ± 37	-27.5 ‰	53 BC– AD 49 (1 sigma) 155 BC–AD 67 (2 sigma)

Site	Lab Code	Context	Years BP	δ13C	Calibrated date ranges
Derrygarriff 2	UBA-12716	Charcoal (alder/hazel) from fill of furnace pit (C5)	2144 ± 21	–30.5 ‰	342–121 BC (1 sigma) 350–100 BC (2 sigma)
Derrygarriff 2	UBA-12715	Charcoal (hazel) from middle fill of charcoal kiln/clamp (C10)	116 ± 19	–28.2 ‰	AD 1691–1922 (1 sigma) AD 1683–1953 (2 sigma)
Sranagalloon 2	UBA-13023	Cremated human bone from pit	2722 ± 20	–23.4 ‰	895–835 BC (1 sigma) 908–821 BC (2 sigma)
Sranagalloon 2	UBA-12727	Charcoal (alder/hazel) from base of water trough	428 ± 21	–32.2 ‰	AD 1439–1459 (1 sigma) AD 1432–1481 (2 sigma)

BIBLIOGRAPHY

Babtie Pettit Ltd 2006 'Chapter 11, Cultural Heritage–Archaeology', *N18 Gort to Crusheen Environmental Impact Statement*. Unpublished report undertaken on behalf of Galway County Council.

Barfield, L & Hodder, M 1987 'Burnt mounds as saunas and the prehistory of bathing', *Antiquity*, 64, 370–9.

Bartlett, A D H 2004 *N18 Gort to Crusheen Road Scheme: Report on Archaeogeophysical Survey of Proposed Route*. Unpublished report for Galway County Council.

Becker, K, O'Neill, J & O'Flynn, L 2008 *Iron Age Ireland: finding an invisible people*. The Heritage Council, Dublin.

Behre, K-E 2008 'Collected seeds and fruits from herbs as prehistoric food', *Vegetation History and Archaeobotany*, 17, 65–73.

Bermingham, N, Hull, G & Taylor, K in press *Beneath the Banner. Archaeology of the M18 Ennis Bypass and N85 Western Relief Road*. NRA Scheme Monographs 10. National Roads Authority, Dublin.

Borlase, W C 1897 *Dolmens of Ireland*, 3 Vols. Chapman and Hall, London.

Brindley, A L, Lanting, J N & Mook, W G 1990 'Radiocarbon dates from Irish *fulachta fiadh* and other burnt mounds', *Journal of Irish Archaeology*, 5, 25–33.

Brück, J 1999 'Houses, lifecycles and deposition on Middle Bronze Age settlements in southern England', *Proceedings of the Prehistoric Society*, 65, 145–66.

Canny, N 1989 'Early Modern Ireland c. 1500–1700', *in* R F Foster (ed.), *The Oxford Illustrated History of Ireland*, 104–60. Oxford University Press, Oxford.

Carlin, N 2008 'Ironworking and production', *in* N Carlin, L Clarke & F Walsh, *The Archaeology of Life and Death in the Boyne Floodplain: the linear landscape of the M4*, 87–112. NRA Scheme Monographs 2, National Roads Authority, Dublin.

Carroll, J 2000 'Report on the glass beads from a ringditch at Ferns, Co. Wexford', *in* F Ryan, *Excavation of a Ringditch at Ferns, Co. Wexford*. Unpublished excavation report, National Monuments Service, Department of the Environment, Heritage and Local Government.

Carroll, J 2007 'Glass bead report', *in* P Stevens, *Preliminary Report on Archaeological Excavation at Ask, Co. Wexford, Site 42–44 (A003/020)*. Unpublished excavation report, National Monuments Service, Department of the Environment, Heritage and Local Government.

Carroll, J 2010 'Report on the glass beads from a ringditch at Donacarney Great, Co. Meath', *in* A Giacometti, *Excavation of a Ringditch at Donacarney Great, Co. Meath (09E0451)*. Unpublished excavation report, National Monuments Service, Department of the Environment, Heritage and Local Government.

Case, H 1961 'Irish Neolithic pottery: distribution and sequence', *Proceedings of the Prehistoric Society*, 9, 174–233.

Case, H 1993 'Beakers: deconstruction and after', *Proceedings of the Prehistoric Society*, 59, 241–68.

Case, H 1995 'Irish Beakers in their European Context', *in* J Waddell & E Shee Twohig (eds), *Ireland in the Bronze Age*, 14–29. Stationery Office, Dublin.

Clarke, D L 1970 *Beaker Pottery of Great Britain and Ireland*. Gulbenkian Archaeological Series, Cambridge University Press, Cambridge.

Clarke, D V 1970 'Bone dice and the Scottish Iron Age', *Proceedings of the Prehistoric Society*, 36, 214–32.

Clarke, L & Carlin, N 2009 'From focus to locus: a window upon the development of a funerary landscape', *in* M B Deevy & D Murphy (eds), *Places Along the Way. First findings on the M3*, 1–20. NRA Scheme Monographs 5, National Roads Authority, Dublin.

Coffey, T 1993 *The Parish of Inchicronan (Crusheen)*. Ballinakella Press, County Clare.

Comber, M 2008 *The Economy of the Ringfort and Contemporary Settlement in Early Medieval Ireland*. BAR International Series 1773. Archaeopress, Oxford.

Corlett, C 1997 'A *fulacht fiadh* site at Moynagh Lough, County Meath', *Ríocht na Mídhe*, 9 (3), 46–9.

Cotter, C 1993 'Western Stone Fort Project: interim report', Discovery Programme Reports 1, 1–19. Royal Irish Academy and Discovery Programme, Dublin.

Coyne, F 2002 '1125 Ballyvollane II. Burnt spread', *in* I Bennett (ed.), *Excavations 2002. Summary accounts of archaeological excavations in Ireland*, 308. Wordwell, Bray.

Crew, P & Rehren, T 2002 'Appendix 1: high-temperature workshop residues from Tara: iron, bronze and glass', *in* H Roche, *Excavations at Ráith na Rig, Tara, Co. Meath 1997*, 83–102. Discovery Programme Reports 6, Royal Irish Academy/ Discovery Programme, Dublin.

Cutler, D F & Gale, R 2000 *Plants in Archaeology – Identification Manual of Artefacts of Plant Origin from Europe and the Mediterranean*. Westbury Scientific Publishing and Royal Botanic Gardens, Kew.

Daly, A & Grogan, E 1993 'Excavations of four barrows in Mitchelstowndown West, Knocklong, County Limerick', *Final Report*, 44–60. Discovery Programme Reports 1, Royal Irish Academy, Dublin.

Delaney, F 2011 'The archaeology of early medieval Uí Fiachradh Aidne', *in* F Delaney & J Tierney, *In the Lowlands of South Galway. Archaeological excavations on the N18 Oranmore to Gort national road scheme*, 45–57. NRA Scheme Monographs 7, National Roads Authority, Dublin.

Delaney, F & Tierney, J 2011 *In the Lowlands of South Galway. Archaeological excavations on the N18 Oranmore to Gort national road scheme*. NRA Scheme Monographs 7, National Roads Authority, Dublin.

Dennehy, E 2002a 'Cloonagowan, Co. Clare', *in* I Bennett (ed.), *Excavations 2002. Summary accounts of archaeological excavations in Ireland*, 39. Wordwell, Bray.

Dennehy, E 2002b 'Cloonagowan, Co. Clare', *in* I Bennett (ed.), *Excavations 2002. Summary accounts of archaeological excavations in Ireland*, 40. Wordwell, Bray.

Dennehy, E & Sutton, B 2002 'Gortaficka, Co. Clare', *in* I Bennett (ed.), *Excavations 2002. Summary accounts of archaeological excavations in Ireland*, 44. Wordwell, Bray.

Doody, M 2000 'Bronze Age houses in Ireland', *in* A Desmond, G Johnson, M McCarthy, J Sheehan & E Shee Twohig (eds), *New Agendas in Irish Prehistory*, 135-59. Wordwell. Bray.

Dowd, M 2007 'Living and dying in Glencurran Cave', *Archaeology Ireland*, 21, 36–9.

Edwards, N 1990 *The Archaeology of Early Medieval Ireland*. B T Batsford Ltd, London.

Eogan, G 1964 'The Later Bronze Age in Ireland in the light of recent research', *Proceedings of the Prehistoric Society*, 14, 268–350.

Eogan, G 1974 'Report on the excavation of some passage graves, unprotected inhumation burials and a settlement site at Knowth, Co. Meath', *Proceedings of the Royal Irish Academy*, 74 C, 11–112.

Eogan, G 1984 *Excavations at Knowth 1*. Royal Irish Academy Monographs in Archaeology, Dublin.

Eogan, G 1998 'Coolnatullagh. Prehistoric cairn and field system', *in* I Bennett (ed.), *Excavations 1997. Summary accounts of archaeological excavations in Ireland*, 5–6. Wordwell, Bray.

Eogan, G 2010 'The small metal tools of the Irish Bronze Age: an outline review', *in* G Cooney, K Becker, J Coles, M Ryan & S Sievers (eds), *Relics of Old Decency: archaeological studies in later prehistory. A festschrift for Barry Raftery*, 107–26. Wordwell, Bray.

Fahey, J A 1893 *The History and Antiquities of the Diocese of Kilmacduagh*. M H Gill & Son, Dublin.

Fanning, T 1994 *Viking Age Ringed Pins from Dublin*. Royal Irish Academy, Dublin.

Farrelly, J & Keane, M 2002 'New barrow types identified in County Sligo', *in* M A Timoney (ed.), *A Celebration of Sligo*, 97–101. Sligo Field Club, Sligo.

Galloway, J A 1991 'Driven by drink? Ale consumption and the agrarian economy of the London region c. 1300–1400', *in* M Carlin & J T Rosenthal (eds), *Food and Eating in Medieval Europe*, 87–100. Hambledon Press, London.

Gevjall, N-G 1948 'Bestämning av de brända benen från gravarna i Horn', *in* K E Sahlström & N-G Gejvall (eds), *Gravfältet på kyrkbacken i Horns socken, Västergötland*, 153–99. Wahlström & Widstrand, Stockholm.

Gibbons, M, Gibbons, M & Higgins, J 2004 'Mapping the Mesolithic in Western Connacht', *Irish Quaternary Association Newsletter*, 32, 4–7.

Gibson, A 1989 'Medieval corn-drying kilns at Capo, Kincardineshire and Abercairny, Perthshire', *Proceedings of the Society of Antiquaries of Scotland*, 118, 219–29.

Gowen, M & Tarbett, C 1988 'A third season at Tankardstown', *Archaeology Ireland*, 8, 156.

Grey, M & McNamara, M (eds) 2000 *Gort Inse Guaire. A journey through time*. Gort Heritage Trust.

Grogan, E 2002 'Neolithic houses in Ireland: a broader perspective', *Antiquity*, 76, 517–25.

Grogan, E 2005a *The North Munster Project. Vol 1. The prehistoric landscape of south-east Clare*. Discovery Programme Monographs 6. Wordwell, Bray.

Grogan, E 2005b *The North Munster Project. Vol 2. The prehistoric landscape of north Munster*. Discovery Programme Monographs 6. Wordwell, Bray.

Grogan, E & Eogan, G 1987 'Lough Gur excavations by Seán P Ó Ríordáin: further Neolithic and Beaker habitations on Knockadoon', *Proceedings of the Royal Irish Academy*, 87 C, 299–506.

Grogan, E, O'Donnell, L & Johnston, P 2007 *The Bronze Age Landscapes of the Pipeline to the West: an integrated archaeological and environmental assessment*. Wordwell, Bray.

Grogan, E & Roche, H 2010 'Clay and fire: the development and distribution of pottery traditions in prehistoric Ireland, *in* M Stanley, E Danaher & J Eogan (eds), *Creative Minds. Proceedings of a public seminar on archaeological discoveries on national road schemes, August 2009*, 27–45. Archaeology and the National Roads Authority Monograph Series No. 7, National Roads Authority, Dublin.

Guido, M 1978 *The Glass Beads of Prehistoric and Roman Britain and Ireland*. Thames & Hudson, London.

Hackett, L 2007 'Diggers find shovel', *Seanda*, 1, 1–7.

Hall, M 2007 *Playtime in Pictland: The material culture of gaming in early medieval Scotland*. Groam House Museum, Rosemarkie.

Halpin, B 2007 'Ballaghfadda West', *in* E Grogan, L O'Donnell & P Johnston, *The Bronze Age Landscapes of the Pipeline to the West*, 169–70. Wordwell, Bray.

Henderson, J 1988 'The nature of the early Christian glass-making industry in Ireland: some evidence from Dunmisk Fort, Co. Tyrone', *Ulster Journal of Archaeology*, 51, 115–26.

Herries Davies, G L & Stephens, N 1978 *The Geomorphology of the British Isles: Ireland*. Methuen & Co. Ltd., London.

Holland, P 1994 'Anglo-Norman Galway: rectangular earthworks and moated sites', *Journal of the Galway Archaeological and Historical Society*, Vol. 46 (1994), 203-11.

Hull, G & Taylor, K 2006 'Archaeological sites on the route of the N21 Castleisland to Abbeyfeale road improvement scheme, Co. Kerry', *Journal of the Kerry Archaeological and Historical Society*, Vol. 6, 5–59.

Jeffrey, S 1991 'Burnt mounds, fulling and early textiles?', *in* M Hodder & L Barfield (eds), *Burnt Mounds and Hot Stone Technology*, 97–102. Sandwell Metropolitan Borough Council, Sandwell, West Midlands.

Jones, C 1998 'The discovery and dating of the prehistoric landscape of Roughan Hill in Co. Clare', *Journal of Irish Archaeology*, 9, 27–44.

Jones, C 2004 *The Burren and the Aran Islands. Exploring the Archaeology*. The Collins Press, Cork.

Jones, C & Gilmer, A 2000 'Clare 153, Roughan Hill, Parknabinnia Court Tomb, *in* I Bennett (ed.), *Excavations 1998. Summary accounts of archaeological excavations in Ireland*, 12–13. Wordwell, Bray.

Jope, E M & Wilson, B C S 1957 'A burial group of the first century AD at Loughey near Donaghadee, Co. Down', *Ulster Journal of Archaeology*, 20, 72–95.

Kelly, F 1998 *Early Irish Farming*. School of Celtic Studies, Dublin Institute for Advanced Studies, Dublin.

Kelly, J 1996 'The politics of Protestant Ascendancy: County Galway 1650–1832', *in* G Moran & R Gillespie (eds), *Galway History & Society*, 229–70. Geography Publications, Dublin.

Kenny, N 2010 'Charcoal production in medieval Ireland', *in* M Stanley, E Danaher & J Eogan (eds), *Creative Minds. Proceedings of a public seminar on archaeological discoveries on national road schemes, August 2009*, 99–115. Archaeology and the National Roads Authority Monograph Series No. 7, National Roads Authority, Dublin.

Kerrigan, A & Gillespie, R F 2010 'Fulachta Fiadh', *in* R F Gillespie & A Kerrigan, *Of Troughs and Tuyères. The archaeology of the N5 Charlestown Bypass*, 45–154. NRA Scheme Monographs 6, National Roads Authority, Dublin.

Killeen, R 1994 *A Short History of Ireland*. Gill & Macmillan, Dublin.

Lanting, J & van der Waals, D 1972 'British Beakers as seen from the Continent', *Helenium*, 12, 20–46.

Lawless, C 1990 'A *fulacht fiadh* Bronze Age cooking experiment at Turlough, Castlebar', *Cathair na Mart*, 10, 1–10.

Lehane, J, Muñiz-Pérez, M, O'Sullivan, J & Wilkins, B 2010 'Three cemetery-settlement excavations in County Galway at Carrowkeel, Treanbaun and Owenbristy', *in* C Corlett & M Potterton (eds), *Death and Burial in Early Medieval Ireland*, 139–56. Wordwell, Bray.

Lennon, A M 2008 *Report on the Archaeological Excavation of Barnasallagh 1, Co. Laois.* Unpublished excavation report for Archaeological Consultancy Services Ltd.

Lennon, C & Gillespie, R 1997 'Part III: Reformation to Restoration', *in* S Duffy (ed.) *Atlas of Irish History*, 50–69. Gill & Macmillan, Dublin.

Lewis, S 1998 *County Clare. A History and Topography.* Clasp Press, Ennis, Co. Clare (originally published in 1837 as part of *A Topographical Dictionary of Ireland*, by the same author).

Lisowski, F P 1968 'The investigation of human cremations', *in* T Bielicki et al. (eds), *Anthropologie und Humangenetik*, 76–83. Gustav Fischer Verlag, Stuttgart.

Liversage, G D 1968 'Excavations at Dalkey Island, Co. Dublin, 1956–1959', *Proceedings of the Royal Irish Academy,* 66 C, 53–233.

Lucas, A T 1965 'Washing and bathing in ancient Ireland', *Journal of the Royal Society of Antiquaries of Ireland*, 96, 65–114.

Lynch, A 1994 'Poulnabrone portal tomb', *in* M O'Connell (ed.), *Burren, Co. Clare*, 18–20. Irish Association for Quaternary Studies Field Guide, 18, Dublin.

Mabey, R 2007 *Food for Free.* Harper Collins Publishers Ltd, London.

McClatchie, M, Brewer, A, Dillon, M, Johnston, P, Lyons, S, Monk, M, Stewart, K & Timpany, S 2007 'Brewing and *fulachta fiadh*', *Archaeology Ireland*, 21, No. 4, 46.

McConnell, B (ed.) 2004 *Geology of Galway Bay: to accompany the Bedrock Geology 1:10,000 Scale Map Series, Sheet 14.* Geological Survey of Ireland. Dublin.

McCracken, E 1971 *The Irish Woods Since Tudor Times: distribution and exploitation.* Queen's University, Belfast.

McKeon, J & O'Sullivan, J (eds) in press *The Quiet Landscape. Archaeological investigations on the route of the M6 Galway to Ballinasloe motorway scheme.* NRA Scheme Monograph Series. National Roads Authority, Dublin.

McKinley, J I 1993 'Bone fragment size and weight of bone from modern British cremations and the implications for the interpretation of archaeological cremations', *International Journal of Osteoarchaeology*, 3, 283–87.

McKinley, J I 1997 'Bronze Age "Barrows" and funerary rites and rituals of cremation', *Proceedings of the Prehistoric Society*, 63, 129–45.

McNeill, T 1997 *Castles in Ireland. Feudal power in a Gaelic world.* Routledge, London.

McQuade, M, Molloy, B & Moriarty, C 2009 *In the Shadow of the Galtees. Archaeological excavations along the N8 Cashel to Mitchelstown Road Scheme.* NRA Scheme Monographs 4, National Roads Authority, Dublin.

Molloy, K 2005 'Holocene vegetation and land-use history at Mooghaun, south-east Clare, with particular reference to the Bronze Age', *in* E Grogan (ed.), *The North Munster Project. Vol 1. The prehistoric landscape of south-east Clare.* Discovery Programme Monographs 6, 255–301. Wordwell, Bray.

Molloy, K, Feeser, I & O'Connell, M in press: a 'A new pollen record from east Galway: fresh insights into farming and woodland dynamics in mid-western Ireland from the Neolithic to recent times', *in* R J Schulting, N J Whitehouse & M McClatchie (eds), *Living Landscapes: Exploring Neolithic Ireland and its Wider Context.* Archaeopress (BAR), Oxford.

Molloy, K, Feeser, I, & O'Connell, M in press: b 'Palaeoecology evidence from Ballinphuill bog', *in* J McKeon & J O'Sullivan (eds), *The Quiet Landscape. Archaeological investigations on the route of the M6 Galway to Ballinasloe motorway scheme*. NRA Scheme Monograph Series. National Roads Authority, Dublin.

Molloy, K & O'Connell, M 1987 'The nature of the vegetational changes at about 5000 BP with particular reference to the elm decline: fresh evidence from Connemara, western Ireland', *New Phytologist* 106, 203–20.

Molloy, K & O'Connell, M 1991 'Palaeoecological investigations towards the reconstruction of woodland and land-use history at Lough Sheeauns, Connemara, western Ireland', *Review of Palaeobotany and Palynology* 67, 75–113.

Molloy, K & O'Connell, M 1995 'Palaeoecological investigations towards the reconstruction of environment and land-use changes during prehistory at Céide Fields, western Ireland', *Probleme der Küstenforschung im südlichen Nordseegebiet* 23, 187–225.

Molloy, K & O'Connell, M 2004 'Holocene vegetation and land-use dynamics in the karstic environment of Inis Oírr, Aran Islands, western Ireland: pollen analytical evidence evaluated in the light of the archaeological record', *Quaternary International* 113, 41–64.

Molloy, K & O'Connell, M 2011 'Boom and bust or sustained development? Fossil pollen records and new insights into Bronze Age farming in County Clare', *in* S Conran, E Danaher & M Stanley (eds), *Past Times, Changing Fortunes: Proceedings of a public Heritage Week seminar, Dublin, August 2010*, 41–64. National Roads Authority Monograph Series No. 8, National Roads Authority, Dublin.

Monk, M A, & Kelleher, E 2006 'An assessment of the archaeological evidence for Irish corn-drying kilns in the light of the results of archaeological experiments and archaeobotanical studies', *Journal of Irish Archaeology* (2005), Vol. 14, 77–114.

Mulloy, S 1996 'The transfer of power: Galway 1642–1702', *in* G Moran & R Gillespie (eds), *Galway History & Society*, 213–28. Geography Publications, Dublin.

Mytum, H 1992 *The Origins of Early Christian Ireland*. Routledge, London.

Needham, S 1996 'Chronology and periodisation in the British Bronze Age', *Acta Archaeologica,* 67, 121–46.

Needham, S, Bronk Ramsay, C, Coombs, D, Cartwright, C & Pettitt, P 1998 'An independent chronology of British Bronze Age metalwork: the results of the Oxford Accelerator Programme', *Archaeological Journal*, 154, 55–107.

Newman, C 1997 *Tara: an Archaeological Survey*. Discovery Programme Monograph 2. Royal Irish Academy, Dublin.

Nicholls, K 2003 *Gaelic and Gaelicized Ireland in the Middle Ages*. Lilliput Press, Dublin.

Ní Lionáin, C 2007 'Life, death and food production in Bronze Age Ireland: recent excavations at Stamullin, Co. Meath', *Archaeology Ireland*, 21, no. 2. 18–21.

Nolan, J 2006 'Excavation of a children's burial ground at Tonybaun, Ballina, County Mayo', *in* J O'Sullivan & M Stanley (eds), *Settlement, Industry and Ritual*, 89–101. Archaeology and the National Roads Authority Monograph Series No. 3, National Roads Authority, Dublin.

O'Brien, E 1992 'Pagan and Christian burial in Ireland during the first millennium AD: continuity and change', *in* N Edwards & A Lane (eds), *The Early Church in Wales and the West*, 130–37. Oxbow Monograph 16, Oxford.

O'Brien, E 2003 'Burial practices in Ireland: first to seventh centuries AD', *in* J Downes & A Ritchie (eds), *Sea Change: Orkney and Northern Europe in the later Iron Age, AD 300–800*, 63–72. Pinkfoot Press, Orkney.

Ó Carragáin, T 2009 'Cemetery settlements and local churches in pre-Viking Ireland in light of comparisons with England and Wales ', *in* J Graham-Campbell & M Ryan (eds), *Anglo-Saxon/ Irish Relations before the Vikings*, 329–66. Oxford University Press, Oxford.

O Carroll, E 2010 'An analysis of the wood excavated from troughs at Caheraphuca 4, 5, 6 and 8', *in* D Bayley, *N18 Gort to Crusheen Road Scheme: Caheraphuca 3–12 (E3653) Burnt Mounds and Pits*, xlviii–lxxvi. Unpublished excavation report for Galway County Council. Irish Archaeological Consultancy Ltd (IAC).

O'Connell, M & Molloy, K 2001 'Farming and woodland dynamics in Ireland during the Neolithic', *Biology and Environment: Proceedings of the Royal Irish Academy,* 101 B, 99–128.

O'Conor, K D 1998 *The Archaeology of Medieval Rural Settlement in Ireland*. Discovery Programme Monograph 3, Royal Irish Academy, Dublin.

Ó Corráin, D 1989 'Prehistoric and Early Christian Ireland', *in* R F Foster (ed.), *The Oxford Illustrated History of Ireland*, 1–52. Oxford University Press, Oxford.

Ó Cróinín, D 1995 *Early Medieval Ireland 400–1200*. Longman, London.

O'Donovan, J & Curry, E 2003 *The Antiquities of County Clare: Ordnance Survey Letters 1839*. Clasp Press, Ennis, Co. Clare.

Ó Drisceóil, D A 1988 'Burnt mounds: cooking or bathing?', *Antiquity*, 62, 671–80.

O'Hara, R 2009 'Early medieval settlement at Roestown 2', *in* M B Deevy & D Murphy (eds), *Places Along the Way. First findings on the M3*, 57–82. NRA Scheme Monographs 5, National Roads Authority, Dublin.

O'Keeffe, T 2000 *Medieval Ireland. An Archaeology*. Tempus Publishing, Gloucestershire.

O'Kelly, M J 1954 'Excavations and experiments in ancient Irish cooking-places', *Journal of the Royal Society of Antiquaries of Ireland*, 84, 105–55.

O'Kelly, M J 1961 'The ancient method of smelting iron', *Internat. Kongress fuer Von u Fruegesschichte*, 459–91. Universitatsbibliothek Basel, Hamburg.

O'Kelly, M J 2005 'Bronze Age Ireland', *in* D O'Cróinín (ed.), *A New History of Ireland*, Vol. 1, 133. Oxford University Press, Oxford.

Ó Murchadha, C 1992 'The Dál gCais and the territory of Tuamhumhain (Thomond)', *in* S Spellissy (ed.) *The Royal O'Briens – A Tribute*, 14–92. O'Brien Clan Association, Co. Clare.

O'Neill, J 2000 'Cherrywood Science and Technology Park, Co. Dublin', *in* I Bennett (ed.), *Excavations 1999. Summary accounts of archaeological excavations in Ireland*, 54–6. Wordwell, Bray.

Ó Néill, J 2004 '*Lapidibus in igne calefactis coquebatur:* the historical burnt mound tradition', *Journal of Irish Archaeology* (2003–04), Vols 12 & 13, 79–85.

O'Neill, J 2006 'Excavation of pre-Norman structures on the site of an enclosed Early Christian cemetery at Cherrywood, Co. Dublin', *in* S Duffy (ed.), *Medieval Dublin VII*, 66–88. Four Courts Press, Dublin.

O'Neill, N 2010 'Bronze Age bathing?', *Seanda*, 5, 38–9.

Ó Ríordáin, S P 1940 'Excavations at Cush, County Limerick', *Proceedings of the Royal Irish Academy*, 45 C, 83–181.

Ó Ríordáin, S P 1954 'Lough Gur excavations: Neolithic and Bronze Age houses on Knockadoon', *Proceedings of the Royal Irish Academy*, 56 C, 297–459.

O'Sullivan, J 2009 'Geophysics, tillage and the ghost ridges of County Galway, c. 1700–1850', *in* M Stanley, E Danaher & J Eogan (eds), *Dining and Dwelling: Proceedings of a public seminar on archaeological discoveries on national road schemes, August 2008*, 29–41. Archaeology and the National Roads Authority Monograph Series No. 6, National Roads Authority, Dublin.

O'Sullivan, M 1994 'Haynestown. Corn-drying kiln and ringbarrow with other features', *in* I Bennett (ed.), *Excavations 1993. Summary accounts of archaeological excavations in Ireland*, 57–8. Wordwell, Bray.

O'Sullivan, M & Downey, L 2009 'Charcoal production sites', *Archaeology Ireland*, 23, 22–5.

Parker, A G, Goudie, A S, Anderson, D E, Robinson, M A & Bonsall, C 2002 'A review of the mid-Holocene elm decline in the British Isles', *Progress in Physical Geography* 26, 1–45.

Patterson, N T 1994 *Cattle Lords and Clansmen. The social structure of Early Ireland*. University of Notre Dame Press, Indiana.

Pearson, K L 1997 'Nutrition and the early-medieval diet', *Speculum*, 72 (1), 1–32.

Peglar, S M & Birks, H J B 1993 'The mid-Holocene *Ulmus* fall at Diss Mere, south-east England—disease and human impact?', *Vegetation History and Archaeobotany* 2, 61–8.

Perrin, P M, Kelly, D L & Mitchell, F J G 2006 'Long-term deer exclusion in yew-wood and oakwood habitats in southwest Ireland: natural regeneration and stand dynamics', *Forest Ecology and Management* 236, 356–67.

Pleiner, R 2000 *Iron in Archaeology: the European Bloomery Smelters*. Archaeologicky, Prague.

Plunkett, G 2009 'Land-use patterns and cultural change in the Middle to Late Bronze Age in Ireland: inferences from pollen records', *Vegetation History and Archaeobotany*, 18, 273–95.

Power, D, Byrne, E, Egan, U, Land, S & Sleeman, M 1997 *Archaeological Inventory of County Cork. Volume III–Mid Cork*. Stationary Office, Dublin.

Quinn, B 2007 *Provisional Report on the Archaeological Testing of a Site at Barnhill Wood, Dromoland, Newmarket on Fergus, Co. Clare (07E0312)*. Unpublished Report by Moore Group on behalf of Clare County Council.

Quinn, B & Moore, D 2007 'Ale, brewing and *fulachta fiadh*', *Archaeology Ireland*, 21, No. 3, 8–11.

Quinn, B & Moore, D 2009 '*Fulachta fiadh* and the beer experiment', *in* M Stanley, E Danaher & J Eogan (eds), *Dining and Dwelling: Proceedings of a public seminar on archaeological discoveries on national road schemes, August 2008*, 43–53. Archaeology and the National Roads Authority Monograph Series No. 6, National Roads Authority, Dublin.

Rackham, O 1980 'The medieval landscape of Essex', *in* D G Buckley (ed.), *Archaeology in Essex to AD 1500*, 103–7. Council for British Archaeology, Research Report No. 34. London.

Raftery B 1984 *La Tène in Ireland. Problems of Origin and Chronology*. Veröffentlichung des Vorgeschichtlichen Seminars Marburg, Sonderband 2, Marburg.

Raftery, B 1995 'The conundrum of Irish Iron Age pottery', *in* B Raftery (ed.), *Sites and Sights of the Iron Age*, 149–56. Oxbow Monograph 56, Oxbow, Oxford.

Raftery, B 1996 *Trackway Excavations in the Mountdillon Bogs, Co. Longford*. Transactions No. 3, Crannog Publications, Longford.

Raftery, B 1997 'The die', *in* D M Waterman, *Excavations at Navan Fort 1961–71*, 95. Northern Ireland Archaeological Monographs 3, Belfast.

Raftery, B 2000 *Pagan Celtic Ireland*. Thames & Hudson, London.

Reimer, P J, Baillie, M G L, Bard, E, Bayliss, A, Beck, J W, Blackwell, P G, Bronk Ramsey, C, Buck, C E, Burr, G S, Edwards, R L, Friedrich, M, Gootes, P M, Guilderson, T P, Hajdas, I, Heaton, T J, Hogg, A G, Hughen, K A, Kaiser, K F, Kromer, B, McCormac, F G, Manning, S W, Reimer, R W, Richards, D A, Southon, J R, Talamo, S, Turney, C S M, van der Plict, J, Weyhenmeyer, C

E 2009 'IntCal09 and Marine09 radiocarbon age calibration curves, 0-50,000 years cal. BP' *Radiocarbon,* No. 51, 1111–50.

Riley, F T 1936 'Excavations in the townland of Pollacorragune, Tuam, Co. Galway', *Journal of the Galway Archaeological and Historical Society,* 17, 44–63.

Roche, H 1999 *Parknabinnia, County Clare (95E061) Pottery Report.* Unpublished specialist report for Carleton Jones & Alix Gilmer, Burren Archaeology Research.

Ryan, F 2008 'Excavation of Iron Age ring ditches, cist burials and features relating to habitation at Glebe South', *in* J Carroll, F Ryan & K Wiggins, *Archaeological Excavations at Glebe South and Darcystown, Balrothery, Co. Dublin,* 107–38. Judith Carroll & Co, Dublin.

Rynne, E 1970 'Oran Beg ring barrow', *in* T G Delaney (ed.), *Excavations 1970. Summary accounts of archaeological excavations in Ireland,* 10. Association of Young Irish Archaeologists and Ulster Archaeological Society, Belfast.

Scholtz, A 1986 *Palynological and Palaeobotanical Studies in the Southern Cape.* MA Thesis of Stellenbosch, South Africa.

Scott, B G 1990 *Early Irish Ironworking.* The Ulster Museum, Belfast.

Sher Dubin, L 1987 *The History of Beads: from 30,000 BC to the present.* Harry N Abrams, New York.

Sheridan, A 1995 'Irish Neolithic pottery: the story in 1995', *in* I Kinnes & G Varndell (eds), *Unbaked Urns of Rudely Shape,* 3–21. Oxbow Monograph 55, Oxford.

Simms, K 1989 'The Norman Invasion and the Gaelic Recovery', *in* R F Foster (ed.), *The Oxford Illustrated History of Ireland,* 53–103. Oxford University Press, Oxford.

Spellissy, S 1999 *The History of Galway: City & County.* The Celtic Bookshop, Limerick.

Spellissy, S 2003 *A History of County Clare.* Gill & Macmillan, Dublin.

St George Gray, H 1966 *The Meare Lake Village. A full description of the excavations and relics from the eastern half of the West Village, 1910–1933,* Vol. III. Taunton.

Stout, G 1982 *Preliminary Report on the Excavations at Ballymount Great, Co. Dublin.* Unpublished excavation report for the Office of Public Works, Dublin.

Stout, G & Stout, M 2008 *Excavation of an Early Medieval Secular Settlement at Knowth, Site M, County Meath.* Wordwell, Bray.

Stout, M 1997 *The Irish Ringfort.* Four Courts Press, Dublin.

Stuijts, I 2005 'Wood and charcoal identification', *in* M Gowan, J Ó Néill & M Phillips, *The Lisheen Mine Archaeological Project 1996–8,* 137–85. Wordwell, Bray.

Stuiver, M, Reimer, P J & Reimer, R 2005-06 *CALIB Radiocarbon Calibration.* http://radiocarbon. pa.qub.ac.uk.calib

Sweetman, D 1999 *The Castles of Ireland.* The Collins Press, Cork.

Teagasc 2006 (Unpublished) *Soil Survey of Ireland.* Department of Agriculture and Food, Dublin.

Tierney, J, Sternke, F & Johnston, P 2009 'Early Mesolithic finds from Barnacragh and Urraghry, east Galway', *Journal of the Galway Archaeological and Historical Society,* 61, 13–15.

Tierney, M & O'Dowd, J 2008 *Archaeological Excavations at Ballynaclogh, Co. Galway (E3874): Galway to Ballinasloe Road Scheme Draft Final Report.* Unpublished excavation report (draft) by The Archaeology Company for N6 Construction Ltd.

Timson, J 1966 '*Polygonum hydropiper* L', *The Journal of Ecology,* 54 (3), 815–21.

Tourunen, A 2007 'No bones about it: burnt mounds along the N9/N10', *Seanda,* 2, 70–1.

Tylecote, R F 1986 *The Prehistory of Metallurgy in the British Isles.* The Institute of Metals, London.

van der Verf, S 1991 'The influence of coppicing on vegetation', *Vegetatio*, 92 (2), 97–110.

Waddell, J 2000 (first edn; third edn 2010) *The Prehistoric Archaeology of Ireland*. Wordwell, Bray.

Wallace, A & Anguilano, L 2010 'Iron-smelting and smithing: new evidence emerging on Irish road schemes', *in* M Stanley, E Danaher & J Eogan (eds), *Creative Minds. Proceedings of a public seminar on archaeological discoveries on National Road Schemes, August 2009*, 69–84. Archaeology and the National Roads Authority Monograph Series No. 7, National Roads Authority, Dublin.

Walsh, C 1990 'A medieval cooking trough from Peter Street, Waterford', *in* V Buckley (ed.), *Burnt Offerings: international contributions to burnt mound archaeology*, 47–8. Wordwell, Bray.

Walsh, F 2008 'Killickaweeny 1: high-class early medieval living', *in* N Carlin, L Clarke & F Walsh, *The Archaeology of Life and Death in the Boyne Floodplain. The linear landscape of the M4*, 27–53. NRA Scheme Monographs 2, National Roads Authority, Dublin.

Waterman, D M 1997 *Excavations at Navan Fort 1961–71* (completed and edited by C J Lynn). Environment and Heritage Service, Department for the Environment, Northern Ireland, Dublin.

Wheeler, R E M 1943 *Maiden Castle, Dorset*. Reports of the Research Committee of the Society of Antiquaries of London 12, London.

Whelan, K 1997 'The modern landscape: from plantation to present", *in* F H A Aalen, K Whelan & M Stout (eds), *Atlas of the Irish Rural Landscape*, 67–103. Cork University Press, Cork.

INDEX